Creative Women
of Korea

The editor and publisher of this volume gratefully acknowledge the generous support of the Korea Foundation. The opinions, findings, and conclusions or recommendations expressed in this publication are those of the authors and do not necessarily reflect the views of the Korea Foundation.

Creative Women of Korea

of Korea

The Fifteenth Through the Twentieth Centuries

Young-Key Kim-Renaud

Editor

An East Gate Book

M.E.Sharpe
Armonk, New York
London, England

An East Gate Book

Copyright © 2004 by M. E. Sharpe, Inc.

The EuroSlavic fonts used to create this work are © 1986–2002 Payne Loving Trust.
EuroSlavic is available from Linguist's Software, Inc.,
www.linguistsoftware.com, P.O. Box 580, Edmonds, WA 98020-0580 USA
tel. (425) 775-1130.

Library of Congress Cataloging-in-Publication Data

Creative women of Korea: the fifteenth through the twentieth centuries / edited by Young-Key
Kim-Renaud.
    p. cm.
"An east gate book."
Includes bibliographical references, glossary, and index.
ISBN 0-7656-1189-9 (alk. paper) ; ISBN 0-7656-1188-0 (pbk: alk. paper)
    1. Women authors, Korean. 2. Women and literature—Korea—History. 3. Women
artists—Korea. 4. Creative ability—Korea. 5. Women—Korea—History.
    I. Kim-Renaud, Young-Key.

PL957.9 .C74 2003
895.7′0099287—dc21

                                        2002030854

Printed in the United States of America

BM (c) 10   9   8   7   6   5   4   3   2   1
BM (p) 10   9   8   7   6   5   4   3

Contents

List of Illustrations

*Illustration numbering corresponds to the panels of the original screens.

Preface

All but one chapter in this volume originate from the papers presented at the Fifth Annual Hahn Moo-Sook Colloquium in the Korean Humanities at The George Washington University (hereinafter, GW), which was held on 24–25 October 1998.[1] Originally the colloquium started as an academic activity of GW's East Asian Languages and Literatures Department and the Sigur Center for Asian Studies. Its main goal was to provide a forum not only for Korean-studies specialists but also for anyone who would like to know about Korea in relation to the rest of East Asia and the world abroad, both in traditional and contemporary contexts.

The initial format was to have two leading scholars, if possible with differing but complementary views, introduce some particular aspect of the Korean humanities—not necessarily presenting controversial or novel ideas—to an international audience and engage all of the participants in common reflection. The response to this program, which brought people together for an educational and enjoyable dialog in a relaxed atmosphere, was so positive from the beginning that it became an ongoing event. A generous grant from the Hahn Moo-Sook Foundation in Korea, which established an endowment at GW upholding her spirit of openness, civility, curiosity, and education, helped to make this dialog an annual event.

In 1998 a special conference, rather than the usual colloquium format, was organized for at least three reasons. First, the conference would commemorate the eightieth birthday of Hahn Moo-Sook, the namesake of the colloquium series. That year also marked the fifteen-year anniversary of the Korean language and culture program at GW. Finally, the topic chosen under the title of "Sparks of Creativity: Women in the Korean Humanities" covered a much different terrain and called for much more original research on the part of the presenters than usual.

Some highly illuminating collected papers have appeared on Korean women in English.[2] However, in those cases, more emphasis was placed upon gender issues, including women's status, role, treatment, and significance in terms of family, society, polity, and history. The current volume is not really about "women's studies" per se, although it could be used as a sourcebook. Rather, the book considers the creativity manifest by a few known and many unknown women of Korea over the past five centuries and more. Women's works, albeit minimal in quantity compared to men's, are extremely diverse and in many cases remarkably original. These creative thinkers and artists have caught the attention of the literary and artistic connoisseurs, and a strange force unifies their creation. By the very varied and common artistic responses to the human drama of life, encompassing people's beliefs, emotions, and also a need for survival, this book aims at demonstrating how Korean women have tried to make sense of their lives and lead a meaningful existence over the years.

Young-Key Kim-Renaud
Washington, D.C.

Notes

1. The chapter by Kevin O'Rourke was written at the invitation of the editor after the conference. The editor is most grateful to Professor O'Rourke for his essential contribution and particularly for having undertaken the work, under pressure, and with such grace and alacrity.

2. See for example, Kim, *Women of Korea*; Mattielli, *Virtues in Conflict*; Sunoo and Kim, *Women in a Struggle for Humanization*; Kendall and Peterson, *Korean Women*; and Park, *Women of the Yi Dynasty*.

References

Kendall, Laurel, and Mark Peterson, eds. *Korean Women: View from the Inner Room* (New Haven, CT: East Rock Press), 1983.

Kim, Yung-Chung, ed. and tr. *Women of Korea: A History from Ancient Times to 1945* (Seoul: Ewha Woman's University Press), 1976/1979 (revised edition).

Mattielli, Sandra, ed. *Virtues in Conflict: Tradition and the Korean Woman Today* (Seoul: Royal Asiatic Society, Korea Branch), 1977.

Park, Younghai, ed. *Women of the Yi Dynasty* (Seoul: Research Center for Asian Women, Sookmyung Women's University), 1986.

Sunoo, Harold Hakwon, and Kong Soo Kim, eds., *Women in a Struggle for Humanization* (Memphis, TN: Korean Christian Scholars), 1978.

Acknowledgments

The George Washington University Colloquium series in the Korean Humanities and the proposed topic for the 1998 conference won approval and confidence from many colleagues and different organizations. First of all, the International Circle of Korean Linguistics became a co-sponsor of the conference, and the Korean Culture and Arts Foundation in Korea offered major financial support for the two-day meeting. Professors from four major universities of the Washington, D.C., area joined hands in organizing the whole conference, and the Consortium of Universities of the Washington Metropolitan Area provided a generous subsidy. My special thanks go to the organizing committee: R. Richard Grinker of GW; Bonnie B. C. Oh of Georgetown University; Byung-Soo Park, then president of the International Circle of Korean Linguistics; S. Robert Ramsey of the University of Maryland; and Young-chan Ro of George Mason University. At GW, then-Dean Lester A. Lefton of the Columbian College of Arts and Sciences; Dean Harry Harding of the Elliott School of International Affairs; Dr. Bruce Dickson, then-director of the Sigur Center for Asian Studies; and Dr. Barbara Miller, then-head of the Women's Studies Program provided financial help. Members of GW's Korean Student Association and Korean-American Student Association worked tirelessly to help with meeting logistics. Stephen Bennett of GW's International Services Office offered his customary essential help in facilitating the matters involved in inviting foreign guest speakers. The Korean ambassador to the United States, Lee Hong-Koo, and Mrs. Lee, honored the colloquium by inviting the speakers and other participants to a sumptuous dinner at their lovely residence in Washington during the evening of the first day of the conference. I also thank student volunteers Joseb Gim, Ellie Hurey, Raymond Lee, Casey Reivich, Shari Sames, and Chusam Yi. I am greatly indebted to my longtime friend, Lindsey Eck, who read the entire book manuscript with a critical eye and provided invaluable comments and suggestions. I also thank my family, especially my father, Jin-Heung Kim, chairman of the Hahn Moo-Sook Foundation, my husband, Bertrand M. Renaud, and my daughter, Nicole K. Renaud, who have always believed in a woman's potential and fully supported all my endeavors. Thanks to the generous support of these individuals and groups, the conference participants could meet in comfort and style for two days, and the publication of this volume became possible. Without their material and moral support, I would not have had the courage and perseverance to plan this book.

Finally, I want to thank the Korea Foundation for the generous publication grant, which helped produce this book in a form that would not have been otherwise possible. I am grateful to various individuals at M.E. Sharpe, Inc., whose professionalism has consistently impressed me. In particular, acquiring editor Patricia Loo's enthusiastic interest in this work and her efficient and pleasant management of the publication process have lifted my spirit. Senior production editor Angela Piliouras' cordial and meticulous treatment of the manuscript in its final production stage has been exemplary. I will be even more blessed if friends, family members, and colleagues find this book worthy of their support.

Creative Women
of Korea

1
Introduction

Young-Key Kim-Renaud

This book, *Creative Women of Korea: The Fifteenth Through the Twentieth Centuries*, was conceived with the specific aim of filling a certain gap in available Western-language materials on Korean women's contributions to the humanities. It introduces to the English-speaking world aspects of important contributions by women in traditional and modern Korea, from the fifteenth through the twentieth centuries. From the outset, three questions were posed:

(1) Have Korean women, especially those in the Confucian Korea of the Chosŏn dynasty (1392–1910), been passive recipients of the subservient status imposed by that society, or have they had their own agency?
(2) In what historical and social context did some of the most creative women achieve their artistic triumphs?
(3) What are the key characteristics of their creativity? Are there any shared traits in their creativity?

Creative Women of Korea consists of nine chapters that discuss literary and artistic works by women that may be considered Korean classics. Most of the women included in this book lived during the Chosŏn dynasty, with the exception of two moderns whose work presents contrasting reactions to past conventions in the wake of Korea's modernization. I excluded living artists, many of whom are among the top literary and artistic figures of contemporary Korea.

The names of most women artists in traditional Korea are unknown to us because their creative activities were not meant to be publicized beyond the world of women. A small number of women—Queen Sohye, Sin Saimdang, Hŏ Nansŏrhŏn, Hwang Chini, and Lady Hyegyŏng of Chosŏn-dynasty Korea, and Kim Iryŏp and Hahn Moo-Sook of modern Korea—have achieved great fame. Their works occupy a public space, each by different circumstances.

All the women discussed in *Creative Women of Korea* are from the upper class (*yangban*), with the exception of Hwang Chini, a courtesan entertainer, or *kisaeng*, who, according to legend, was at least partially noble in origin. It is no coincidence that what literary and artistic works by women have survived are by noblewomen. They were the educated ones, with enough leisure and presence of mind to participate in creative endeavors, unlike lower-class women for whom education was thought useless as they would be too busy tending to daily chores. There may have been exceptions, but even if lowborn women did write and create, their productions were probably considered too unimportant for anyone to preserve whatever they left behind.

Propriety demanded that the literature and works of art by noblewomen not be publicized, even if these women, in their hearts, wished for their works to be discovered. In premodern times, therefore, among creative pieces by female authors and artists, anonymous works far exceed in number those whose creators are known. Women's work was meant to circulate among their own gender, although circumstances made some of their works known among the general public. So, the creative women discussed in this book may share similar backgrounds, but their individual works are extremely varied in their originality and provenance. Thus, while those works represent the range of Korean women's achievements, in no way is their presentation here meant as a characterization of Korean women in general.

Nevertheless, the force behind their creation is very much of one thread. Creative activity was the road to self-discovery. Each artist possessed a clear sense of self-confidence and an urge to express her creativity. Each wrote, painted, and made objects from a sincere and genuine desire to express deep emotions, trying to lead a life of harmony, good taste, and beauty emanating from within (*mŏt*), while guarding her personal creed, integrity, and dignity, in her own particular ways. These women occupied unmistakable spaces of their own in traditional Korea; they often challenge the view of Korean women of the past commonly held today.

How did a woman of traditional Korea feel about herself? Was she miserable about her wretched "life of bondage" in the service of men? Conventionally, a traditional Korean woman has been considered as powerless under the burdens and abuses inflicted upon her by the patriarchal norms of Confucian society. An "ideal" woman was one of noble birth, who remained cloistered within the inner quarters (*anch'ae*). In fact, the higher her status, the more she was sequestered.[1] The assumed inferior position of women in human relationships and the presumed paucity of women's works in pre-modern Korean literature and art would seem to attest to the verisimilitude of such preconceptions.[2] Women had no room of their own in the sense of Virginia Woolf, the English writer, as they were ostensibly silenced into non-existence.[3]

The Neo-Confucian politico-moral system supposedly was adopted as the set of governing principles of the Chosŏn dynasty at its founding. And current scholarship informs us that, as the dynasty progressed, women—especially of the *yangban* class—gradually became less publicly visible.[4] Under a dogmatic interpretation, the "proper" place for women was narrowly defined in terms of the physical and abstract sphere they occupied. A wellborn woman belonged to the inner quarters behind the thick walls of her family's house—and those of her husband's abode after marriage. In Confucian Korea, the world of a decent woman was private; the public sphere belonged to men only. An ideal woman was neither to be visible to, nor to communicate with, the opposite sex, with the exception of male servants, who were "less than normal" human beings. She was modest, diligent, frugal, faithful, docile, patient, and, above all, discreet. A system of female doctors, chosen from the lower classes, was created because aristocratic women refused to see male doctors.[5]

Among the key characteristics of Korean civilization are rites, lineage structure, literature, and education. In a Confucian society, rites are of the utmost importance, because "correct" acts are considered crucial for enhancing harmony among the members of society.[6] In an ideal Confucian state, the moral conduct of the people was thought to contribute directly to the health of society and the vigor of the nation. Three cardinal human relationships (*samgang*) and five moral imperatives (*oryun*) were the inviolable creed, which regulated people's behavior in minute detail. *Samgang* concerned the relationships between ruler and subject, father and son, and husband and wife. *Oryun*, reinforcing and clarifying *samgang*, prescribed righteousness between ruler and subject, affinity between father and son, separation of functions between husband and wife, proper order of birth between elder and younger brother, and fidelity between friends.[7]

To maintain proper human relationships, ritual and etiquette were mandated. Of the Four Rites (*sarye*)—adulthood, nuptials, funeral, and ancestor worship (or the remembrance ceremony)—the institution of ancestor worship brought about the most profound change in Korean society. Ancestral worship categorized members of the descent group into a hierarchy. In the early Chosŏn dynasty, well before the seventeenth century, when Korea was completely Confucianized, women were equal participants in ancestral rites, but gradually the main line of the eldest sons came to assume the heaviest responsibility in ritual obligations. The system of primogeniture was thus solidified, and unequal inheritance customs ensued. Patriarchy was considered the most natural requirement for an orderly life. Women's participation in ritual gradually but surely came to be limited to the preparation of sacrificial foods and proper ceremonial garb for men.

On the surface, a woman's status seemed to be determined uniquely by the men in her life. The "etiquette of Three Dependencies" (*Samjong chi ŭi*) meant that a woman obeyed her parents as a child, her husband as a wife, and her son as a widow. With the wholesale Confucianization of society, women seemed to lose their identity completely. However, in contrast to most patrilineal systems, in Confucian Korea the old custom of women playing a pivotal role in determining the social status of their offspring persisted. It is well known that the issue of illegitimate or secondary consorts met with discrimination. Protest literature, such as the *Hong Kiltong chŏn* (The Tale of Hong Kiltong) by Hŏ Kyun, attests to the unhappiness felt by victims of the system and their sympathizers.[8]

However, there has been substantial variation and complexity even in the matter of gender and class in traditional Korea, depending on the historical period, personal life cycles, and, finally, individual qualities and talents of the person in question. With the common belief of *pubu ilch'e* ("a couple is one body"), even in the worst period for women, a woman received due respect from all who respected her husband. For the same reason, filial piety did not apply only to one's father, but to both parents. This is well reflected in linguistic protocol. Due to an elaborate honorific system in the Korean language, the choice of the appropriate forms of address and referent honorifics is the most overt representation of interpersonal relationships. A husband and a wife have not used equal speech levels to each other of late, but early twentieth-century novels indicate that, until quite recently, aristocratic couples used to address each other by equal-in-level polite forms. A mother may use a formal speech style to a grown son (or daughter), especially if he (or she, as is manifest in Lady Hyegyŏng's memoirs) attained high social status, but in no way would a son "talk down" to his own mother or elder sister, however high a position he or she may have reached.

Recent studies have shown that the social institutions affecting women in the gravest ways were fully implemented only by the seventeenth century.[9] Even in the most unfavorable times for women, a noblewoman often exercised considerable power by virtue of her birth, station, and upbringing. Her ancestry bestowed privilege upon her. Married, she became an opposing but complementary half in the *yin* and *yang* whole, playing a key role in establishing the legitimacy of a noble lineage. In other words, although one's aristocratic lineage was through one's father, one's mother's aristocratic origin was equally important in confirming one's nobility in the Korean tradition. At a certain stage of her life cycle, a woman would even become a lead manager of not only the inner quarters but of the entire household. Thus, Korean "women opened up arenas of freedom for themselves without directly challenging the ideal norms promulgated by the official ideology."[10]

There is a clear parallel here to Dorothy Ko's portrayal of traditional Chinese women:

> [I]f the assumptions of patriarchy were not being challenged outright in the seventeenth century, in practice they were being constantly mitigated. Although men still claimed legal rights over family property and fathers enjoyed authority over women and children, the housewife as de facto household manager, mother, and educator of children had ample opportunities to influence family affairs. In the context of everyday life, women were hardly outsiders to the family system.[11]

Indeed, stories abound about virtuous Asian women who lectured their corrupt (official) and undiscerning husbands. The quantity of known women's writings and artwork in Korea is minimal compared to men's, as women were not supposed to be visible in the first place. However, a few works by identifiable women authors, and by countless anonymous others who are clearly women, allow us a glimpse of the world of women and an idea of their sensibility, intelligence, and dignity. In almost every work, there is a surprising sense of self-confidence or self-awareness on the part of the author or creator as an important and often daring and innovative participant in artistic life, even when some women may have been lamenting their destiny.

Women wrote mainly in *han'gŭl*, the Korean alphabet invented in the mid-fifteenth century. Only men held public office, and official positions were filled through the civil-service examination, which was based mainly on the Confucian classics. Therefore, it was mandatory for men to study literary Chinese. In fact, "literacy" meant familiarity with Chinese classics. All official documents and much of the nation's literature continued to be written in Chinese.[12]

Men preferred to write in Chinese to lend their writing an air of officiality, formality, intellectualism, and, of course, prestige, because literary Chinese was far more difficult to master than writing in the vernacular and in *han'gŭl*, the simple alphabetic Korean writing system. In written language, at least, all educated men were completely bilingual in Chinese and Korean, and, in some cases, monolingual only in literary Chinese, that is, they did not know *han'gŭl*.

The Korean language, which shares numerous typological similarities with Japanese, is syntactically very different from Chinese. After trying for centuries to use the essentially nonphonetic Chinese characters to transcribe the polysyllabic vernacular with myriad affixes and other grammatical markers, many Korean writers just wrote in classical Chinese. Most of them, however, did not know any spoken Chinese. The literati wrote mainly in Chinese except when writing *sijo* or *kasa* poetry, mundane notes, casual records, and the like. Thus, as in Japan, true writing in traditional Korea meant literary Chinese. As such, the act of writing was in itself foreign and the style was always formal and classical. There was a great distance between the spoken and written forms of language in space and time, much as with Europeans' use of Greek and Latin during the eighteenth century.[13]

Teaching women Chinese was considered a waste of time, not only because they were thought inferior but also because they did not need literacy to fulfill their womanly tasks. However, if learning Chinese was perhaps considered futile or impertinent, it was not actually banned for women. On the contrary, those who managed to acquire a "masculine" education were highly respected. As a consequence, some women managed to become literate; they learned Chinese classics "over the shoulder" (ŏkkae nŏmŏ), as their brothers and fathers recited in a loud voice, which was a common way of reading and learning books. Some fathers and brothers, as well as mothers, actually instructed their daughters and sisters who showed exceptional intelligence. Such women certainly earned the respect and praise of all, so long as they did not neglect womanly duties.

Even those women who did learn Chinese, however, used it only for certain poetic works; mostly they opted to use han'gŭl. In fact, han'gŭl was nicknamed amk'ŭl ("female writing"), a term almost always used pejoratively.[14] Thus, unlike Chinese—and more like Japanese—women, Korean women wrote in what they viewed as their own medium of writing, thus empowering themselves.

Writing in the conveniently easy alphabet gave them a crucial tool for literary creations, which were at times spiritual and reflective, at times spontaneous, playful, and frank. Consequently, women's works reveal thought and inner feeling more directly and powerfully than men's, because women were speaking both their mind and heart in their own language.

"Virtuous women" were thought by many to be vital to an ideal Confucian society. Moral conduct was prescribed in the Chinese classics. Though a few Korean women were well versed in the classics, most did not read Chinese. Many scholars have pointed out that one motive for Sejong's invention of the Korean alphabet in 1443 or 1444[15] may have been to enhance literacy; but the ultimate goal was moral education.[16] When the Chinese classics became accessible to commoners, women, and children with the help of an easy writing system—Sejong may have thought, according to these scholars—the basic moral principles of the Three Bonds (samgang) could be upheld, and everyone could live in harmony with the "natural" order of the Confucian universe.

Various circumstances served to elevate the queen to an extraordinarily powerful position, far above any other woman in fifteenth-century Korea. The well-educated Queen Sohye, mother of King Sŏngjong, took upon herself the task of women's education by compiling a textbook entitled the Naehun ("Instructions for Women," 1475), which included quotations from various Chinese classics. Queen Sohye was from an illustrious family, her close relatives were politically mighty, and she was chosen as a royal consort, enjoying the status of "mother of the nation." Hers thus became the voice of authority beyond the sphere reserved for women, even as Chosŏn *yangban* women were gradually being deprived of the social and economic equality enjoyed by their foremothers.

However, what distinguished the queen even more impressively was the fact that she was educated in the Confucian classics. Her privileged station allowed her to compile selections in literary Chinese, the "male language of public business," with a *han'gŭl* translation—in a manner reminiscent of moral primers authored by men of the time.

In his chapter entitled "The *Naehun* and the Politics of Gender in Fifteenth-Century Korea," Professor John Duncan (hereinafter, all honorific titles will be omitted) investigates "how elite women of the Chosŏn period sought, within the strictures of the Confucian gender system, to define a space wherein they could play meaningful social, cultural, and political roles" (in this volume, p. 27; further cross-references given simply with *p.*). Maintaining her discourse at men's level, Sohye strove to claim important social, cultural, and even political roles for women, as "exemplars of ritual propriety and as confidants and advisers to their husbands" (p. 53). Sohye was an extraordinary woman possessing considerable self-assurance and a sense of responsibility for her country's destiny. In the final analysis, Sohye was pleading for education for women so that they could fulfill proper roles within the Confucian system. No one had ever done this publicly, and eloquently, before her.

Even when Korean families were restructured according to the Confucian patrilineal descent group, and women's status in family and society was transformed from adviser and helpmate to submissive spouse and dutiful caregiver, Koreans continued to be conscious of the centrality of women's roles and the importance of their wise judgment in fulfilling those roles.[17] Education, formal and public, was neither accessible nor considered relevant for women; its purpose was the preparation of scholar-officials. However, women's wisdom and proper upbringing were still considered important, because Koreans believed that the vicissitudes of a family and a society crucially, if not primarily, depended on them.

Another woman enjoying privilege and high acclaim was Sin Saimdang (1504–1551), the subject of Yi Sŏng-mi's chapter "Sin Saimdang: The Foremost Woman Painter of the Chosŏn Dynasty." Sin Saimdang was born into the illustrious family of Sin. Like her mother, she was taught to read the Chinese classics by her father, who gave her the pen name *Saimdang*. Again like her mother, Lady Sin stayed with her natal family for many years, even after her marriage, before joining her husband's family, in accord with the custom of uxorilocal residence.[18] This living arrangement is likely to have given her the freedom, away from her husband's family and from all the responsibilities of a daughter-in-law, which must have been a huge contributing factor toward her growth as an artist.

Sin Saimdang is known for having been a good wife and the wise mother of Yulgok, also called Yi I (1536–1584), one of the two most eminent Neo-Confucian philosophers in Korean intellectual history. Lady Sin was known for her exquisite paintings, embroidery, calligraphy, and poetry. Yi Sŏng-mi, however, strongly believes that Saimdang's social and intellectual position as the mother of the prominent and influential thinker helped create a new image for her, creating what Yi terms a "Saimdang myth." Many works of uneven quality thus came to be attributed to Sin Saimdang on account of her fame. Yi's research offers hope not only in identifying some important characteristics of Saimdang's artistry but also in clarifying her contribution to the development of Korean art.

Although Lady Sin is famous for her embroidery, her ink paintings fall within the general framework of literati painting of her time, according to Yi Sŏng-mi. Yi's research on Sin Saimdang and her art suggests that an important link exists between the Korean and Chinese painting traditions prior to the sixteenth century, and what we have of works attributed to Saimdang, in some cases, serves to fill in the missing links in the chain of stylistic development of painting in the Chosŏn period.

Hŏ Nansŏrhŏn (1563–1589) is another talented woman from a distinguished family whose many members were known for scholarship and literary creativity. In his chapter entitled, "Hŏ Nansŏrhŏn and 'Shakespeare's Sister,'" Kichung Kim compares an imaginary gifted sister of Shakespeare—reconstructed by Virginia Woolf in her classic work, *A Room of One's Own*—with Hŏ Nansŏrhŏn who lived in Korea, also in the sixteenth century. In Kim's view, the two women would have had much in common as victims of male-dominated societies. Unlike Shakespeare's sister, however, Lady Hŏ's birth and circumstances gave her educational opportunities to become literate. She was surrounded by a loving, talented family and by a library of "10,000 books."[19] Her cultural foundation and her personal sensitivity are two crucial ingredients of her poems; her work has been anthologized and praised in China and Japan as well.

The unsheathed sorrow in many of Lady Hŏ's poems as well as some remarks on her brief life by others, including her brother Hŏ Kyun, has led scholars and readers to speculate about the origin of her melancholy. Kim, like many researchers on Hŏ Nansŏrhŏn, finds the source of her agony in her sense of failure as a woman, notwithstanding her talents and position, in light of what was expected of a virtuous lady of her time. Kichung Kim, at the same time, embraces as plausible the hypothesis—proposed by scholars such as Martina Deuchler, Mark Peterson, and John Duncan—that women may have been relatively less confined at the time of Hŏ Nansŏrhŏn. Kim thus suggests that Lady Hŏ might have been able to write the kind of poetry she did—both in quantity and quality—because she had probably been allowed to remain with her own family for some time after her marriage.

The sense of alienation and loneliness expressed in Hŏ Nansŏrhŏn's works may not all derive from her actual experiences, warns Kichung Kim. They could have originated in books or the people around her. She also empathized with people suffering from analogous feelings of loneliness and unhappiness, such as fishermen's wives and unmarried seamstresses. These intense feelings, whatever their reason or origin, made Lady Hŏ want to write, not necessarily for others but for herself. Writing about her sadness sublimated her worldly misery to spiritual joy. That is probably why she wished her work to be burned after she died—not because she did not want to have another woman poet ending up as miserable as she was, as some researchers have claimed.[20]

Kichung Kim invites us to ponder the relationship between Hŏ Nansŏrhŏn's realistic sad poems and her fantastic dream poems: two very different modes, both in form and content, of Hŏ Nansŏrhŏn's art. By expressing frankly her mind and heart, she sought to experience catharsis. By freely traveling into the world of immortals, she tried to find philosophical meaning and peace in her life. In both cases, her urge to create, to turn her feelings into an aesthetic experience, is evident. Kichung Kim's essay suggests that Hŏ Nansŏrhŏn, in spite of her sad, short life, was luckier than Shakespeare's sister.

In traditional Korea, especially in the late Chosŏn, a noblewoman's physical place was within the inner quarters. However, most women from the lower classes were free to appear in public. Servants, commoners, women doctors, shamans, and *kisaeng* (women entertainers or courtesans) were officially allowed into the public space, but that space was not an honorable one for women. In the case of *kisaeng*, their space was different from other women's in that they mingled with men, if only

as their playmates. Even though from a lower class, the *kisaeng* under-
went strict, formal training in etiquette, poetry, painting, calligraphy,
singing, dancing, games, and so on, in an effort to emulate the education
of the noblemen whom they would eventually entertain. Nevertheless,
"repeated attempts to cleanse official society of these women indicate
that the kisaeng were viewed as being subversive of proper decorum."[21]

Hwang Chini (1502–?) is an eternal name in Korean literary history.
Her works are limited to six *sijo* poems and seven poems in Chinese.
Hwang Chini is unlike most of the *kisaeng* poets: Most songs and poetry by these women tend to express their longing for an absent lover,
their lament for a lost love, or their nostalgia for the days of their youth
and glory.[22] Hwang Chini's poems present her as a secure woman—
strong, confident, forthright, playful, decisive, and in control of her emotions, one who knows her own mind, who seeks perfection in herself
and in her company, and who could laugh at her own foibles as well as
the foibles of others. More important, her poems evince a poet with a
refined sensibility and remarkable literary talents.

Hwang Chini's identity remains obscure. This has provided ample
opportunity for admirers of her poems to create the "Hwang Chini myth."
Kevin O'Rourke's chapter, "Demythologizing Hwang Chini," espouses
the need for separating the historical and the mythical Hwang Chini for
the sake of proper evaluation of her artistic achievement.[23] O'Rourke
examines her work against the canvas of her times and the work of her
peers, male and female. He points out that the early sixteeenth century
was not a great time for poetry in general in Korea, and he carefully
avoids superlatives in describing her works because he does not believe
there is evidence to support such qualitative judgments. He believes that
hyperbolic expressions, in fact, are part of the myth that he sets out to
debunk.

O'Rourke's analyses of Hwang Chini's poems in Chinese and of her
Korean *sijo* poems, however, make evident her genius, her clearly thorough literary education, and her keen sense of beauty in nature and in
human relationships. Hwang Chini's poems evoke traditional Korean
and East Asian literary traditions, but her artistic skills of expressing in
lyrical language her true feelings, while being able to detach herself
from them using irony and contrasting imagery, are distinctive.

In the chapter entitled "Private Memory and Public History: The
Memoirs of Lady Hyegyŏng and Testimonial Literature," JaHyun Kim
Haboush contemplates the works of an eighteenth-century princess.

Lady Hyegyŏng (1735–1815) was the wife of Crown Prince Sado, whose tragic life and death have become known thanks to her writings.[24] Haboush discusses *Memoirs* in the context of testimonial literature. She analyzes how Lady Hyegyŏng organizes memory to construct her narratives, thus turning private memory into public history. Haboush also reflects on the gendered sense of self represented in her memoirs, and investigates the relationship between such a sense and genres of testimonial literature, noting the preponderance of women writers in this category of writing.

Haboush distinguishes testimonial narratives written in *han'gŭl* from official petitions-memorials written in classical Chinese, which are legal documents. Lady Hyegyŏng, writing private narratives in vernacular Korean, thus unofficially contests the official historiography on Sado's death and the events leading to it—a subject of the highest sensitivity and importance touching on dynastic legitimacy, and taboo for discussion. Haboush investigates cultural imperatives that led Lady Hyegyŏng to write her memoirs and the cultural context in which she wrote them.

Lady Hyegyŏng wrote the history of a king and his heir as the story of a father and son. Her remarkable achievement in this testimony, according to Haboush, was how she could turn her private memory into public history, in a way no man, let alone any woman, was to do.

Lady Hyegyŏng's testimony was as much for herself as for history. She clearly wrote to keep the record straight; however, what essentially drove her creativity was her quest for self-identity. Like Hŏ Nansŏrhŏn, by relating what had happened and entering it into the written record, she could come to terms with her own self and with her destiny. That is, at a most personal level, she could finally mourn the loss by recognizing that it had happened, thereby bringing it to closure. She was at last free from the cords of life that had bound her.

It is noteworthy that just as Korean women, especially noblewomen, were effectively marginalized and segregated, more of them participated in literary activities. Because of their invisible status, most of their names are not known but, from content and other circumstantial evidence, their gender is certain. In a completely Confucianized Korea, even noblewomen were no longer educated in Chinese classics. Therefore, almost all writings by women were in vernacular Korean. Chŏng Pyŏng'uk notes, "From the Korean literary historical point of view, a 'fortunate consequence' of women's segregation was that Korean literature was no longer bound by the narrow definition of writing in classical Chinese."[25] Lady

Hyegyŏng's memoirs, together with *Hunmin chŏng'ŭm*, the proclamation document of the Korean alphabet of 1446—whose scientific, philosophical and humanistic qualities are now well established—surely belong among the great literary works of human civilization.[26]

A traditional noblewoman, especially in Confucianized late-Chosŏn Korea, was not supposed to express her feelings. The creative urge, however, can be even more intense when a person is so confined. These women saw opportunities for creativity in ordinary customs and mores involving themselves. Women wrote letters by obligation and of their own accord. A *yangban* woman was required to write salutary letters to her parents-in-law, if they were away. These letters were strictly formulaic, and not writing exactly as required was a sign of bad upbringing. Personal letters between a woman and a confidant were another matter. It is not surprising that many moving narratives are written in the form of letters. A particular form of poetry called *kasa* (literally, "prose song"), possibly developed as a form of letter, was the favorite literary genre chosen by *yangban* women of this period.

In the chapter entitled "*Kyubang kasa:* Women's Writings from the Late Chosŏn," Sonja Häußler discusses works by anonymous women writing in *kasa*, which are long poems written in the Korean vernacular with a set rhythmic pattern. *Kyubang kasa* ("*kasa* of the inner chambers") were written on rolls of paper (*turumari*) and handed down from woman to woman. Some *kyubang kasa* were written collectively, and became quite long, as women kept adding to the received text. Häußler's study features some poignant examples that help us understand the nature and origin of this genre.

Häußler observes that *kyubang kasa* originated directly from the Confucianization of Korea and its effect on women. *Kasa* probably started as a cycle of personal missives filled with moral and psychological encouragement from a mother to her daughter leaving the natal home for her affine family. These poems were also a part of the home she was leaving behind that the marrying daughter carried with her: "Touching the scroll and looking at the calligraphy of her beloved, she would be with them."

Kyubang kasa, therefore, may belong to the category of didactic literature, and literature for women at that. However, with time, the range of subjects expanded to encompass all forms of ceremonial greetings and wishes including homilies, travelogs, and, finally, fiction. In a crucial manner, writes Häußler, women tried to emulate men by writing poems on Chinese and Korean history, thus penetrating men's jealously guarded domain. In contrast to *kasa* by male poets, women's historical narratives included accounts of queens, upholding female virtues. Then followed women's involvement in political life, and their vision soon extended to the world beyond Korea. *Kyubang kasa* thus truly came to present "a kaleidoscopic view of Korean life."[27] More important, they give a glimpse of the inner thoughts and feelings of wellborn women of the late Chosŏn. *Kyubang kasa* provide authentic sources for studying the intellectual and psychological state of many Korean women of the past.

The effort to render the life of the inner room more meaningful and beautiful was not limited to literary creation. An important aspect in the life of good taste and style was the visual. One of the imperatives for a traditional woman was to keep herself and her surroundings as clean and beautiful as possible. If frugality was praised and extravagance looked at askance, a beautiful object created from meager means received utmost respect. One area in which Korean women of the past showed remarkable ingenuity is in some highly original designs that embellished daily necessities, as well as in purely decorative small embroidered ornaments called *kwebul*. One of the objects in which women demonstrated their refreshing creativity is *pojagi* (wrapping or covering cloth), which had a particular significance in the Korean cultural context.

Kumja Paik Kim, in the chapter entitled "A Celebration of Life: Patchwork and Embroidered *Pojagi* by Unknown Korean Women," discusses the nature, meaning, and art of *pojagi* (covering), with illustrations of some of the most exquisite examples. Kim believes that the custom of *pojagi*-making started at the court, where the rules of proper conduct had to be strictly adhered to. Later it not only became an integral part in the protocol of the court (*kung po*) but also in the daily life of ordinary people (*min po*).

Covering expressed respect for the objects covered, seriousness toward the occasion, and esteem for the receiver of the items covered. People believed, too, that by wrapping something they would capture good fortune (*pok*) to be associated with the enclosed object. Naturally, women made them with the seriousness and care any precious object required. Kumja Paik Kim also discusses spiritual aspects of *pojagi*-making. Virtues of patience, frugality, and devotion would add to the good luck of the user and blessings of the object to be covered. What is unique in this endeavor, however, is that Korean women did not just follow templates to produce them mechanically, but demonstrated their creativity by designing and making original pieces. *Pojagi*, although all by anonymous women, represent the ethos and distinct, sophisticated aesthetic sensibilities of traditional Korea.

The traditional Confucian social and political order came to be seriously challenged in the nineteenth century. As early as the late eighteenth century, a group of scholars of Qing studies known as Northern Learning (*Pukhak*) within the Practical Learning (*Sirhak*) movement had advocated foreign trade with Western nations and enlightened reform embracing Western technology.[28] Unfortunately, the regent Taewŏn'gun's isolationist policy—made even fiercer following the destruction of an American merchant ship, the *General Sherman*, in 1866, which gave him a misguided sense of superiority—led the country to constant predicaments in its transactions with other, more powerful nations. Korea, hopelessly weakened by many ills toward the end of the Chosŏn dynasty, succumbed to the ambition of Japan and became its colony in 1910. It would regain its independence only in 1945.

In a rapidly declining nation, the Reform of 1894 (*Kabo kyŏngjang*) brought about extensive changes that affected all aspects of the political, economic, and social life of Koreans. The reform touched on vital issues in various social practices and conventions, including those involving women. The existing social class system was totally eradicated.

In 1895 King Kojong issued an edict emphasizing the importance of education in preserving national sovereignty. Already in 1883, the first modern private school, Wŏnsan Haksa (Wŏnsan Academy), was founded in Wŏnsan, a port city whose residents wished to establish the school to meet the challenge from abroad. In 1886, American missionary organizations established private schools. Among these was Ewha Women's School, Korea's first educational institution for women. The zeal for education was quite high among the public at large, and many more schools for young women as well as for men were founded, responding to public interest in the education of the younger generation. The number of private schools reached some 3,000 before Korea became completely dominated by the Japanese.[29] These schools not only offered a Western curriculum but also became breeding grounds for the patriotic movement. At first the *yangban* were not interested in mass public education, especially for women. Thus, in the beginning, these private schools were attended mostly by children of non-*yangban* (including some Christian) families.

One of the most devastating effects of the failed March 1 Independence Movement of 1919 was a terrible sense of frustration, hopelessness, resignation, decadence, and escapism. Korean literature truly joined the modern era in this grim situation. Earlier writers engaging in "new literature" wrote didactic material with a politico-social agenda to enlighten the people with a view to the country's salvation. As the new "art for art's sake" trend started, a pathetic mood reigned as writers experimented with various types of realism and naturalism, inspired by European and American writers whose works in translation became increasingly available. Many of these writers went to study in Japan, and were also influenced by Japanese colleagues who were drawing upon Western examples. A handful of·women writers joined this group of writers, but much of their attention was given to the social issue of women's liberation. Bonnie B. C. Oh's chapter entitled "The Conflicting Worlds of Kim Iryŏp" is about one of these women, Kim Wŏnju. Kim Wŏnju is better known by the pen name Iryŏp (One Leaf) she used before joining the Buddhist order, rather than by Hayŏp (Lotus Leaf), her Buddhist name.

Kim Iryŏp (1896–1971) is well known in Korea, but remains an intriguing and controversial personage. Iryŏp is most unusual in that "her thinking, lifestyle, and personal conduct in the 1920s clearly verged on moral anarchism by the standards of her time, and perhaps even by those of today."[30] For many, Iryŏp was a revolutionary thinker and an activist who tried to elevate women's status in the arts and letters in the early years of Korean modernization.[31] Like two of her close contemporaries, Kim Myŏngsun and Na Hyesŏk, she was ridiculed and denounced by Korean society. It seemed as if they did a disservice to the true women's liberation movement by being such "bad" examples. However, unlike her colleagues, Kim Iryŏp eventually came to be at peace with herself and with those surrounding her. Kim Iryŏp sought and found a place for herself to make a difference in this world, which gave her renewed creative energy. The place she found was seemingly antithetical to her earlier life—one of total abstinence, calm, and meditation. However, even as a born-again Buddhist, she would not just seek her personal salvation. Unlike the usual Sŏn or Zen Buddhist, she continued to work for the multitude, especially the women, sacerdotal as well as lay.

Indeed Kim Iryŏp's life seems to lie in the confluence of two conflicting worlds. And yet, somehow, the two worlds are closely interconnected: It is as if her unhappy experiences and bold experimentation in her secular life were some kind of preparation for her reincarnation as a Buddhist cleric, karma of a sort. Bonnie Oh's essay introduces the basic nature of Kim Iryŏp's Buddhist thought and literary creativity. Iryŏp's joy and urge to spread her newly discovered faith were so strong that she continued to write even after becoming a cleric, violating her vow not to write after entering the monastery. She eventually secured a place of respect for herself, and in some sense for her depàrted colleagues who were not as fortunate.

It is true that women's status in general improved greatly over the years. Because mass education became available only rather recently in Korea even for men, women had equal opportunity in public education and voting from the start of the modern era. The word *suffragette* does not evoke any feeling among Koreans. Women's legal status also improved: Widows could remarry, and women could divorce their husbands. Economically, women took charge of household finances.

In practice, however, old habits die hard. An ideal woman was still a *hyŏnmo yangch'ŏ* (a wise mother and a good wife) whose place was at home. A sonless woman was still to be pitied, and inheritance law discriminated against women until very recently. Even after the law provided equal inheritance, people managed to override the principle by various means to maintain primogeniture or at least to usurp the daughters' inheritance. Furthermore, rule by the Japanese, in whose culture women were assigned a definitely inferior position, put an unfortunate brake on Korea's modernization as far as women were concerned. Traditionally, as noted before, noblemen used to address their wives with respect. However, even former aristocrats began to speak down to their wives in a way their ancestors did not, but more like the way Japanese husbands spoke to their wives. However, modern Korean women, equipped with modern education and with increased communication with the outside world, have come to participate in public affairs, except perhaps in the arena of politics and public finance, still viewed essentially as masculine spaces.

In this climate, a new profile of an ideal modern woman has emerged. Today the powerful Korean Housewives' Club annually chooses a woman of the year with a huge celebration in Tŏksu Palace in central Seoul. The award is named after the celebrated Sin Saimdang. The Sin Saimdang Award is given to "a professionally successful woman who is first and foremost a good mother and wife." In 1973 the Club chose as its fifth Sin Saimdang laureate Hahn Moo-Sook (Han Musuk, 1918–1993), a writer who had had a 30–year literary career while carrying out all her duties as an "exemplary" mother, wife, and daughter-in-law, considered still a difficult feat for a career woman to attain. Such an award might not necessarily have been viewed positively in the literary circles of the time, and might even have adversely affected her image in the general field of literature. However, such a goal is not unrelated to what Hahn tried to pursue in her life as a writer and as a person.

Yung-Hee Kim, in her chapter "Dialectics of Life: Hahn Moo-Sook and Her Literary World," examines how Hahn Moo-Sook's views of life and human existence are articulated in three of her narrative works.

Kim identifies Hahn as a perceptive literary mediator, who sought harmony and balance between contrasting forces, seeing human existence in terms of "dialectic interactions of [these] seemingly binary opposites" (p. 196). Kim adds that the distinguishing hallmark of Hahn Moo-Sook is her acute awareness of the enduring presence of Korean traditional culture which operates in the lives of modern Koreans. Hahn, viewing Korean culture as threatened with extinction, seems to have devoted her energy to its preservation, along with the national language, affirming and fostering a literature consonant with the modern Korean history.

Many critics agree with Yung-Hee Kim who observes that Hahn's works are informed by "the need for negotiating a felicitous balance between tradition and change, past and present, each illuminating the other rather than negating each other." Her "eclecticism or integrative stance," however, "is not limited simply to Hahn's embracing of the indigenous and foreign cultural traditions. It extends to many other areas of concerns in her works, which deal with different conceptual dyads such as love/hate, joy/sorrow, happiness/misery, the sacred/the profane, transgression/redemption, past/present, life/death" (p. 195). Life's meaning is in "accepting, and ultimately celebrating them as interlocked and integral parts of human existence" (p. 196).

Yung-Hee Kim's critical framework is helpful for understanding the way in which the binary opposites of rationality and spirituality are resolved in the figures of Tasan and his nephew Hasang in Hahn's novel *Encounter*, according to JaHyun Kim Haboush.[32] Haboush then proposes an interesting analysis of Tasan's progression from Confucian rationality to Catholic spirituality, noting: "Confucianism, which represents rationality, is in this sense affirmed as a preparatory stage for modernity rather than rejected as a past to be overcome."[33] Don Baker also supports Yung-Hee Kim's critical apparatus, observing how Hahn "accommodates the Western concept of sin within a dialectic of binary opposites provided by Korean tradition," often with an "explicit presentation of the complementary nature and interchangeability of sin and sanctity."[34] Popular writer Ch'oe Inho offers a similar comment about Hahn's motivation in writing *Encounter*. Ch'oe says, "In meeting her God who dwelled deep in the abyss of her heart, she [Hahn Moo-Sook] made an apology for her own human weaknesses through the character of Chŏng Yagyong, while expressing her passionate fervor for God through the martyrdom of his nephew Chŏng Hasang."[35]

A remark by Hahn Moo-Sook herself seems to support Yung-Hee Kim's critical device. In the epilogue to the Korean original of *Encounter*, she wrote:

> This gigantic but lonely soul [Tasan Chŏng Yagyong], paradoxical and impregnated with human weaknesses, has long captivated me. His very human faults and trespasses came to move me just as deeply as his greatness. Another personage that I have adored is Tasan's nephew, St. Paul Chŏng Hasang, who unlike Tasan trod the road of unwavering faith, for which he willingly sacrificed his life. St. Paul Hasang's immaculate life has always cleansed my soul. These two souls, contrasting as they are, have filled my heart, one just as dearly as the other . . . (translation, Young-Key Kim-Renaud)

Ironically, it was not her meeting with the West but her arranged marriage into an archconservative Korean family that shocked her the most. What really struck her, however, was her discovery that the differences she observed were only superficial, and that the two families shared the same, deep-rooted cultural values. Her Korean sense of identity, grown faint after years of Japanese schooling, now solidified. Silently but forcefully she said to herself, "I want to write!"

It is such creative urges that inspired the women discussed in this book. The creativity manifested by these women is varied in the themes, style, spirit, and messages they convey, in spite of the limited quantity of their works in comparison with men's. Through these sparks of creativity, we have a glimpse of the fire that has been burning within, the fire that has warmed our hearts and bodies, the fire that has made our nourishment, the fire that has brightened our paths, the fire that has given birth to many other sparks still to be discovered and to be studied.

Special circumstances have enabled each of these women to occupy a visible space. Even though the goal of this book is not to essentialize what Korean women were or are, there is a certain pattern that all the creative women of Korea show. Traditionally they have considered *han'gŭl* their own writing system, enabling them to express themselves more freely than men with their Chinese. They all speak from their heart and with confidence. Their works manifest self-assurance and enjoyment in innovative work; all have endeavored to be different from ordinary beings, all the while pursuing "authenticity." Far from being passive and pessimistic about the societal norms that constrained women, they have a clear sense of themselves, and each occupies a clear space in the life of family and society. They are strong.

As mentioned before, this book is rather limited in its scope in that almost all the women discussed are from the aristocratic *yangban* class. Because professional artists were viewed as artisans and craftsmen and given low status, especially in Confucian Korea,[36] most women's works have gone unnoticed and often are completely lost. Such is the case particularly for lower-class women. Because of the easy Korean writing system, however, there must have been at least some lower-class women who wrote and made beautiful objects. We really know very little about commoners' lives and their creative activities. Therefore, sparks to be studied more seriously include songs and tales handed down to us through *p'ansori* singers, *kisaeng*, shamans, beggars, grandmothers, and children, as well as those material and spiritual objects that have embellished our lives but that we have taken for granted, because they are such an integral part of our lives—like *pojagi*. From what little is visible, one notices a strong vitality and creativity in the works of marginalized people, too. They are beyond the realm of this book, but they certainly demand their own space.

Notes

1. Kendall and Peterson, *Korean Women*, 5.

2. Mattielli, *Virtues in Conflict*, ix; Chung, *A Korean Confucian Encounter with the Modern World*, 182–83.

3. Woolf, *A Room of One's Own*.

4. However, more recent scholarship (for example, Haboush, "Gender and the Politics of Language in Chosŏn Korea"), suggests that women have played an important role even in the latter part of the Chosŏn dynasty, departing from what was previously proposed.

5. Hong and Kim, "King Sejong's Contribution to Medicine," 103–10. A Chosŏn dynasty official, Hŏ To, wrote on March 15, 1406, "Ladies, who beget an illness, are shamed to consult with a doctor, which leads to death in extreme cases. Therefore, if dozens of girls are educated about acupuncture and examination for ladies, they will

greatly help their cure." Hŏ's proposal was apparently accepted and the female-doctor institution was created (Yang Sung-jin, http://english.gija.com/click17.htm).

6. Deuchler, *The Confucian Transformation of Korea*, 25.

7. Deuchler, "Rites in Early Chosŏn Korea," 38.

8. Hŏ Kyun's authorship of *Hong Kiltong chŏn* is seriously questioned by such scholars as Paik in "Kososŏl Hong Kiltong chŏn ŭi chojag-e taehan chae kŏmt'o," 307–31. Most scholars, however, agree with Kim, in *Chosŏn Sosŏlsa*, 70–82, who first proposed it. These scholars give as evidence a statement left by a near contemporary Yi Shik (1584–1647), who commented that Hŏ Kyun wrote the novel emulating the Chinese *Shui Hu Zhuan* (Tale of the Water Margin), which he supposedly admired (Paik, 310).

9. See, for example, Deuchler, *The Confucian Transformation of Korea*; Kendall and Peterson, *Korean Women*.

10. Ko, *Teachers of the Inner Chambers*, 11.

11. Ibid.

12. Lee, Introduction to *The Traditional Culture and Society of Korea*, 3.

13. Jones, "The Power of Reading," 175. As Sonja Häußler [personal communication] notes, this statement probably should not be limited to the eighteenth century, because the same could already be said about the medieval age in Europe.

14. The Korean morpheme *amh-* is a biological term meaning "female," usually referring to animals.

15. Which year depends on how the date is calculated according to the Western calendar.

16. See, for example, Ledyard, *The Korean Language Reform of 1446*, 131, and Ramsey, "The Korean Alphabet," 49.

17. Haboush, "Women's Education," 46.

18. We now know from recent studies that uxorilocal residence among well-to-do women of the yangban class was not so unusual during her lifetime.

19. As Sonja Häußler [personal communication] notes, 10,000 was a symbolic number for the expression of "many" in East Asia and should not be taken literally.

20. See, for example Hŏ, *Han'gug yŏryu munhangnon: kojŏnp'yŏn*, 52.

21. McCann, "Formal and Informal Society," 134.

22. For example, most of about ninety poems left by Xue Tao, one of the two most distinguished women poets of the Tang dynasty, are love poems addressed to her male patrons in their absence, or occasional poems celebrating their brief unions, and many critics apparently dismiss her poetry as mere erotic and occasional verse of no significance. See Nienhauser, *The Indiana Companion to Traditional Chinese Literature*, 439. I am indebted to Jonathan Chaves for this reference.

23. In his chapter, Kevin O'Rourke refers to Hwang Chini as "Chini." Widely used in the popular literature, this appellation evinces the kind of affection Koreans feel toward her. Her low social status might also have something to do with the usage of the given name, which is a condescending term of reference in Korean. However, "Chini" seems merely to be perceived or transformed as a kind of pen name by many literary critiques.

24. Lady Hyegyŏng wrote four memoirs, together known as *Hanjungnok* (Records Written in Silence) or *Hanjungmallok* (Memoirs Written in Silence), at separate occasions for different purposes, from 1795 to 1805, the last one at the age of seventy. The most recent and acclaimed translation appeared in a book by Haboush,

The Memoirs of Lady Hyegyŏng, 1996. Other translations include Grant and Kim, *Han Joong Nok*, and Choi-Wall, *Memoirs of a Korean Queen*.

25. See Chŏng, Pyŏng'uk, and Yi Ŏyŏng, *Kojŏn ŭi pada*, 321.

26. See Kim-Renaud, *The Korean Alphabet*.

27. Expression used by Kongdan Oh when she commented on Häußler's paper during the 1998 GW-HMS Conference, "Sparks of Creativity: Women in the Korean Humanities."

28. See Lee, tr., Wagner with Shultz, *The New History of Korea*.

29. Lee, *The New History of Korea*, 332.

30. Commentary on Bonnie Oh's paper made by Yung-Hee Kim during the 1998 GW-HMS Conference, "Sparks of Creativity: Women in the Korean Humanities."

31. Commentary on Bonnie Oh's paper made by Kongdan Oh during the 1998 GW-HMS Conference, "Sparks of Creativity: Women in the Korean Humanities."

32. Hahn, *Encounter*.

33. For a discussion of *Encounter*, see Haboush, "In Search of HISTORY in Democratic Korea," 189–214.

34. Commentary on Yung-Hee Kim's presentation made by Don Baker during the 1998 GW-HMS Conference, "Sparks of Creativity: Women in the Korean Humanities."

35. Ch'oe In-ho, "Literature as Encounter and Discovery," 3.

36. Lee, *Introduction to The Traditional Culture and Society of Korea*, 11.

References

Ch'oe In-ho. "Literature as Encounter and Discovery, as exemplified by Hahn Moo-Sook's novel *Encounter*." In *Creation and Re-Creation: Modern Korean Fiction and Its Translation*, Young-Key Kim-Renaud and R. Richard Grinker, eds. *The Sigur Center Asia Papers* 8 (Washington, DC: The George Washington University, 2000), 1–4.

Choi-Wall, Yang-hi, ed., tr., and introduction to *Memoirs of a Korean Queen*. London: KPI, 1985.

Chŏng, Pyŏng'uk, and Yi Ŏyŏng. *Kojŏn ŭi pada* (The Sea of Classics) Seoul: Hyŏnamsa, 1977.

Chung, Chai-sik. *A Korean Confucian Encounter with the Modern World: Yi Hang-no and the West*. Berkeley, CA: U.C. Berkeley Institute of East Asian Studies, Center for Korean Studies, 1995.

Deuchler, Martina. *The Confucian Transformation of Korea: A Study of Society and Ideology*. Cambridge, MA: Council on East Asian Studies, Harvard University, 1992.

———. "Rites in Early Chosŏn Korea." In Kim-Renaud 1992/97: 35–40.

Grant, Bruce K. and Kim Chin-man, trans. *Han Joong Nok: Reminiscences in Retirement*. Larchmont, NY: Larchwood, 1980.

Haboush, JaHyun Kim. *The Memoirs of Lady Hyegyŏng: The Autobiographic Writings of a Crown Princess of Eighteenth-Century Korea*. Berkeley and Los Angeles: University of California Press, 1996.

———. "Gender and the Politics of Language in Chosŏn Korea" (paper presented at the conference "Rethinking East Asia: Gender, the Body and Confucianism," UCLA, April 25, 1999).

————. "Women's Education." In *Sources of Korean Tradition, Volume II: From the Sixteenth to the Twentieth Centuries*, 2d ed., edited by Yong-ho Ch'oe, Peter H. Lee, and Wm. Theodore de Bary. New York: Columbia University Press, 2000, 46–60.

————. "In Search of HISTORY in Democratic Korea: The Discourse of Modernity in Contemporary Historical Fiction." In *Constructing Nationhood in Modern East Asia*, edited by Kai-wing Chow, Kevin M. Doak, and Poshek Fu. Ann Arbor: University of Michigan Press, 2001, 189–214.

Hahn, Moo-Sook. *Encounter*, a novel translated from the Korean original entitled *Mannam* by Ok Young Kim Chang. Berkeley: University of California Press, 1992.

Hŏ, Mija. *Han'gugyŏryu munhangnon: kojŏnp'yŏn* (Study of Korean Women Writers: Classical Era). Seoul: Sŏngshin Woman's University Press, 1991.

Hong, Wŏn Sik, and Quae Jung Kim. "King Sejong's Contribution to Medicine." In Kim-Renaud 1992/97, 103–10.

Jones, Sumie. "The Power of Reading: Women and the Postmodern in Eighteenth-Century Literature." *Asian Women* 8 (1999): 165–76.

Kendall, Laurel, and Mark Peterson, eds. *Korean Women: View from the Inner Room*. New Haven, CT: East Rock Press, 1983.

Kim T'aejun. *Chosŏn Sosŏlsa* (The History of Fiction in the Chosŏn Dynasty). Seoul: Hagyesa, 1939.

Kim-Renaud, Young-Key. *King Sejong the Great: The Light of Fifteenth-Century Korea*. Washington, DC: International Circle of Korean Linguistics, 1992/97.

————, ed. *The Korean Alphabet: Its History and Structure*. Honolulu: University of Hawaii Press, 1997.

Ko, Dorothy. *Teachers of the Inner Chambers: Women and Culture in Seventeenth-Century China*. Stanford, CA: Stanford University Press, 1994.

Ledyard, Gari. *The Korean Language Reform of 1446*. Seoul: Shin'gu Munhwasa, 1998.

Lee, Ki-baek, trans., Edward W. Wagner with Edward J. Shultz. *The New History of Korea*. Cambridge, MA: Harvard University Press, 1984.

Lee, Peter H., ed. Introduction to *The Traditional Culture and Society of Korea: Art and Literature*. Occasional papers 4:1–14. Honolulu: The Center for Korean Studies, 1975.

Mattielli, Sandra, ed. *Virtues in Conflict: Tradition and the Korean Woman Today.* Seoul: The Royal Asiatic Society, Korea Branch, 1997.

McCann, David R. "Formal and Informal Society: A Reading of Kisaeng Songs." In Kendall and Peterson, 129–37.

Nienhauser, William H., Jr., comp. and ed. *The Indiana Companion to Traditional Chinese Literature*, vol. I. Bloomington: Indiana University Press, 1985.

Paik, Sungjong. "Kososŏl Hong Kiltong chon ŭi chojag-e taehan chae kŏmt'o" (Fabrication of Ancient Novel *Hong Kiltong chŏn* Revisited). *Chindan hakpo* 80 (1995): 307–31.

Peterson, Mark A. *Korean Adoption and Inheritance: Case Studies in the Creation of a Classic Confucian Society.* Ithaca, NY: Cornell University East Asia Program, 1996.

Ramsey, S. Robert. "The Korean Alphabet." In Kim-Renaud, 1992/97, 41–50.

Woolf, Virginia. *A Room of One's Own*. London: Hogarth, 1929.

2

The *Naehun* and the Politics of Gender in Fifteenth-Century Korea

John Duncan

Introduction

The *Naehun* (Instructions for Women), compiled in 1475 by Queen Sohye (1437–1504), is a morality handbook composed of mostly selections taken from various Confucian sources and accompanied by translations into vernacular Korean. The *Naehun*, with the exception of a few pieces of poetry, is the oldest known surviving work by a woman writer in Korea. However, it has attracted little scholarly attention, getting only passing mention in works dealing with women's and social history of the Chosŏn period.[1] It has been examined by at least one historical linguist interested in what it can tell us about women's language in early Chosŏn Korea,[2] as well as by a few scholars concerned with the effects of Confucian social values on women's status.[3] But the *Naehun* has been almost totally ignored by mainstream historians preoccupied with the male, public realm depicted in official histories. Even those few scholars who have looked at the *Naehun* have tended to use it to demonstrate how Confucianism segregated and oppressed women.

There is no reason to doubt that Confucianism played a part in the way which Chosŏn women were increasingly excluded from public life and, by the seventeenth century, deprived of many privileges—including inheritance of property and participation in ritual—they had enjoyed in earlier times.[4] However, what is problematic is the way in which women have often been depicted as simply objects, victims with no voice of their own. A recent study of elite woman in premodern China pointed out the dangers in the tendency among Westernizing modernizers, beginning with the May Fourth movement, to accept normative prescriptions for female behavior as accurate descriptions of premodern social reality. It also showed how some Ming dynasty women, a privileged group of an educated elite, were able to exercise agency within the Confucian gender system to further their perceived interests.[5]

From the time Korea "opened" itself to direct Western influence in the late nineteenth century, observers have presented contradictory images of Korean women: Korean women were often depicted as victims, as the "wretched and deprived product of oppressive patriarchy," while at the same time being portrayed as forceful, outspoken, and more capable than the men who were their nominal superiors.[6] This polarity in views of women in Korea has continued to the present day. Some scholars continue to stress the way women have been oppressed and to assign to Confucianism a primary role in that oppression;[7] others, while recognizing the strictures of Confucian gender roles, have sought to show how the Confucian system allows women some degree of authority within the family.[8] A recent study shows how elite Chosŏn-era women were indoctrinated in a "painful process of adjustment" to their deprivation by the new social mores of much of the economic security and social prestige they had previously enjoyed—nonetheless, they continued to receive some degree of education and to exercise considerable authority as stewards of family affairs.[9] What I hope to do in this examination of Queen Sohye and the *Naehun* is to explore how elite women of the Chosŏn period sought, within the strictures of the Confucian gender system, to define a space wherein they could play meaningful social, cultural, and political roles.

The circumstances surrounding the publication of the *Naehun* were exceedingly complex. In society at large, the legislative campaign to transform Korea into a patrilineal society, which began with the founding of the Chosŏn nearly a hundred years earlier, gained new momentum after Queen Sohye's son, Sŏngjong (r. 1469–95), took the throne and featured, among other things, a new emphasis on the seclusion of women and the ideal of *yŏllyŏ* (the chaste woman). At the same time, however, supreme political authority in Korea was in the hands of a woman, Queen Chŏnghŭi (Sejo's primary consort), mother of King Yejong (r. 1468–69) and grandmother of Sŏngjong, who acted as regent during the first seven years of Sŏngjong's reign. At court, there was an ongoing controversy over the relative status of Yejong's primary consort—Queen Ansun—and Queen Sohye, while within the palace there was growing tension over the selection of a primary consort for Sŏngjong, a choice with important political considerations for the state as well as for the inner palace. It is clear, therefore, that any attempt to gauge the historical significance of the *Naehun* will have to consider its relationship to a variety of larger societal and political issues as well as to a number of more immediate concerns of the inner palace and royal household.

My essay attacks the problem of understanding what kind of agency Queen Sohye could have employed, and how she could have employed it, by following the approach of the French sociologist Pierre Bourdieu. Bourdieu, who is clearly aware of the way that conventional rationalist, or objectivist, explanations reduce human behavior to the mechanistic application of rules, strives to maintain a socially grounded understanding of practical actions by arguing that all individuals have a set of dispositions, or habitus, that inclines them to act in certain ways. These dispositions are inculcated through training and education from childhood; structured in ways that reflect social conditions; ingrained, preconscious, and lasting; and generative and transposable, that is, capable of generating a multiplicity of practices and perceptions in various contexts. Habitus, which gives individuals a "feel for the game," is not just a state of mind but rather more a question of how the body is deployed in postures, gestures, and ways of speaking. Bourdieu contends that actions always take place in specific social contexts, and thus they must be seen as interactions between habit and social contexts, or "fields." He defines a "field" as a structured space of positions within which individuals seek to deploy various kinds of social, political, cultural, and linguistic resources, or "capital," in order to enhance their relative status or position within that field.[10] My purpose here is to construct an understanding of what kind of habitus Sohye might have had, what her relative position was in various fields, and how she sought to deploy her not inconsiderable resources in those fields.

Text and Author

The Text

The *Naehun* is composed of Queen Sohye's preface, an epilogue by Cho ssi, another royal consort, and seven chapters: "Speech and Comportment"; "Filial Piety"; "Marriage"; "Husband and Wife"; "Motherhood"; "Amiability"; and "Thrift." In her preface, Sohye tells us that the *Naehun* is made up of selections from four basic Confucian primers: the *Nüjiao* (K. *Yŏgyo*, "Teachings for Women"); the Lienü (K. *Yŏllyŏ*, "Faithful Women"); the *Xiaoxue* (K. *Sohak*, "Lesser Learning"); and the *Mingjian* (K. *Myŏnggam*; presumably, the *Mingxin baojian*, "Precious Mirror for Illuminating the Mind"). The *Naehun* also includes occasional brief comments by Sohye herself. The chapter "Husband and Wife," which features some lengthy discussions of Chinese empresses, is the longest, accounting for nearly half the entire text; other comparatively long chapters include "Speech and Comportment" and "Motherhood." The last two chapters, "Amiability" and "Thrift," are the shortest.

Three versions of the *Naehun* are still extant. The original appears to have been lost; the oldest surviving version is in the Hosabunko in Nagoya, Japan, thought to have been printed in the mid-sixteenth century and taken to Japan at the time of Hideyoshi's invasions near the end of that century.[11] The second oldest is the 1611 version housed at Seoul National University's Kyujanggak; and the third version was printed in 1736. Although all three versions contain the same seven chapters, the number of *kwŏn* (fascicles/volume), the proportion of Chinese characters to vernacular script, and the orthography of the vernacular script vary from one to the next. In all three versions the preface and the epilogue are written in literary Chinese. The absence of the original makes it impossible to do a close linguistic analysis of the text as Sohye prepared it; the consensus of modern scholars is that the seven chapters were written in Chinese and translated into vernacular Korean.

The publication of Queen Sohye's *Naehun* came several decades after the publication of a text by the same name (*Neixun*, in Chinese) by Wen Huanghou (d. 1407), consort of Emperor Chengzu, of the Ming dynasty. The timing, the use of the same title, and the lengthy discussion Sohye devotes in the chapter on husband and wife to imperial consort Gao Huanghou (d. 1382), consort of Ming Taizu, whose teachings Wen Huanghou compiled in her *Neixun*, all suggest that Sohye may have been influenced by the Ming text. A comparison between the organization and the content of the two, however, suggests little direct connection. Whereas the *Naehun* is made up of seven chapters, some quite long, the *Neixun* is composed of no fewer than twenty chapters, all quite brief.

Whereas the *Naehun* begins with a practically oriented chapter on "Language and Comportment," the *Neixun* starts off with philosophically oriented chapters on moral nature (*dexing*, K. *tŏksŏng*) and self-cultivation, before taking up such mundane issues as language, comportment, and frugality. Furthermore, although Sohye draws from a wide range of Chinese texts for the *Naehun*, not once does she quote from, or even mention, the *Neixun*. Sohye may have been aware of the *Neixun*, and may even have been inspired to name her work after it, but it is clear that she did not model her text after that of Wen Huanghou. Rather, Sohye most likely had her own set of concerns when compiling the *Naehun*, concerns derived from the social, political, and cultural context of late-fifteenth-century Korea.

This becomes even more evident when we compare the prefaces of the two works. Wen Huanghou begins her preface:

> Boys begin studying the Lesser Learning at eight and girls learn from women teachers at ten. We do not have a complete text for teaching women, even though texts for teaching women have recently become popular.
>
> These texts mostly use the *Zhouli* and the *Neize*,[12] poetry, and biographies.
>
> I think the teachings of our Gao Huanghou are much better, so I have compiled them to teach the women of the court.[13]

Wen Huanghou then explains the sequence of her twenty chapters, saying that fostering moral nature and cultivating the self are taken up in the first two chapters because they are the most important virtues. She then states that language and comportment are taken up in the third and fourth chapters because they are central to cultivation of the self; she continues with a similar process of linkage for the remaining sixteen chapters. Nowhere in her preface does she take up such issues as the specific roles of women or the reasons for the importance of women's education.

Sohye starts off her preface with a statement that echoes Wen Huanghou's emphasis on self-cultivation, but then moves into a discussion of the important roles women play and of the need for educating women:

> All persons at birth receive the spirit of Heaven and Earth, and all are endowed with the virtues of the Five Relations. There is no difference in the principle of jade and stone, but yet how is it that orchids and mugwort differ? It depends on whether one has done one's utmost in fulfilling the Way of cultivating the self. The civilizing transformation of King Wen of Zhou was enhanced and broadened by the brightness of his consort Taisi and the hegemony enjoyed by King Zhuang of Chu was largely due to the efforts of his consort Fanji; who could do more to serve her king or her husband? The order and disorder, the rise and fall of a country are related to the wisdom and ignorance of men, but are also closely tied to the goodness and badness of women, so women must be taught.
>
> Generally, the minds of men move amid the broad flowing power and they develop their will from mysterious sources so that they can, on their own, distinguish between right and wrong and sustain themselves; how could they possibly wait for my teachings before acting? Women, however, are different. They know only the thickness and thinness of thread and do not know the urgency of virtuous action; this is my constant regret. Also, a person with even an originally clear nature who has not seen the teachings of the sages will, if elevated to high station, be like a monkey wearing a crown or a person standing in front of a wall. Such a person will find it difficult to behave appropriately or speak properly. . . .
>
> The great sages Yao and Shun each had sons, Danju and Shangjun, repectively. Despite the teachings of their strict fathers, Danju and Shangjun did not become good sons. Yet I, a widow, hope to have a daughter-in-law with a mind like jade. Thus, although there are texts— such as the *Sohak, Yŏllyŏ, Yŏgyo,* and *Myŏnggam*—which are highly appropriate and clear, they contain too many fascicles and would be hard to master, so I have chosen important passages from those four texts and written the seven chapters which I give to you. Ah, the learning of one body is all here. Once you lose the Way, you may repent but how can you recover? Inscribe these teachings in your hearts, engrave them on your bones and strive everyday to follow the sages. A bright mirror has great luster; how can you not take heed?[14]

In contrast to Wen Huanghou's somewhat narrow and cautious preface, Sohye here expresses a strong sense of the importance of women in

the realms of society, culture, and politics, accompanied by an unequivo-
cal assertion of the need to educate women so that they may fulfill their
proper roles in the Confucian scheme of things. Although Sohye does
seem to describe a secondary role for women, the forcefulness of her
statement about the importance of women and women's education runs
counter to the popular image derived largely from normative models of
the late Chosŏn period, of *yangban* women as passive, oppressed, and
retiring. It is also clear from the preface, however, that Sohye's concerns were not limited to the larger issue of constructing a positive
sociopolitical role for women within the Confucian model of gender
relations. Her reference, for example, to what she hoped for in a daughter-in-law suggests that she also had more immediate domestic concerns, as well. Thus a reading of the *Naehun* should take into
consideration its status as a text that was put into play in more than one
field and for more than one reason.

The Author

Key to constructing an interpretation of Queen Sohye's purposes in publishing the *Naehun* is an understanding of her background and the positions she occupied in various fields. Let me begin with Sohye's childhood.
It is almost certain that she was born and raised in the capital. Her family, as is discussed below, had a history of providing royal and imperial
consorts, so it is likely that she received an early, and thorough, indoctrination in Confucian behavioral norms; indeed, we are told that King
Sejo praised her as a filial daughter-in-law (*hyobu*).[15] How she obtained
her familiarity with the classics and her literacy in classical Chinese is
not known, but it is probable that she—like many other literate women
of the Chosŏn—learned the basics alongside her brothers (given her
family's scholarly traditions and the fact that she was raised in a household with three brothers.) At any rate, after she entered the palace, she
became known for her intense devotion to the education of the royal grandsons,[16] which suggests that she may have gotten a strong sense of the
importance of education from her upbringing. This leaves us with a picture, admittedly sketchy, of a young woman in whom were inculcated
Confucian notions of proper comportment and respect for education.

Concerning her social standing. Queen Sohye was a daughter of the
Ch'ŏngju Han, an aristocratic descent group that had placed male members in high offices generation after generation since the mid-thirteenth

century and that ranked among the most prominent *yangban* families of the early Chosŏn.[17] The Ch'ŏngju Han's fortunes waxed even stronger after Sejo (r. 1455–68) took the throne. Three Han men were made merit subjects by Sejo, including Sohye's father, Han Hwak (1403–1456), and her third cousins, Han Myŏnghoe and Han Myŏngjin. Han Hwak and Han Myŏnghoe both held positions at the highest level of the dynastic government; so did Sohye's three brothers, Han Ch'iin, Han Ch'irye, and Han Ch'iŭi; her first cousin, Han Ch'ihyŏng; and her third cousin, Han Paengnyun.

The family's prestige was further enhanced by its status as provider of imperial consorts: Two of Han Hwak's sisters (Sohye's aunts) were selected as consorts for the Ming emperor Chengzu. Also, Sohye was only one of four Ch'ŏngju Han women chosen as consorts for Chosŏn kings and crown princes in the second half of the fifteenth century. Sohye herself was consort to Sejo's eldest son and crown prince, known posthumously as Tŏkchong (Yi Chang, 1438–1457), who died before he could take the throne. Two of Han Myŏnghoe's daughters, Queens Changsun (1445–1461) and Konghye (1456–1474), were consorts to Kings Yejong and Sŏngjong, respectively, while Han Paengnyun's daughter, Queen Ansun (?–1498), was a consort to Yejong.

Sohye's maternal kin were equally illustrious. Her mother was a daughter of the Namyang Hong, another old aristocratic descent group that traced its presence in the central bureaucracy back to the eleventh century and was among the two or three most prominent descent groups of the late Koryŏ period. Among the late Koryŏ members of the Hong was Queen Myŏngdŏk (Myŏngdŏk *wanghu*), who, as the mother of King Kongmin (r. 1351–74), participated actively and openly in court politics from Kongmin's ascension up to the time of her death in 1380.[18] Although the Namyang Hong suffered some diminution of their political power in the waning years of the Koryŏ, by the mid-fifteenth century they had made a strong recovery and had several members in high office, including such merit subjects and state councilors as Hong Ŭng and Hong Kyŏngson. In short, in an aristocratic society such as the fifteenth-century Chosŏn, Queen Sohye's family, with its illustrious ancestors and highly placed officials as well as its links with the Ming imperial court, provided her with a strong relative position in the field of society.

This position was undoubtedly enhanced by Sohye's selection as a royal consort. It is not clear when Sohye first entered the palace, but a

Sillok (Veritable Records) entry from 1453 shows Han Hwak referring to himself as father-in-law to Prince Towŏn (title held by Tŏkchong before he was named crown prince).[19] In 1454, she bore a son, Prince Wŏlsan. In 1455, after Sejo became king, Prince Towŏn was elevated to crown prince and she was named his primary consort (*seja pin*).[20] Subsequently, Sohye had a daughter (Princess Myŏngsuk, ?–1482) and another son, Prince Chasan (Sŏngjong, 1457–1495). Thus, by the age of twenty, Sohye had attained, as the primary consort of the crown prince and the mother of two royal grandsons, a strong position in the inner palace.

Two months after the birth of her second son, however, Sohye's husband died and his younger brother, Yejong, became the new crown prince. Although this turn of events meant that Sohye would never become the queen of a reigning king, she remained a personal favorite of King Sejo, who entrusted her with the care of the new crown prince, Yejong.[21]

After Yejong died without leaving an heir, her son Sŏngjong took the throne. The next year her husband was enshrined as a deceased king under the funerary name Tŏkchong, and she received the title of *Insu wangbi* (Queen Insu).[22] Five years later her title was changed to Insu *taebi* (Queen Dowager Insu), a title more commensurate with her official status as the primary consort of a deceased king.[23] After the death of King Sŏngjong, her title was changed to Insu *taewang taebi* (Grand Queen Dowager Insu),[24] and finally, after her own death in 1504, she was given the title Sohye *wanghu* ("deceased" Queen Sohye). Although these titles may seem, to the casual observer, to be empty formalities, they can also be seen as indicators of Sohye's relatively strong position in the inner palace at a time when, as is discussed below, the inner palace exercised considerable political authority.

Queen Sohye had many resources, or capital, which she could employ. Her aristocratic family background gave her no small amount of social capital; her several close male relatives in high office, as well as her position in the inner palace, gave her a great deal of potential political capital; and her status as royal consort/queen and as mother of King Sŏngjong gave her a great deal of symbolic capital. But these kinds of resources were not unique to Sohye; most other royal consorts came from similar backgrounds and some were also mothers of kings. Queen Chŏnghŭi, for example, was a daughter of the P'ap'yŏng Yun, a descent group with a history as illustrious and a political presence just as strong as the Ch'ŏngju Han; Chŏnghŭi was the primary consort of Sejo, the mother of Yejong, and the grandmother of Sŏngjong. What set Sohye apart from the other consorts was her knowledge of the Confucian classics and her literacy in classical Chinese. In other words, even as a woman she had social, political, and cultural capital equivalent to the elite males of her time. In the remainder of this essay, I try to show how she was able to deploy this capital in various fields from her particular relative position as a woman. In the process I hope to show how she exercised certain kinds of agency as a woman and to contribute to the effort to correct the widely held perception of Chosŏn-era women as passive victims.

The *Naehun* and the Politics of Gender

The time when Queen Sohye compiled the *Naehun* was a complex period in the Chosŏn dynasty's political history. Conventional, male-centered political and social histories focus almost exclusively on the building conflict between the meritorious subjects (*hun'gu*) and the rusticated literati (*sarim*) or on institutional conflict between the State Council and the censoring bodies.[25] Rarely do these histories touch on issues related to women except insofar as they are deemed relevant to the political struggles being waged among male protagonists. This is, of course, a reflection of the Confucian bias of the historical sources, but it is also a result of the widely held notion that women, and particularly the women of the Chosŏn dynasty, were powerless private creatures excluded from any meaningful participation in politics, which itself was understood as a public, male-dominated realm. What I hope to do here is to bring issues of gender back into the political history of the early Chosŏn and, at the same time, to show, through Sohye, how women could pursue their own interests within the admittedly limiting strictures of the Confucian system. I will achieve this through an examination of Sohye and the *Naehun* in relation to such issues as the seven-year (1469–76) regency by Queen Chŏnghŭi, linguistic practices related to classical Chinese versus the vernacular script, and the renewed oppression of Buddhism during Sŏngjong's reign.

The Regency

The regency of Queen Chŏnghŭi was the first of five instances of formal regency by queens dowager in the Chosŏn; the others were those of Queen Munjŏng (eight years for King Myŏngjong, 1545–53), Queen Insun (one year for King Sŏnjo, 1567–68), Queen Chŏngsun (four years for King Sunjo, 1800–4), and Queen Sunwŏn (two years for King Ch'ŏlchong, 1849–51). Thus it provides us with a rare opportunity to see women openly involved in the political decision-making process.

Shortly before he died, Sejo, who had seized the throne from his nephew Tanjong and who was undoubtedly worried about ensuring his own posterity, began to make preparations for handing the throne over to his son Yejong. One thing he did was to select a number of high-ranking officials from the Royal Secretariat (*Sŭngjŏngwŏn*), known collectively as the *wŏnsang*, to act as advisers and protectors for his successor. When Yejong died without an heir in the eleventh month of 1169, it fell to Queen Chŏnghŭi to select a successor. When she named the twelve-year-old Sŏngjong the new king, the *wŏnsang* asked her to act as regent until the young king was old enough to handle affairs himself. Chŏnghŭi demurred, but the *wŏnsang* persisted until she finally agreed.[26] It was determined that, although the young king was to hear court affairs on a regular basis, no decisions were to be put into effect until they were approved by Queen Chŏnghŭi.[27]

Although Chŏnghŭi remained regent for seven years, one would hardly know it from looking at the *Sillok*. There are only eighteen instances during those seven years in which Chŏnghŭi was identified as the decision-maker on issues other than those concerned with affairs of the inner palace or royal family where, as the senior female, she would be expected to have some say.[28] Nonetheless, those eighteen instances, covering such issues as litigation regarding the ownership of lands and people,[29] personnel decisions,[30] border defense,[31] and construction projects,[32] serve to remind us that it was she who had the final say on policy decisions. By omitting reference to Chŏnghŭi's role in day-to-day governance, the *Sillok*, and presumably the daily court records from which it was compiled, appear to minimize, if not disguise, the role that Chŏnghŭi played in the political decision-making process.

This sense of deliberate elision is strengthened when we consider the issue of language. Although Chŏnghŭi was not literate in classical Chinese, all her edicts during her regency are presented in the sources in classical Chinese. It was only when she decided to step down as regent that the *Sillok* states that her instruction was written in vernacular Korean (*ŏnmun*). As JaHyun Kim Haboush argues, this in effect means that "by presenting her as another Chinese-writing person amidst Chinese-writing males, the *Sillok* degenders and depowers her. She is allowed to enter into the public space of the all male court but in the guise of a male with no real power. Only when she leaves this space, is she re-gendered through the restoration of her language."³³ In short, what we have is a picture of a court and a government that were extremely uncomfortable with the idea that a woman could, or should, play a public role in the political process.

What does all this mean for Queen Sohye? Although Chŏnghŭi, as the senior woman in the palace, was chosen to be regent for Sŏngjong, Sohye was Sŏngjong's mother. It can be surmised, therefore, that Sohye had some influence on Sŏngjong's decision-making. Given the way that the *Sillok* almost completely effaced Chŏnghŭi's role as formal regent, it is highly unlikely that it would have depicted Sohye as exercising any political authority. That she did, however, is suggested by one *Sillok* entry from 1474 (the fifth year of Sŏngjong's reign) where some high-ranking eunuchs are shown attempting to enlist her aid in overturning a decision made by the Board of War denying them the right to have personal guards, an instance that was recorded only because the eunuchs' request was deemed improper.³⁴ Though this suggests that Sohye was perceived by the eunuchs as having influence over Sŏngjong, it is difficult to gauge the extent to which Sohye's status as the king's mother endowed her with political authority within the palace.

On the other hand, we know that Queen Chŏnghŭi, when first offered the regency, attempted to decline it in favor of Sohye, saying:

> I have had little good fortune and have lost my sons, so I wish to go to a detached palace and recuperate. Furthermore, I am not literate and it will be difficult for me to make decisions on political affairs. The mother of the successor, Subin (Sohye), is literate and knows the way of affairs; she should be in charge.³⁵

Although the *wŏnsang* rejected Chŏnghŭi's plea and prevailed on her to assume the regency, two months later she revived the idea, arguing:

> Although I have no choice but to make decisions together (with the *wŏnsang*) on the business of the state, what I have done is not in accord with the mind of Heaven and has brought drought. I do not know what to do. Queen Insu (Sohye), however, is intelligent, versed in the way of affairs, and knows the essence of things. I wish to turn important issues over to her; is this acceptable?

This, too, was rejected by the *wŏnsang* on the grounds that even sage kings experience droughts.[36] Although the *wǒnsang*'s insistence on Chǒnghǔi as regent may have reflected the belief that the senior palace woman should be in charge, I cannot help but wonder, in light of the argument about gendered linguistic distinctions, if the *wǒnsang* were not more comfortable with the illiterate (in Chinese) Chǒnghǔi than they would have been with Sohye. All memorials and other official documents would have been presented to Chǒnghǔi, either orally or in vernacular translation, and all of her decisions would have had to have been rendered back into Chinese in a process that gave men a high degree of control; had Sohye been regent, she would have been able to handle affairs directly and thus would have had a much more immediate and visible public presence. At any rate, even though the *wǒnsang* rejected any formal role for Sohye, it is almost certain that Chǒnghǔi relied heavily on Sohye in making major decisions.

Thus Sohye compiled the *Naehun* in a situation wherein the considerable political authority that her mother-in-law, Queen Chǒnghǔi, and (highly likely) she herself exercised, was masked and kept largely informal by the Confucian sensibilities of fifteenth-century public life. This situation was reflected in complex and subtle ways in the organization and contents of the *Naehun*.

The *Naehun* presents itself as a morals handbook for women, a primer teaching women how to conduct themselves properly according to the ideals of a male-dominated society, and that is how it has often been received by modern scholars. To quote Kim Chonggwǒn, the *Naehun* "taught women to live valuable lives by cultivating their minds and bodies on the basis of women's virtue, to be correct in language and comportment, to be filial to their parents, to support and love their husbands after marriage, and to bring up and teach their children well while maintaining harmony with their husbands' families and managing their households diligently and frugally."[37] In short, the *Naehun* is often seen as a text whose purpose is to train women to fulfill supportive roles in the private, or domestic, sphere.

There is much in the *Naehun* to justify this understanding. For example, the third entry in the first chapter ("Speech and Comportment") stresses the Confucian value of separation, saying, "Men and women should not sit together; they should not hang their clothes together; they should not use the same washcloth or comb; and they should not be familiar with each other."[38] Regarding womanly behavior before men, the *Naehun* states: "The *Xiaoyi* (a book of the *Liji*) says, 'When eating in the company of a superior man (*junzi*), taste the food before he eats; do not use chopsticks to eat your rice; do not slurp your soup noisily; eat lightly and swallow quickly; and do not stuff your mouth.'"[39] Again: "The *Analects* say, 'When presenting food to the king, you must have proper posture and taste the food first; if the king gives you some raw meat, you must cook it before you present it to him; and if the king gives you something living, you must raise it well.'"[40] Or: "The *Neize* says, 'When you are with your parents-in-law and they give you an order, you must diffidently answer yes; you must be careful when entering or leaving their presence, walking around the side; when you enter or leave their room, you must bow; while in their presence, you dare not hiccup, sigh, cough, sneeze, or yawn, nor should you stretch yourself, lean to one side, or look out of the corners of your eyes.'"[41]

Elsewhere, however, Sohye sounds a somewhat different note. In the second entry of the second chapter ("Husband and Wife"), she stresses the importance of the relationship between spouses and makes a strong argument for the need to educate women so that they can fulfill their roles as wives.

> The Way of husband and wife joins in the harmonization of yin and yang and reaches to the spirits. It truly embodies the broad intent of Heaven and Earth and constitutes the essence of human morality. Thus the association of men and women is held high in the Book of Rites, and the intent of Guanzhu (a poem celebrating love and fidelity between man and woman) is written in the *Book of Poetry*. This tells us that we must not take lightly the way of husband and wife. If a husband is not wise, then he cannot lead his wife and if a wife is not wise, she cannot serve her husband. If a husband cannot lead his wife, he loses dignity and if a wife cannot serve her husband, she loses righteousness; these two things are of equal value but their function (*yong*) is one. Looking at the superior men of today, all they know is that they must lead their wives and not lose their dignity. For this reason they train only men and transmit book learning only to men, and they do not know that women must serve their husbands and that women must know ritual propriety. Thus they teach men and do not teach women because they have not taken both into consideration. The Liji says to start studying at eight and to set one's mind on learning at fifteen; does this mean that women alone should not do so?[42]

In the second entry of the fifth chapter ("Motherhood"), Sohye elaborates on the kind of education she thought important for women:

Lord Sima Wen said, "At six, a daughter should learn the small things of women's work. At seven, she should memorize the *Classic of Filial Piety* and the *Analects*. At nine, she should be able to discuss the *Analects*, the *Classic of Filial Piety* and the various writings for training women and explain their general meaning. But nowadays people often teach their daughters only how to write songs and poetry or popular music. This is very inappropriate."[43]

In both entries, Sohye is clearly protesting men's indifference toward the importance of women's role and their refusal to train women in the classics and ritual propriety. But it is also clear that she is arguing that women must be trained so that they can fulfill their proper gendered roles in the Confucian scheme of things.[44]

It appears that Sohye's view of the proper role of the educated woman was not limited to preparing food properly and tasting before serving it to men, nor to maintaining proper decorum before her in-laws. Let me consider what Sohye relates about Fanji.

Fanji was the wife of King Zhuang of Chu. After Zhuang took the throne, he spent his time hunting. Fanji protested but he paid her no heed. When Fanji then refused to eat meat, the king reconsidered and devoted himself to political affairs. One day when the king finished the court session late, she waited for him at the foot of the palace stairs and asked him, "Why did you finish so late? Are you not tired and hungry?" The king responded, "I forgot hunger and fatigue because I was talking with a wise man." Fanji asked, "Who is this wise man of whom you speak?" The king answered, "I speak of Wu Zixu." Fanji covered her mouth and laughed, so the king asked her, "Why do you laugh?" Fanji said, "Wu Zixu may be a wise man, but I think he is not a loyal man." The king asked, "Why do you say that?" Fanji replied, "I have served the king for eleven years; during that time I have sent agents to such countries as Zheng and Wei to bring back beautiful women to present to the king. As a result, there are now two consorts more worthy than me and seven others of the same quality as me. Of course, I would like to monopolize the king's favor, but I have heard that one can tell the capability of a man by the number of women he has in his household. Thus I cannot let my personal desires take precedence over the public good. Wu Zixu has served this country of Chu for ten years, but all the men he has recommended have been his sons and his brothers. I have never heard anyone say that he has brought in worthy men and chased out unworthy men; this means that he has deceived the king and blocked the path of worthy men.

Knowing but not bringing in worthy men is disloyal, and not knowing who the worthy men are is unwise. Why should I not laugh?" King Zhuang was delighted. The next day, when he told Wu Zixu what Fanji had said, Wu could find no answer and avoided the king.

Wu hid in his house and sent a man out to take Sunshu Ao to the king. The king gave high office to Sunshu and within three years became hegemon. The History of Chu says that King Zhuang owed his hegemony to the efforts of Fanji.[45]

Here Sohye is depicting a consort as a woman who accepts an inferior position vis-à-vis her husband, as seen in the way she waits upon him and the way she brings in other consorts, but who also plays a vital role as a wise confidant and counselor to her king.

All told Sohye gives six examples of royal and imperial consorts in the chapter "Husband and Wife," all of which depict their subjects as having provided valuable counsel to their husbands. That Sohye believed that an education in the classics was necessary for women to fulfill their role as advisers to the husbands is illustrated in several of the entries in this section. For example, Sohye relates the following regarding Empress Gao, consort of Ming Taizu, an emperor notorious for his harsh treatment of officials who had committed what he perceived as *lèse majesté*.

As a child the empress was chaste, clean, filial, respectful, and benevolent. She was brighter than others and liked the *Book of Poetry* and the *Book of Documents*. After she became consort to Emperor Taizu, her sincere and respectful comportment moved others and won her much praise. . . . Once the empress told Taizu, "Even though the Emperor has the quality of a sage, you cannot rule all under heaven by yourself. You must strive to rule by selecting worthy men. However, as the generations pass, it becomes more and more difficult to find capable men, so what you must do is to employ men according to their strengths and weaknesses. But, what is more important is to forgive minor trespasses and preserve your men." The emperor was delighted and praised her.[46]

An even clearer example is Sohye's presentation of the case of Empress Deng of the Later Han. Sohye describes the young Empress Deng as an avid learner.

At six, she was competent in the histories and at twelve she was conversant with the *Book of Poetry* and the *Analects*. When her brothers were reading the classics, she would respectfully ask them the meanings of difficult passages. She was only interested in books and asked no questions about household management. Her mother scolded her, saying, "You do not learn women's work and do not make clothing, but devote yourself only to study, so perhaps I should make you an erudite." Realizing she should heed her mother's words, the empress learned women's work during the day and memorized the classics at night. Members of the household called her a scholar. Her father thought highly of his daughter, taught her all things, great and small, and discussed affairs with her.[47]

Sohye goes on to discuss Empress Deng's selection as consort and relates at some length a number of episodes illustrating the empress's qualities. When the emperor died in 105, he left behind only two sons, the elder quite ill and the younger not even 100 days old. When the younger reached 100 days, Empress Deng named him emperor and then assumed duties at court as his regent. Sohye goes on to give examples of Empress Deng's wise disposition of household affairs, including her treatment of other consorts and the way she won great praise for resolving a difficult case involving the theft of valuables from the palace.[48]

It is interesting to note that, while Sohye lays a great deal of stress on the educational attainments of various consorts and on the importance of their roles as advisers to their husbands, she avoids any mention of Empress-regent Deng's handling of political affairs. Given that the *Naehun* was published just one year before Queen Chŏnghŭi was forced to step down as regent,[49] it is tempting to speculate that Sohye, by omitting any discussion of the "public" political activities of female regents, may have been attempting indirectly to pressure Chŏnghŭi to step down, perhaps in hopes that she, as the king's mother and as a woman who was literate and well versed in the Confucian classics, would then have a bigger voice in political decision-making. There is, however, no evidence of any conflict between Chŏnghŭi and Sohye. Furthermore, although Sohye talks a great deal about the importance of wives as advisers to their husband kings, she makes no mention of mothers as advisers to their son kings in her chapter on motherhood. Indeed, if Sohye had been trying to push Chŏnghŭi out, she might have noted Empress Deng's notorious refusal to step down even after her son had reached his majority.[50] Indeed, given the apparent sensitivity the male officials had regarding Chŏnghŭi's regency, one might imagine that

Sohye was actually trying to support Chŏnghŭi by eliding the negative aspects of Empress Deng's regency.

However, the issue is probably more closely related to Sohye's view of what constituted proper gender roles. It might be easy for us, in the third millennium, to think that Sohye's emphasis on women's education and on the wisdom of such consorts as Fanji amounted to some sort of protest against or resistance to what we perceive as unilaterally oppressive Confucian gender-role constructs. In the fourth chapter on husband and wife, however, Sohye introduces the *Yan Family Instructions.*

> A wife should generally focus on the work of preparing food. She should devote herself only to the arts of liquor, food, and clothing and should not involve herself in political affairs, nor should she dispose of family affairs. Even though she might be bright, talented, and knowledgeable and versed in affairs both old and new, she should only assist her husband and advise him of his deficiencies. She should never be like the hen that crows at dawn and brings disaster.[51]

Whether Sohye actually believed wholeheartedly in this differentiation of male/female roles, or whether she simply deemed it as an unavoidable reality, it seems clear that she accepted the general framework of Confucian inner-outer gender constructs and sought to work within them to gain some agency for women like herself. This was a tricky business at a time when supreme political authority was vested in a woman, when the dominant males were clearly uncomfortable with the idea of women engaging in any public role or exercising any kind of open political power. Her strategy was to argue that women should be literate and should be educated in the Confucian classics in order to fulfill their duties of serving their husbands and observing ritual propriety. But, just as Queen Chŏnghŭi's political authority was masked and degendered through the use of literary Chinese, so was the wisdom and knowledge of Sohye's women to be kept out of the public realm through the device of relegating them to the status of private, personal confidants and advisers to their husbands. Nonetheless, this assertion that women have to help their husbands from the inside (*naejo*), a theme frequently voiced throughout the Chosŏn period, could in effect extend women's agency, albeit indirectly, into the political arena.[52]

The Discourse on "Faithful Women" (Yŏllyŏ)

Let me turn next to the issue of the discourse on "Faithful Women." As is widely known, one of the goals of the Confucian reformers of the early Chosŏn was to do away with the old Korean practice of allowing divorced women and widows to remarry. They sought to achieve this goal through a variety of means, including applying economic sanctions, enacting legislation that discriminated against the children of remarried women, and publishing and circulating morals handbooks depicting ideal models of virtuous women.[53] It is this latter category that interests us here, because it is the group into which the *Naehun* would seem to fall.

The first morals handbook to deal with the issue of faithful women was the *Samgang haengsilto* (Illustrated Exemplars of the Three Bonds), first published in 1431. Although subsequent editions were translated into vernacular Korean, this first version was published prior to the promulgation of *Hunmin chŏng'ŭm* (Correct Sounds for the Instruction of the People) and thus was presented entirely in literary Chinese. As suggested by the title, the *Samgang haengsilto* covered the Three Bonds— filial piety, loyalty, and faithfulness—and did so evenhandedly, presenting 110 examples of each in three separate sections. The section on faithful women is of interest for two reasons: First, only fifteen of the exemplars were drawn from Korean history; the rest came from Chinese sources. Second, the faithful woman was depicted in a variety of ways: Tomi of Paekche was honored for remaining faithful to her husband despite the king's efforts to sleep with her; Baiji of Song China was lauded, for example, for her willingness to die in a fire rather than leave her house unaccompanied at night; Madame Dong of the Yuan was praised for shielding her mother-in-law from the swords of invading soldiers; Mujiang of Han China was honored for raising her husband's sons from a previous wife as though they were her own; and an unnamed woman of Han China was cited for sacrificing her life when she went back into a burning house in an effort to save her drunken husband.[54] The use of these varying exemplars suggests that the early fifteenth-century conception of a faithful woman was quite broadly defined.

There was, however, a clear shift in emphasis with the publication of the *Sok samgang haengsilto* (Continued Illustrated Exemplars of the Three Bonds) in 1514. This book abandoned the equal treatment of all three bonds: It gave thirty-six examples of filial children, only five examples of loyal subjects, and twenty-eight examples (of which twenty-six are legible) of faithful women. Another difference from the fifteenth-century *Samgang haengsilto* is the way in which the *Sok samgang haengsilto* defines the faithful woman of Korea—the central issue now has become chastity. In the *Samgang haengsilto*, examples of Korean women defending their chastity were limited to stories of women who killed themselves rather than submit to rape by foreign soldiers; in the *Sok samgang haengsilto*, all twenty-six examples depict widows or abandoned wives who never remarried but chose instead to live with and take care of their husbands' parents. Many of these widows were shown as adhering rigidly to the three-year graveside mourning requirements. Furthermore, in eight cases women were depicted as killing themselves to avoid remarriages arranged by their natal parents, who pitied their sad situation as young widows.[55] Thus, by the early sixteenth century, the definition of a faithful woman had narrowed to an almost exclusive focus on chastity, on the idea that a woman should only have one husband throughout her entire life and that she owed first duty to her husband's family.

This emphasis on chastity as the hallmark of the faithful woman entailed a fundamental contradiction with the other key Confucian value of filial piety. Filial piety was, according to Confucian teachings, an expression of the special and spontaneous love that one naturally feels for one's birth parents. The cultivation of this natural emotion was allowed, or rather encouraged, for sons, but the ideal of the chaste faithful woman demanded that daughters, once married, transfer their primary filial allegiance to their husbands' parents,[56] even to the extent of disobeying their natal parents and committing suicide in order to avoid remarriage. Inhered in the emphasis on chastity for women was the notion that women's filial piety was somehow different; whereas men's feelings were consistent with the natural moral order, women's feelings were not, and thus could, and should, be redirected and subordinated to a higher value.

My examination of the *Sillok* and other sources indicates that the emphasis on women's chastity began during Sŏngjong's reign. There are no entries regarding faithful women in the *Sillok* for Sejo's and Yejong's reigns, but shortly after Sŏngjong was enthroned there was a spate of memorials celebrating the deeds of widows who fulfilled the three-year graveside mourning requirements and rejected their natal parents' entreaties to remarry; this kind of memorial, which usually called for the awarding of *chŏngp'yo* ("honorary gates") continued to appear regularly throughout Sŏngjong's years on the throne.[57] Sŏngjong's reign also saw a number of reprints of the *Samgang haengsilto*, including a full reprint in 1471, a vernacular translation of the faithful-woman section

(*Ŏnmun samgang haengsilto yŏllyŏdo*) in the 1481 reprint, and a shortened version of the whole text, with vernacular translation, giving thirty-
five examples for each section in the 1490 edition.

Although the upsurge in interest in the ideal of the faithful woman
and the effort to stress chastity as its key feature at that time may be seen
simply as a consequence of the gradual spread of Confucian social values among the early Chosŏn elite, there is more to the story. One scholar
has argued that there was a close relationship between male efforts to
regulate female sexuality and issues of political power and sovereignty
in early modern France, that the increasing legal subjugation of wives to
their husbands was seen as a guarantee of the obedience of both men
and women to the slowly centralizing state.[58] Inasmuch as fifteenth-
century Chosŏn Korea was in the process of creating a more centralized
polity, like early modern France, there is a certain rough parallel. But
what strikes me as more immediate is the timing of this shift—within a
few months after Queen Chŏnghǔi became regent—toward an emphasis
on chastity in the discourse on the faithful woman. In other words, it
seems possible that the emphasis on female chastity may have been born
of male anxiety, as seen in the efforts to mask Chŏnghǔi's role, over
issues of political sovereignty or dynastic legitimacy at a time when a
woman was exercising supreme political power.

How, then, do Sohye and the *Naehun* fit into this situation? At least
one author has speculated, based on Sohye's reputation as a filial daughter-in-law and a strict teacher of royal grandsons: "Sŏngjong's strict
policy of moral suasion for women may have been the result of his
mother's influence."[59] A consideration of the contents of the *Naehun*,
however, suggests that Sohye may not have been an enthusiastic supporter of the new discourse on chastity. Sohye does at one place make a
statement that, although men can remarry, women cannot,[60] but there is
a marked absence of any examples of women observing the three-year
graveside mourning or of women refusing to remarry and remaining
with their in-laws. Instead, as noted before, the emphasis is on the way
in which wives provided counsel and assistance to their husbands.

Regarding differences in filial piety, JaHyun Kim Haboush has noted
that the *Naehun* treats a woman's filiality to her natal parents and her
parents-in-law as equal, that a woman "naturally remains devoted to her
own parents" even after she marries.[61] Indeed, my own examination of
the *Naehun*'s section on filial piety reveals that it begins with several
male examples of filial piety drawn from Mencius and Confucius, then

switches to several instructions, dealing with how to behave toward in-laws, drawn from writings for women such as the *Nüjiao* and the *Neize*, before returning to several more examples of male filial piety. The implication here is that not only is there no difference between the filial piety women owed to their natal parents and their husbands' parents, but also that there is no fundamental difference between male and female filiality to begin with.

The Persecution of Buddhism

Buddhism had been under periodic attack from the late fourteenth century, but had enjoyed something of a revival under King Sejo, who relied on monk advisers and expended considerable resources on Buddhism-related projects. During Sŏngjong's reign, however, Buddhism came under increasing attack by Confucian ideologues, due in part to Sŏngjong's own basic antipathy to the religion.

Although Buddhism was still widely practiced by large numbers of ruling-class males, as the comments of contemporary observers such as Sŏng Hyŏn make quite clear,[62] the *Sillok* presents belief in Buddhism as basically a female problem, as seen in the various restrictions against women visiting Buddhist temples or in the 1492 affair when Confucian scholars attacked palace women, including Sohye, for their role in dissuading Sŏngjong from enacting stringent measures prohibiting men from becoming Buddhist monks.[63]

There is no question that Sohye was a devout believer in Buddhism and that she occasionally intervened to protect Buddhist interests. In addition to the 1492 affair, Sohye also weighed in against censorate attacks of a proposal to build a new temple in 1490.[64] There is no doubt that she resented the attacks on Buddhism. In 1477, when she was attacked by the censorate for sponsoring the copying of Buddhist sutras, she responded:

> Generally, the reason why Confucians have from old rejected Buddhism is nothing other than their concern that if kings worship Buddha, they will neglect the affairs of government, inflict hardship on the people by building temples, and waste funds feeding monks. . . . Although I am making these sutras with private funds and feeding the monks with private grain so that it has nothing to do with the state, the protests of the censors is such that I don't know what to do. Furthermore, when King

Munjong [r. 1450–52] was in mourning, he made many sutras and Buddhist statues, but I have heard nothing about even a single person remon-
strating. Is that because there were no ministers and no censors then? If
the Way of Buddha is empty and false, how is it that masses were conducted for the kings and queens of old, and how is it that sacrificial rites
were carried out for famed mountains and large rivers?[65]

Although Sohye is obviously sensitive to concerns about Buddhist influence on governance and about charges that state funds were being used
to promote Buddhism, she is also clearly presenting Buddhism as a religion of both kings and queens, as a belief sanctioned by hoary precedent.
One question that arises here is how to reconcile the strongly Confucian
content of the *Naehun* with Sohye's personal devotion to Buddhism.

It is likely that Sohye's position was the same as that taken by many
scholar-officials in the Koryŏ period and even by such Buddhist-believ-
ing early Chosŏn officials as Kim Suon (1407–1481),[66] as well as by
Chosŏn-period monks such as Hyujŏng, that Confucianism's proper
sphere of authority was social ethics and governance while that of Buddhism was spiritual cultivation, and that ultimately the two resolved to
the same truth. Sohye, by holding herself to the highest standards of
Confucian conduct and by emphasizing Confucian social values in the
Naehun, may have been presenting herself as an example of how one
could hold Buddhist beliefs and still live up to Confucian standards of
moral conduct. Also, to the extent that the anti-Buddhist activists of the
late fifteenth century may have been employing a rhetorical strategy of
weakening Buddhism by depicting it as a religion of women, Sohye
may have been trying to counter it by intervening to ensure a continuing
replenishment of the ranks of male Buddhist monks and by stressing the
historical status of Buddhism as a religion for both kings and queens.
Thus, for her the battle over Buddhism may not have been simply a question of culture and religion; it may very well have seemed to her a crucial
contest in the field of gender politics, a field in which she sought to prevent the further marginalization of women by bringing to bear her status
as queen and her assets as a woman well versed in the Confucian classics.

Summary

What I have reviewed to this point indicates that Sohye pursued a variety of strategies in dealing with the politics of gender. She stepped forth
as a positive advocate for educating women and for the importance of

women as personal advisers for their husbands. She apparently refused to participate in the chastity-centered discourse on faithful women of the late fifteenth century, and she took a somewhat defensive posture regarding the feminization and persecution of Buddhism. In all three cases, however, she appears to have been striving to create and maintain a certain space in which women could exercise some agency within the constraints of Confucian-constructed gender roles.

Some Final Remarks

It is difficult to fathom the extent of Sohye's influence on elite women's efforts to maintain a space in which they could play meaningful social, cultural, and political roles. Certainly we know that the *Naehun* was reprinted several times, either separately or as part of an anthology of women's handbooks, in the sixteenth, seventeenth, and eighteenth centuries. Thus it seems likely that large numbers of women and men read Sohye's work throughout the Chosŏn period.

The general impression today is that women of the Chosŏn period did not receive training in the Confucian classics and were not literate in classical Chinese; even the education of women of socially and politically elite families is often assumed to have consisted of nothing more than indoctrination in basic morals primers and literacy in the phonetic script. The few women, such as Sin Saimdang (1504–1551) or Hŏ Nansŏrhŏn (1563–1589), known to have been well educated and literate in Chinese, are seen as the rare exceptions who prove the rule. There is, however, some evidence to suggest that other, less well-known women had similar educational backgrounds and intellectual attainments.

There were a few mid-sixteenth-century women whose poetry and other achievements were briefly evaluated by the mid-Chosŏn literus Ŏ Sukkwŏn,[67] but the limitations of the source materials available to us today, compounded by the pervasive assumption that women were not educated in the Chosŏn period, make it difficult to gauge how many women were conversant in the classics and literate in Chinese. The cases of several women of the sixteenth and seventeenth centuries have been examined—including those of the elder sister of the famed poet Chŏng Ch'ŏl (1536–1593) and of the aunt of the renowned scholar and official Song Siyŏl (1607–1689), who were literate and well read in the classics—suggesting that the degree of women's educational attainments "largely depended on the scholarly milieu of their natal homes."[68]

One particularly interesting case I have managed to stumble upon of an educated sixteenth-century woman is that of Madam Song (1521–1578), the wife of Yu Hŭich'un (1513–1577), a prominent official and well-known Confucian scholar. Yu left behind a diary, *Miam ilgich'o*, in which he recorded many details of his private life, details which give us some sense of the relationship he had with his wife and of the kind of person she was. The diary frequently depicts the exchange of letters between Yu and Song; it contains three written by Song in classical Chinese.[69] The diary also shows Yu and Song enjoying the exchange of poetry and contains an entry where Song reads and critiques one of Yu's poems.[70] Yu's writings leave little doubt about what he depended heavily on his wife for: counsel (as in the entry where he describes Song as giving him valuable advice about the education of their son)[71] and management of practical affairs (as in the entry where he discusses her efforts in keeping up the household while overseeing a construction project on their estate in Haenam).[72] Madam Song, who was well read in the classics and histories and whose writings were compiled in an (apparently no longer extant) literary collection,[73] would appear to have been the kind of woman Sohye had in mind when she compiled the *Naehun*.

Particularly interesting in this regard is Yu Hŭich'un's responsibility for editing and distributing a new printing of the *Naehun*, which unfortunately is no longer extant, sometime around 1569 or 1570.[74] It is not clear what role Yu may have played in the decision to reprint Sohye's work, but given the kind of wife he had and the nature of their relationship, there is no doubt that he would have appreciated the message of the *Naehun*. Yu was also a close associate of Hŏ Nansŏrhŏn's family,[75] and was the teacher of her elder brother, Hŏ Pong (1551–1588),[76] who, as Kichung Kim points out in his contribution to the volume, did much to develop Nansŏrhŏn's literary talent. It is not difficult to imagine, therefore, Yu Hŭich'un sanctioning, if not actively encouraging, his sister Hŏ Pong's intellectual development. This suggests that there were certain circles forming a kind of subculture, among the early Chosŏn *yangban,* that appreciated the value of education for women and respected the intellectual attainments of their wives, sisters, and daughters. It is clear that these *yangban* were aware of, and influenced by, Sohye's *Naehun*.

The chastity-centered discourse on faithful women gathered strength as time went by. The early seventeenth-century *Tongguk sinsok samgang haengsilto* (New Continued Illustrated Exemplars of the Three Bonds in Korea) perpetuated, in both space allocation and content, the emphasis of the *Sok samgang haengsilto* on chaste women. One of the features of the *Tongguk sinsok samgang haengsilto* is that the number of examples of women who died defending their chastity during the Hideyoshi invasions of the late sixteenth century was three times the number of examples of loyal subjects and filial sons combined. This may have been a reflection of male perceptions of the invasion of their country being like the rape of their women, of male insecurity in the wake of their failure to repel the Japanese invaders, but at any rate it is clear that the ideal of the chaste "faithful women" remained strong well into the second half of the dynasty.

Although little substantial research has been done on Chosŏn-period Buddhism, it appears Sohye was fighting a losing battle there, too. We know that belief in Buddhism remained strong among palace women until at least the mid-sixteenth century and that Buddhism enjoyed something of a philosophical revival under Hyujŏng (Sŏsan taesa, 1520–1604) in the late sixteenth and early seventeenth centuries. But—pending further study of Buddhism in the mid and late Chosŏn—all that can be said is that the Confucian ideologues appear to have succeeded in feminizing and marginalizing Buddhism.

Thus, the focus of my inquiry remains on Sohye and on how she belies the stereotype of the Chosŏn woman as a passive, helpless victim of patriarchical Confucian social values. Though Confucian gender constructs did impose limits on what Sohye could do and how she could do it, it is clear that she sought to work within those constructs to advance her interests as a woman, to exercise agency in ways that could be justified by Confucian learning.

That Sohye was able to do so was due in large measure to the high status she enjoyed in the Chosŏn as the daughter of one of the greatest aristocratic descent groups of her time, a descent group among which the prestige of women was enhanced by its position as providers of consorts of Ming emperors. It is highly doubtful that a woman from a lesser family, not to mention a commoner, could possibly have dared to challenge *yangban* men's notions of proper education for their daughters and proper roles for women. There were, however, many women from elite family backgrounds in the early Chosŏn. What gave Sohye a particular advantage was the cultural capital she brought to bear. Sohye, in a move that Bourdieu would have appreciated, began the *Naehun* as an extended discussion of speech and comportment, or what Bourdieu calls habitus, those habits of speech and posture that enable individuals to "know how to play the game." Sohye did not just write about speech and comportment. The praise she won from Sejo as a filial daughter-in-law and the reputation she had as a strict observer of Confucian propriety—attitudes ingrained in her from her upbringing—show that she was able to use speech and comportment to gain for herself a relatively powerful position in the royal family. But it also is likely from the way in which she emphasized Confucian womanly virtues in the *Naehun* that she calculated that strict adherence to the forms of Confucian propriety would deflect criticism from males and allow women to exercise substantial authority within the domestic sphere.

Sohye had another advantage beyond the traits of speech and comportment she learned as a child. That was her command of literary Chinese, the male language of public business, as well as her knowledge of the Confucian classics. Sohye's educational attainments were certainly equal, if not superior, to those of many ruling-class males in the late fifteenth century. That may have been cause for alarm among some men, but it also certainly would have made other men, at least those not sure of the superiority of their own learning, cautious in attacking Sohye and her ideas. The epilogue to the *Naehun* states that she presented the work as a compilation of selections in literary Chinese with an accompanying vernacular Korean translation.[77]

Because this format was the common practice with such male-authored morals handbooks of the late fifteenth and early sixteenth centuries as the abbreviated *Samgang haengsilto*, the *Iryun haengsilto* (Illustrated Examples of Relations Between Elder and Younger and Between Friends), the *Chŏngsok ŏnhae* (Vernacular Translation of Correcting Customs), or the *Kyŏngminp'yŏn* (Warning the People), can this not be seen as constituting a direct challenge to the linguistic foundations of male superiority? Would it not have been more acceptable for Sohye to have written her work in the vernacular? Perhaps so, but that would have undermined the essential message about the need to educate women in the classics and in literary Chinese. Here it may be useful to consider another feature of the *Naehun*: All of the examples Sohye presented of educated women were drawn from Chinese history, and all of the Confucian male scholars she quoted regarding the importance of educating women were Chinese. The implication is that, if literary Chinese was appropriate for both men and women in China and for men in Korea, then it would have been appropriate for women in Korea as well. By drawing exclusively on Chinese sources, Sohye was using the *yangban* male perception of the superiority of Chinese culture to legitimize her use of literary Chinese.

Thus Sohye appears to have done a masterful job of exercising her cultural and social capital to delineate a space for women to exercise some agency within the limits of Confucian gender constructs. In other words, Sohye's literacy in Chinese and her knowledge of the Confucian classics, coming from a member of one of the greatest early Chosŏn aristocratic families and a close relative of women chosen as Ming imperial consorts, provided her with substantial resources. These she deployed in the field of gender relations against the apparent majority of ruling-class men who, as she described them, thought only of their dignity and had no appreciation of the important role educated women could play as exemplars of ritual propriety and as confidants and advisers to their husbands.

In closing, it is important to note that Sohye's ability to draw from the Confucian tradition to make her arguments for education for women and for a vital role for women as counselors to their husbands suggests that, even as Chosŏn *yangban* women were losing much of the social and economic privilege enjoyed by earlier Korean women, they nonetheless were still striving to use the Confucian gender system to allow them to fulfill important—even if largely private—social, cultural, and even political roles.

Notes

1. Examples include Kim, ed., *Han'guk yŏsŏngsa*, 576, 590; and Deuchler, *Confucian Transformation*, 257.

2. Yi, "*Naehun* ŭi ŏnŏ pŏpto yŏn'gu," 73–94.

3. Kim Chiyong, "*Naehun* e pich'uŏjin Yijo yŏindŭl ŭi saenghwalsang," 334–366; Kim Jin-Myung (Kim Chinmyŏng), "Kabujang tamnon kwa yŏsŏng ŭi ŏgap, 61–74.

4. See Deuchler, *Confucian Transformation*.

5. Ko, *Teachers of the Inner Chambers*, 1–26.

6. Kendall and Peterson, "Introduction," in *Korean Women*, 1–17. The quotation is from page 6.

7. Kim Jin-Myung, "Kabujang tamnon kwa yŏsŏng ŭi ŏgap."

8. See, for example, Cho, "Male Dominance and Mother Power," 187–207.

9. Deuchler, "Propagating Female Virtues in Chosŏn Korea."

10. Bourdieu's approach is laid out in several works, including: *Outline of a Theory of Practice*; *The Logic of Practice*; and *Language and Symbolic Power.*

11. One scholar speculates that the Hosabunko version may be the 1475 original. See Kim Chiyong, "*Naehun*," 340.

12. Two chapters from the *Book of Rites*.

13. Ming Renxio Wen huanghou, *Neixun xu*, 709:1a.

14. Sohye wanghu, *Naehun sŏ* (Introduction).

15. Sugŭi Cho-ssi, *Naehun pal* (Epilogue).

16. Ibid. Sohye was jokingly referred to as the "p'okpin" (tyrant consort) for her stern and demanding manner of teaching.

17. See Duncan, "Social Background," 74–75, for discussion of the Ch'ŏngju Han in the late Koryŏ and early Chosŏn dynasties.

18. See Queen Myŏngdŏk's biography at *Koryŏsa* (hereafter KS) 89:19a ff. See also KS 111:9a and 111:27a–27b for examples of Myŏngdŏk's political activities.

19. *Tanjong sillok* (Veritable Records of King Tanjong) 8 (01/10/11).

20. *Sejo sillok* (Veritable Records of King Sejo) 1 (01/07/26).

21. *Sŏngjong sillok* (Veritable Records of King Sŏngjong) 15 (03/02/20).

22. *Sŏngjong sillok* 2 (01/01/22).

23. *Sŏngjong sillok* 51 (06/01/06) and 55 (06/05/12).

24. *Yŏnsan'gun ilgi* (Veritable Records for Yŏnsan'gun) 1 (00/12/29)

25. Kibaik Lee (Yi Kibaek) gives a good summary of South Korean historical scholarship on the Meritorious Elite and the Rusticated Literati in *Han'guksa sillon*, 269–74. For discussion of institutional conflict, see Wagner, *The Literati Purges*, 23–31.

26. *Sŏngjong sillok* 1 (00/11/28).

27. Haboush, "Gender and the Politics of Language," 6–7.

28. Those were cases when the *Sillok* used the terms "taewang taebi chŏn," "taebi chŏn," or "ŭiji," which specifically indicated that the decision was Chŏngghŭi's. Most other decisions were simply called "chŏn," or royal edicts.

29. *Sŏngjong sillok* 4 (01/03/09).

30. *Sŏngjong sillok* 29 (04/04/09).

31. *Sŏngjong sillok* 41 (05/04/01).

32. *Sŏngjong sillok* 55 (06/05/27).

33. Haboush, "Gender and the Politics of Language," 8.

34. *Sŏngjong sillok* 45 (05/07/25).

35. *Sŏngjong sillok* 1 (00/11/28).

36. *Sŏngjong sillok* 4 (01/04/20).

37. Kim Chonggwŏn, Introduction to *Naehun/Kyenyŏsŏ*, 1986), 2.

38. Sohye wanghu, *Naehun*, 17.

39. Ibid., 20.

40. Ibid., 21.

41. Ibid., 49.

42. Ibid., 79.

43. Ibid., 164.

44. As Professor Young-chan Ro of George Mason University pointed out (in his comments on the draft version of this paper), Sohye's vision of the relationship between husband and wife was based in the complementary polarity of Confucian cosmology. Thus, in comparing husband and wife to yin and yang, Sohye was going beyond immediate issues of ameliorating the position of women within the elite family and constructing a philosophical argument about mutual correspondence among women's position, the social order, and the cosmic order.

45. Sohye wanghu, *Naehun*, 90–91.

46. Ibid., 145, 147.

47. Ibid., 78–79.

48. Ibid., 121–23.

49. Chŏnghŭi decided to step down after an unsigned missive appeared at court accusing her of misgovernment and of giving preference to her relatives. Although she protested her innocence, and had some support from high officials, including Chŏng Ch'angson and Han Myŏnghoe, those accusations clearly made it impossible for her to continue on as regent. See the entries at *Sŏngjong sillok* 62 (06/12/13) and her letter of resignation at *Sŏngjong sillok* 63 (07/01/13). Also, Professor Sonja Häußler of Humboldt University, in her comments on the first draft of this paper, pointed out that the time when Sohye compiled the *Naehun* was a critical time for her son, King Sŏngjong. Not only was the regency of Queen Chŏnghŭi about to come to an end, but also a search was underway to find a consort for the young king. Professor Häußler suggests that Sohye—who was concerned that the early deaths of both her husband, Tŏkchong, and his brother, Yejong, may have been due to the vengeful spirit of Tanjong's mother—was seeking to stabilize the inner court and return order and harmony to the state and the cosmos, which had been disrupted by the interference of such a harmful female element.

50. See Chŏng Ch'angson's comment on Empress Deng at *Sŏngjong sillok* 6 (06/12/13).

51. Sohye wanghu, *Naehun*, 86.

52. I am indebted to Martina Deuchler for bringing to my attention the discourse on naejo and its implications for women's agency in the political arena.

53. See Deuchler, *Confucian Transformation*, 276–81.

54. Kim, Sonja, "'Fierce Women,'" 15–20.

55. Ibid., 21–22.

56. Haboush, "Filial Emotions," 132–37.

57. See, for example, *Sŏngjong sillok* 3 (01/02/07), 15 (03/02/09), 15 (03/02/18), 72 (07/10/07), 117 (11/05/19), 128 (12/04/12), and 134 (12/10/25).

58. Davis, *Society and Culture in Early Modern France*, 124–28.

59. Kim Okkil, ed., *Han'guk yŏsŏngsa*, 576.

60. Sohye wanghu, *Naehun*, 83.

61. Haboush, "Filial Emotions," 137.

62. Sŏng Hyŏn (1439–1504), among others, comments frequently on the persistence of Buddhist beliefs among late fifteenth-century officials. For example, he speaks of many sadaebu participating in Buddhist rituals in order to gain earthly blessings and also notes that Confucian students of the Sŏnggyun'gwan (Royal Confucian Academy) were consecrating Buddha's bones. See Sŏng's *Yongjae ch'onghwa*, 195.

63. See Wagner, *The Literati Purges*, 34–36.

64. *Sŏngjong sillok* 236 (21/01/17).

65. Ibid., 78 (08/03/07).

66. Kim Suon makes a clear statement in favor of a Buddhist/Taoist/Confucianist eclecticism in his *Sigu chip* (literary collection) 2: 4a.

67. Ŏ Sukkwŏn, *A Korean Storyteller's Miscellany*, 249–50.

68. Deuchler, "Propagating Female Virtues in Chosŏn Korea," 11–15.

69. Yu Hŭich'un, *Miam ilgich'o*, vol. 5, 319–20, 326–27.

70. Ibid., 5: 290. Several of the poems exchanged between Yu and Song are contained in vol. 5, 321–26.
71. Ibid., 5: 111.
72. Ibid., 5: 100.
73. Ibid., 5, "Kaisetsu," 19.
74. Ibid., 3: 45–57. See also *Sŏnjo sillok* 7 (06/03/17).
75. See the exchange of visits and written communications between Yu and various members of Hŏ Nansŏrhŏn's family, including her father Hŏ Yŏp, and her brother Hŏ Pong, described in the *Miam ilgich'o*, vol. 1, 6–17 passim.
76. Yi et al., *Han'guk inmyŏng taesajŏn*, 100.
77. Sohye wanghu, *Naehun* 216.

References

Bourdieu, Pierre. *Outline of a Theory of Practice*. Tranlsated by Richard Nice Cambridge, UK: Cambridge University Press, 1977.
———. *The Logic of Practice*. Translated by Richard Nice. Stanford, CA: Stanford University Press, 1990.
———. *Language and Symbolic Power*. Translated by Gino Raymond and Matthew Adamson. Cambridge, MA: Harvard University Press, 1991.
Cho, Haejoang. "Male Dominance and Mother Power: The Two Sides of Confucian Patriarchy in Korea." In *Confucianism and the Family*, ed. Walter H. Slote and George A. De Vos (Albany, NY: SUNY Press), 1998.
Davis, Natalie Zemon. *Society and Culture in Early Modern France*. Stanford, CA: Stanford University Press, 1975.
Deuchler, Martina. *The Confucian Transformation of Korea: A Study of Society and Ideology*. Cambridge, MA: Harvard University Press, 1992.
———. "Propagating Female Virtues in Chosŏn Korea," unpublished paper.
Duncan, John B. "The Social Background to the Founding of the Chosŏn Dynasty: Change or Continuity?" *Journal of Korean Studies* 6 (1988–89).
Haboush, JaHyun Kim. "Filial Emotions and Filial Values: Changing Patterns in the Discourse of Filiality in Late Chosŏn Korea." *Harvard Journal of Asiatic Studies* 55 (1995).
———. "Gender and the Politics of Language in Chosŏn Korea"(Paper presented at the workshop on "Rethinking East Asia: Gender, the Body and Confucianism," UCLA, April 25, 1999).
Kendall, Laurel, and Mark Peterson, eds. *Korean Women: View from the Inner Room*. New Haven, CT: East Rock Press, 1983.
Kim Chiyong. "*Naehun* e pich'uŏjin yijo yŏindŭl ŭi saenghwalsang" (The Life of Chosŏn Korean Women Reflected in the Naehun), *Yijo yŏsŏng yŏn'gu* (Chosŏn Women), edited by Sungmyŏng Women's University, Asia Women's Affairs Research Institute. Seoul: Sungmyŏng yŏja taehakkyo Asea yŏsŏng munje yŏn'guso, 1976. 334–366.
Kim Chonggwŏn. Introduction to *Naehun/Kyenyŏsŏ*. Seoul: Myŏngmundang, 1986.
Kim Jin-Myung (Kim Chinmyŏng). "Kabujang tamnon kwa yŏsŏng ŭi ŏgap: *Naehun* sŏ mit *Ŭirye* sŏ ŭi punsŏk ŭl chungshim ŭro" (Patriarchal Discourse and Repression of Women: An Analysis of *Naehun* and the *Ŭirye*). *Asea yŏsŏng yŏn'gu* (Asian Women) 33 (1994).

Kim Okkil, ed. *Han'guk yŏsŏngsa* (The History of Korean Women) vol. I. Seoul: Ewha Woman's University, 1972.

Kim, Sonja. "'Fierce Women': The Discourse on Female Chastity in Early Chosŏn." (Paper presented for the seminar on Chosŏn Dynasty history at UCLA, June 1998).

Kim Suon. *Sigu chip* (Literary collection).

Ko, Dorothy. *Teachers of the Inner Chambers: Women and Culture in Seventeenth-Century China.* Stanford, CA: Stanford University Press, 1994.

Koryŏsa (History of Koryŏ).

Lee, Kibaik (Yi Kibaek). *Han'guksa sillon* (A New History of Korea) *chungsup'an* (revised edition). Seoul: Ilchogak, 1990.

Ming Renxiao Wen huanghou. *Neixun,* in *Yingyin wenyuan ge Siku quanshu* (Photolithographic reprint of the *Siku quanshu* from the Pavilion of Erudite Literature). Taibei: Taiwan shangwu yinshuguan, 1983.

Ŏ Sukkwŏn. *A Korean Storyteller's Miscellany.* Translated and edited by Peter H. Lee. Princeton, NJ: Princeton University Press, 1989.

Sohye wanghu, *The Naehun.* Translated and edited by Yi Sumin. Seoul: Myŏngmundang, 1986.

Wagner, Edward W. *The Literati Purges: Political Conflict in Early Yi Korea.* Cambridge, MA: East Asian Research Center, Harvard University, 1974.

Yi, Hŭisŭng et al., eds. *Han'guk inmyŏng taesajŏn* (Korean Biographical Dictionary). Seoul: Sin'gu Munhwasa, 1986.

Yi Ŭrhwan. "*Naehun* ŭi ŏnŏ pŏpto yŏn'gu" (Linguistic Propriety According to *Naehun*). *Asea yŏsŏng yŏn'gu* (Asian Women) 19 (1980).

Yu Hŭich'un, *Miam ilgich'o* (Diary of Yu Hŭich'un). Keijo: Chosenshi Henshukai, 1938.

3

Sin Saimdang

The Foremost Woman Painter
of the Chosŏn Dynasty

Yi Sŏng-mi

In documentary sources from the Chosŏn dynasty (1392–1910), only seventeen women painters have been recorded in a period that spans more than five centuries.[1] Of these, only five have extant paintings credited to them. The earliest and the most prominent painter in this group, and the first female painter in recorded Korean history, is Sin Saimdang (1504–1551).[2] The other four are Yi Maech'ang (1529–1592), Sin Saimdang's daughter; Lady Yi (1584–1609), Saimdang's granddaughter; Hŏ Nansŏrhŏn (1563–1589), a well-known poet; and Chukhyang, a courtesan of the nineteenth century.[3]

Considering the kind of social restrictions placed upon most women during the period, the fact that so few female artists have been recorded for the Chosŏn dynasty is not surprising. Under the strict code of conduct within Chosŏn Neo-Confucian society, the activities of women of the *yangban* class were circumscribed by the inner quarters of their residences. Women were not allowed outside their homes except when visiting relatives or being accompanied by servants. Until the final years of the Chosŏn period, females were not permitted to pursue a formal education. Under those circumstances, it was impossible for a woman to have engaged in activities other than those prescribed for her: being an obedient wife and good mother.

What we know about the life and art of Lady Sin Saimdang is due largely to the recognition she received as the mother of Yi I (1536–1584), also known by his sobriquet, Yulgok, one of the most famous Neo-Confucian philosophers of the Chosŏn dynasty. Even today, she is revered as the model of *hyŏnmo yangch'ŏ*, or "benevolent mother and good wife."[4] For that reason, the circumstances of her life are better documented, and her works better preserved, than those of other women painters of the period. In this respect, her situation is similar to those of the male scholar-official painters whose biographies and paintings are better known, owing to their official careers.

Biographical Sketch

Sin Saimdang was born in Kangnŭng, Kangwŏn Province, on 29 October 1504. She was the second daughter of Sin Myŏnghwa (1476–1522), a descendant of the illustrious Sin family from P'yŏngsan, which produced several generations of high-ranking officials during the late Koryŏ period.[5] Sin Myŏnghwa, also a scholar of high standing who earned the *chinsa* (presented scholar) title in 1516, chose not to serve in the government because of factional strife at court, which ultimately led to a purge of scholars in 1519.[6]

Saimdang's given name was, and still is, unknown, as it was the custom of the Chosŏn period not to record a woman's name in the family register. Saimdang (literally hall of emulating T'aeim) is the sobriquet given to her by her father, who wished her to emulate the mother of King Wen of China's Western Zhou dynasty (ca. 1100–771 B.C.), Tairen (in Korean, T'aeim), who, in Chinese history, was revered as the paragon of a benevolent mother and good wife.

Sin Saimdang's mother was from the Yi family of Yong'in, Kyŏnggi Province, which had established a base in Kangnŭng. She was the only daughter of Yi Saon; he has passed the provincial examinations (*saeng'wŏn*) but did not serve in the government. Like her mother, Saimdang was taught to read the classics by her father. After her marriage to Yi Wŏnsu (1501–1562)[7] of the Tŏksu Yi clan, in 1522, Saimdang complied with her father's wishes and stayed with her parents in Kangnŭng until 1524, when she gave birth to her first son.[8] She had seven children, of which Yulgok, the philosopher, was the third son.[9]

The Tŏksu Yi clan had established a base in Yulgok village, P'aju, Kyŏnggi Province, about fifty-one kilometers (almost thirty miles) north of Seoul. The philosopher Yulgok took his sobriquet from the name of the village, which means "chestnut valley." Tombs of several family members, including those of Lady Sin and Yulgok, are located in the village.

Yulgok inherited his mother's intelligence; two of her other children inherited her artistic talent. Her youngest son, Oksan Yi Wu (1542–1609), was a talented musician, poet, calligrapher, and painter who specialized in the subject collectively known as the Four Gentlemen (bamboo, plum, orchid, and chrysanthemum), as well as paintings of grapes in ink. Her first daughter, Maech'ang (1529–1592), is also known for her paintings in ink of bamboo and plum.

Oksan's daughter, Lady Yi (1584–1609), is also recognized for her ink bamboo paintings. Thus, Sin Saimdang's artistic legacy extends to three generations within the close network of her family and beyond.

Documented sources on Sin Saimdang's paintings fall into two broad groups. The first consists of comments by her son and her contemporaries; the second consists of colophons to the paintings attributed to her, many written by adherents to Yulgok's Neo-Confucian philosophy. As revealed in these colophons, her fame as a talented painter grew with her social and intellectual status as the mother of a prominent thinker with a significant following among politically influential figures in the mid-to-late Chosŏn period. However, it is more important to examine the first group of written sources, as they focus more on her art and less on the myth that grew around her.

The earliest writing on Sin Saimdang is Yulgok's biographical essay of his mother, "Sŏnbi haengjang," in which he remarks:

> When she was young, she mastered the Classics. She had talent in writing and in the use of the brush. In sewing and embroidery, she displayed exquisite skills. . . . From the age of seven, she painted landscapes after An Kyŏn (active ca. 1440–1470), and also painted ink grapes. They were so wondrous that no one could dare imitate them. Screens and scrolls [she painted] are around today.[10]

Ŏ Sukkwŏn (a court translator of Chinese language and the author of the *P'aegwan chapgi* (Storyteller's Miscellanies), wrote of her paintings:

> Today there is Madam Sin of Tongyang[11] who excelled in painting since her childhood. Her paintings of landscape and grapes are so excellent

that people say they come only next to those by An Kyŏn. How can one belittle her paintings just because they were done by a woman, and how can we scold her for having done what a woman is not supposed to do?[12]

Although brief, these comments are valuable in that they were made by people who knew the artist in her lifetime. From them, we know that she executed landscapes in the manner of the then-famous early Chosŏn painter, An Kyŏn, and painted grapes in ink, which, like the Four Gentlemen, was one of the favorite themes of literati painters. We also know from Ŏ Sukkwŏn's remarks that painting was not a prescribed activity for a woman. In this connection, we are reminded of the passage in the sixteenth-century *Manual of the Inner Court* that specifically condemns the writing of poetry and the use of the brush as skills practiced by courtesans trained to entertain men, and, by definition, inappropriate activities for women of scholar-official families.[13]

It is also interesting to note that the two statements quoted above do not mention Saimdang's paintings of grasses and insects, which today are known as the most important genre of painting she produced, as well as being the subject of most of her extant works. In addition to her painting, Yulgok also mentioned his mother's exquisite skill in embroidery, one of the prescribed activities for women of traditional Korea. A screen of embroidery believed to be the work of Saimdang is in Tong'a University Museum, in Pusan, South Kyŏngsang Province. The relationship between her grass-and-insect paintings and the Tong'a University screen is examined later in this essay.

The Paintings of Sin Saimdang

The range of subject matter painted by Sin Saimdang is more varied than that of other known women painters of the period, whose surviving works are confined to only one or two genres. She painted landscapes, grasses and insects, birds and flowers, grapes, bamboo, and plum flowers. The works she left are important in that some can serve as representative examples of painting styles in the early Chosŏn, a period for which there is a dearth of material for the study of painting. However, compared with her male contemporaries she seems to have painted fewer landscapes than grass-and-insect or bird-and-flower themes. Her landscapes, as suggested in the biography written by her son, must have been based on paintings she had seen rather than her own observations of nature. It is almost unthinkable that a woman of her class would be able to sketch actual scenery *en plein air*, as the Chosŏn Legal Code specifically forbid women of status from going outdoors for pleasurable activities.[14]

We find an analogous situation in the subject matter dealt with by the most talented female poet of this period, Hŏ Nansŏrhŏn (1563–89).[15] Her poetry was published by her brother Hŏ Kyun (1569–1618), the author of the well-known Korean novel *The Story of Hong Kiltong*. A survey of the themes of her poems reveals only a handful of poems on nature or scenery. The nature scenes in her poetry consist of either those that she could observe from her home, such as a "lotus pond" or a "moonlit night," or some scenes she had envisioned in her dreams.[16] This confirms how completely a woman's realm of activity was confined to the inner quarters of her home.

Ink Monochrome Paintings

It seems natural that Sin Saimdang, being a lady of the scholar-official class, would have created ink paintings in the spirit of the literati. As noted earlier, the subjects of her paintings, such as landscapes, the Four Gentlemen, and grapes, also fall within the category of themes favored by literati painters. The landscape paintings now traditionally attributed to Sin Saimdang show a variety of styles. Among these, only the two-panel *Screen of Landscapes* (Figure 1; figures follow page 77), now in the National Museum of Korea, Seoul, is plausibly by her.[17]

Each of the two paintings has a fold line down the center, indicating that they were originally leaves of an album. Except for this screen, all other landscape paintings attributed to Saimdang are stylistically similar to Korean landscape paintings dated to the eighteenth century or later; therefore, there is little possibility that those works are actually by the artist. The two-panel screen in the National Museum of Korea, on the other hand, is in the Zhe school style, one of the predominant styles of landscape painting in Korea during the sixteenth and seventeenth centuries. Well-known painters such as the court painters and the brothers Yi Sunghyo (1536–1611) and Yi Hŭnghyo (1537–1593) or the royal clansmen Yi Kyŏng'yun (born 1546) and Yi Yŏng'yun (1561–1611), all painted in the same style.

The Zhe school style is based on the Southern Song (1127–1279) "one corner" composition and characterized by the use of contrasting tones of light and dark ink, as well as the lack of calligraphic brushstrokes. These stylistic features are evident in the paintings of the screen. They display a nearly mirror-image composition, with a foreground placed to one side, a vast expanse of water, and hills in the distance beyond the water. A few trees appear in the foreground, while the distant hills also show some faint images of vegetation. The second panel shows a moon rising above the distant hills. There are poems inscribed in cursive script on the upper part of both paintings. The poem on the first panel (Figure 1), at the upper right, is by Meng Haoren (689–704). It reads:

> Rowing the boat to anchor by the foggy shore,
> At dusk, the traveler's worries deepen.
> Vast is the field, where the treetops touch the sky,
> The moon reflected in the clear river comes close to men.

The second panel[18] bears a poem in the upper left by Li Bo (705–62):

> In the clear sky, a goose flies away to the distance,
> In the vast sea, a lone sailboat floats slowly.
> The sun is about to set,
> When will the apricot tree by the water bloom?

Although the poems are not the artist's own composition, she has faithfully portrayed the scenery described in the poems in keeping with the literati tradition of rendering poetic feelings in a painting.

As mentioned earlier, Sin Saimdang was said to have studied the paintings of An Kyŏn. Yet what we know of An Kyŏn's paintings today is very different from what we see in her landscape screen in the National Museum. An Kyŏn's best-documented work, *Dream Journey to the Peach Blossom Spring*, dated 1447,[19] in Tenri Central Library, Tenri University, Nara, and other paintings attributed to him are mostly in the so-called Li-guo style, named after the two noted Northern Song masters Li Cheng (919–67) and Guo Xi (ca. 1000–90).

A closer look at the literary sources on An Kyŏn, however, reveals that he could well have painted landscapes in the Zhe School style. In his *Collected Writings*, Kim Allo (1481–1537) recorded that An Kyŏn saw many valuable old paintings in the royal collection, and that, had he tried to emulate Guo Xi or any other painter, he could easily have done so.[20] The masters An Kyŏn endeavored to follow also included Ma Yüan (active ca. 1190–1225) of the Southern Song Academy, whose painting style provided the basis for the Zhe School of the early Ming (1368–1644) period. Therefore, it is indeed possible that Saimdang may have taken such a painting by An Kyŏn as her model. Yulgok's comment that his mother followed An Kyŏn may have been based on his belief that An Kyŏn, as the foremost painter of the early Chosŏn period, would have been the logical choice as her model. Still another possibility is that Sin Saimdang indeed painted in the An Kyŏn manner following the Guo Xi style, but no such paintings have survived.

In their subject matter and subdued, expressive manner, the set of four paintings in the Pang Iryŏng collection, *Flowers*, *Grasses*, *Fish*, and *Bamboo*, could also be considered works suitable for a lady of Sin Saimdang's standing. This set of paintings includes a watermelon and plants; a spray of bamboo; a cucumber vine and eggplant; and a fish.[21] Numerous grass-and-insect paintings in color are attributed to Sin Saimdang, but only a handful of ink monochrome paintings depicting plants and waterfowl. Although the condition of the Pang Iryŏng paintings is rather poor, they seem to be the best works by Saimdang in that category in terms of delicate handling of ink and brush and the realistic rendering of forms based on observation.[22]

The first leaf, depicting a watermelon and plants (Figure 2), shows a well-balanced, asymmetrical composition with the large, globular fruit occupying the lower left corner; the rest of the space is filled with delicate stalks of plants. A faint ground line is indicated by lightly shaded ink just above and to the right of the watermelon. The brushstrokes depicting the two sprays of foxtails in the upper left corner are extremely delicate, creating an impression of the plants swaying gently in space. The other plant to the right also conveys, in its thin, coiling vines, a feeling of light movement in space.

The second leaf, a spray of bamboo (Figure 3), is a valuable example of mid-sixteenth-century bamboo painting in ink. Another bamboo image of a similar type and style can be found in the lower right corner of *Gathering of Scholars Who Passed the Chinsa Examination in the Same Year* (artist unknown), a hanging-scroll painting in the National Museum in Seoul.[23] Because the latter painting can be dated to around 1542 in accordance with the date of this particular gathering (Ahn 1975: 117–23), the Pang Iryŏng bamboo leaf can likewise be dated to the mid-sixteenth century, during Sin Saimdang's later years.

Compared with a sixteenth-century ink bamboo painting by Yi Chŏng (1554–1626),[24] *Windblown Bamboo* (Figure 4), Saimdang's ink bamboo does not show emphatic swelling of the bamboo joints. Instead, like the spray of bamboo in *Gathering of Scholars*, the stems are rather thin and straight, with the joints marked by gently arcing lines. The leaves are grouped in threes or fours, but do not give an impression of the extreme stylization characteristic of late Chosŏn bamboo paintings in ink. Also, the stalk on the right, executed in light ink, looks somewhat like the shadow of the main stalk rendered in dark ink. The manner of depicting bamboo in two contrasting tones of ink is more systematically applied in Yi Chŏng's paintings of the early seventeenth century. Sin Saimdang's bamboo, however, shows a definite change of style from the earlier *Album of Ink Bamboo Paintings* by Sumun, dated 1424 (Figure 5), in which the artist painted the bamboo with thin stalks and long, thin leaves. Although the stalks are still relatively thin in the Saimdang painting, the leaves approach well-balanced proportions in that they are not excessively thin. A painting by Sin Saimdang's daughter, Maech'ang, *Bamboo and Sparrows* (Figure 6), which is now kept in Yulgok Memorial Hall in Kangnŭng, goes one step further in the same direction: The leaves look even more natural and are relatively well proportioned in length and width.[25] This is the style of bamboo painting preferred by Yi Chŏng in the late sixteenth and early seventeenth centuries. Thus Sin Saimdang's bamboo marks a distinct place in the chain of development of bamboo painting from the fifteenth to the seventeenth centuries.

Of the several paintings in ink of plum attributed to her, the *Album of Ink Plum Paintings*, now in Ewha Woman's University Museum, is worth considering as the paintings approach the compositional type prevalent during the sixteenth century.[26] The eight leaves form four sets of compositions of two leaves each. Each composition features several old, thick branches that are abruptly cut at the top and stretch diagonally to the left and right at the point where the two album leaves join together.[27] From these thick branches sprout a few thin sprays rendered in light green strokes. White flowers bloom profusely on the branches as well as the green sprays. Although the composition varies slightly from one set to another, this basic scheme is evident in all four sets.

In the absence of any other paintings in ink of plum by artists who preceded Sin Saimdang, it is difficult to place it in a comparative context.[28] Other plum paintings comparable in composition to those in this album are one by Maech'ang, *Plum and Moon* (Figure 7), and another of the same title attributed to an otherwise unknown painter named Hwaong, now in the National Museum, Seoul. The two paintings include a large moon delineated by the shaded area of the sky around it. A slightly later painting by Ŏ Mongnyong (born 1566), *Plum and Moon* (Figure 8), in the National Museum, also has basically the same arrangement of thick branches and thin sprays, with the moon above. In the early seventeenth century, however, the compositional type shows a marked change as seen in *Ink Plum* by O Talche (1609–1637) (Figure 9), who was a generation younger than Ŏ Mongnyong. In this painting, a large tree trunk pushes diagonally upward to the left, and a branch extends toward the right making a large S curve. Smaller branches and sprays rising vertically from the trunk balance the composition.

As is the case with the artist's bamboo painting, the Ewha University Album of Paintings in ink of plum attributed to Sin Saimdang fits into a stylistic chain of development in painting in ink of plum from the sixteenth to the seventeenth centuries.

Bird-and-Flower and Grass-and-Insect Paintings in Color

Paintings of birds and flowers and grasses and insects executed in color constitute the largest single group of extant works attributed to Sin Saimdang. However, it is very difficult to determine the authenticity of these paintings as no other paintings from the categories remain that can be dated to the period prior to Saimdang or to her contemporaries.

A majority of the artist's grass-and-insect paintings, as exemplified by the screen painting now in the National Museum, Seoul (Figures 10b, 10c, and 10d), or by the screen painting in Yulgok Memorial Hall in Kangnŭng (Figures 11a and 11d), are characterized by a centralized composition dominated by one or more stalks of a plant, such as poppies, cockscombs, eggplants, watermelons, or cucumbers. Butterflies, bees, and other flying insects hover in the air around the plants while grasshoppers and the like crawl on the ground. In many cases, the ground line is not indicated. When shown, it is drawn minimally with ink or color wash. Many sets of paintings which once formed albums survive, but not necessarily in their original format.[29]

The centralized composition seems unique, as no other Korean artist of later periods followed it. Professor Roderick Whitfield contends that Sin Saimdang's composition was based on earlier Chinese models (Whitfield 1993: 56). Indeed, we can find several precedents in Chinese paintings of the Northern Song (960–1125) and later periods. The earliest example is the hanging scroll *Bamboo, Sparrow, and Rabbits*

(Whitfield 1993: 10, pl. 3), recovered in 1974 from a tenth-century Liao dynasty (907–1125) tomb (Tomb No. 7) at Yemao-tai, Liaoning Province. Another is a pair of hanging scrolls by Lü Jingfu (Whitfield 1993: 48, pl. 13a-b), a little known painter from Biling, Jiangsu Province. These paintings, which bear Lu's seals and are now in Manju-in, Kyoto, depict grasses and insects. Although his dates cannot be determined, it is known that Lü was a disciple of the Northern Song monk-painter Juning, also a native of Biling.[30]

The fact that Lü Jingfu's paintings made their way to Japan might indicate that such a compositional type could also have come to Korea prior to Sin Saimdang's time. If we could find a similar composition in a late-Koryŏ dynasty (918–1392) painting, that would be a perfect link in a chain of transmission. Unfortunately, however, aside from the bamboo or peony motifs inlaid on the surface of celadon vessels, no other Korean flower paintings of such a compositional type have survived. Nevertheless, it is well established that artistic contacts had long existed between China and Korea through which techniques, motifs, styles, and compositional types were transmitted. We should admit, however, that Sin Saimdang's grass-and-insect paintings are more sensitive representations of a smaller, more intimate world than that depicted so luxuriously by Lü Jingfu.[31]

Of the numerous paintings of this type attributed to Sin Saimdang, perhaps the best known are two screen paintings, one in the National Museum, Seoul (Figures 10b, 10c, and 10d), and the other, in the Yulgok Memorial Hall, Kangnŭng (Figures 11a and 11d). However, these two screens, each consisting of eight paintings on paper, show somewhat different styles. The Kangnŭng paintings are done in lighter colors, almost like watercolor, whereas the National Museum paintings are executed in opaque color, with many traces of retouching. Also, some of the panels in the Kangnŭng screen display more spontaneity than the panels on the National Museum screen. The Kangnŭng paintings each measure 48.5 x 36 centimeters; the National Museum paintings, which measure 33.3 x 28.5 centimeters, are slightly smaller, indicating that they could originally have formed an album.

The Kangnŭng screen is allegedly from the Songdam Academy, in Kangnŭng.[32] Dedicated to Yulgok, the academy was built in 1624 and was forced to close in 1871 by the order of Taewŏn'gun, Regent and father of King Kojong (r. 1863–1907). The screen is said to have been in a Pak family in Kangnŭng for four generations before it was given to the

Yulgok Memorial Hall. However, the Kangnŭng local gazetteer records that, in 1804, a fire at the Songdam Academy destroyed everything there. It is not clear whether the screen was saved from the disaster.

The National Museum screen, on the other hand, has two colophons now mounted as the last two panels of the screen, thus forming a ten-panel screen. The first colophon is by a former owner of the screen, Sin Kyŏng (1696–1766), a descendant of Sin Saimdang. According to him, the screen's provenance goes back to Yi Yangwŏn (1529–1592), a high official and contemporary of Yulgok. The second colophon, dated 1946, was written by O Sech'ang (1864–1953), author of the *Biographical Dictionary of Korean Painters and Calligraphers* (1928). In the colophon, he pronounced the paintings, which he referred to as an "album," as genuine works by Sin.

Despite the high praise given to the National Museum screen by O Sech'ang, a comparison of the two sets of paintings shows the National Museum's to be more rigid in composition (the handling of forms in space). The second panel (10b), for example, depicts two stalks of eggplant, and insects and grasses. Two butterflies are shown with wings spread flat, as if pasted on a wall instead of hovering in space; other insects and grasses are likewise placed close to the surface of the picture plane. In another panel (10d), in which a poppy flower occupies the center of the composition and a few dianthus and morning glories fill the lower part of the outspread poppy plant, two butterflies, one on either side of the poppy, appear flat and almost lifeless. In all eight panels, the ground lines are indicated by ink dots, which seem quite out of place among the plants and insects rendered in opaque colors.

The Kangnŭng screen displays a subtlety in its color tones that is analogous to the variations in ink tones in the set of paintings in the Pang Iryŏng collection. In particular, the first panel, composed of a cucumber vine with a few stalks of dianthus, comes close to those paintings in its delicacy of the brushstrokes as well as in the subtle gradation of tones. The ground line, a low mound on the left, is a line drawn in light ink wash, and the composition is not as centralized as in the other panels. In contrast to the rigid and stationary butterflies in the National Museum screen, two butterflies fly toward the center of the painting, fluttering their wings.

The degree of subtlety differs a great deal from panel to panel on the Kangnŭng screen. The fourth panel (11d), with two eggplant stalks and butterflies, displays none of the delicacy and suppleness of the first panel's brushstrokes and color gradations. One possible explanation for the uneven quality of this screen is that the set might have been painted by another artist as a replacement after the fire at the Songdam Academy in 1804.[33]

An examination of the embroidery screen now in Tong'a University Museum, Pusan (Figures 12d and 12f), is useful in understanding the composition of the paintings attributed to Sin Saimdang. The screen is said to have been handed down to the descendants of Yi Wu, Sin Saimdang's youngest son and himself a talented painter.[34] The fourth panel of the Tong'a University screen (Figure 12d) and the second panel of the National Museum screen depicting eggplants (Figure 10b) are almost identical in composition. Even one of the flatly "pinned" butterflies in the painted panel appears in the embroidery panel. Surprisingly, the overall composition of the embroidered version looks less rigid, depicting more freely scattered insects in the air and thin grasses around the central group of eggplant stalks that seem to sway gently in light wind. Several small eggplant flowers blooming on the upper parts of the stalks also evoke the feeling of naturalness inherent in an original composition.

The same is true of another similar set of compositions, namely, the sixth embroidered panel (Figure 12f) and third painted panel (Figure 10c), both of which depict cucumber vines and a frog. The painted panel shows a nearly symmetrical arrangement of bunches of millet in the center, while the embroidered version presents a somewhat asymmetrical arrangement of the cucumber vine and small white flowers along with thin strands of grasses overlapping one another. A small cucumber, partly hidden behind a large leaf, still has the flower hanging at its tip while more flowers bloom on the vine.

Of all three works discussed here, it is the embroidered version that shows the characteristic indications of an original; the painted versions lack such salient qualities.[35] Sin Saimdang, who is said to have excelled in embroidery, could have composed her own underdrawings for her embroidery, which, in turn, could also have been used for her flower-and-insect paintings. Whether the paintings are indeed by her is not such a significant issue here. More important is their value as a compositional type that links sixteenth-century Korean paintings with earlier Chinese treatments of the same subject. In this regard, like the ink bamboo or the painting in ink of plum, the flower-and-insect and grass-and-insect paintings attributed to Sin Saimdang mark a certain place in the history of Korean painting.

The Creation of the Saimdang Myth

As we have seen, there are more problems than answers concerning Sin Saimdang's oeuvre, especially the grass-and-insect paintings attributed to her. It is not easy to determine why so many of these types of paintings have been attributed to her. Was she really perceived in her lifetime as an accomplished painter commensurate with all the respect now accorded her? When did this phenomenon begin to occur? A chronological survey of the documentation of Sin's life and art, including the colophons to paintings in which the respective writers attribute the work to her, will shed some light in attempting to answer such questions. The following is a list of those materials:

1. Yi I (1533–1584), "Sŏnbi haengjang" (Biographical Notes on Deceased Mother).
2. Ŏ Sukkwŏn (active sixteenth century), *P'aegwan chapki* (Storyteller's Miscellany).
3. Yi Chŏnggu (1564–1635), *Wŏlsa-jip* (Collected Writings).
4. Song Siyŏl (1607–1689), *Songja taejŏn* (Complete Works of Master Song).
5. Yun Kye (1622–1689), colophon (dated 1660) to a twelve-leaf album of bird-and-flower paintings, National Museum, Seoul.
6. Chŏng Sisul (active during the reign of King Hyŏnjong, 1660–1674), *Haedong hobo* (Catalog of Sobriquets of Koreans).
7. Chŏng Ho (1648–1736), colophon datable to 1715, now mounted on the first panel of the ten-panel, painted grass-and-insect screen (eight paintings) in the Yulgok Memorial Hall, Kangnŭng.
8. Kwŏn Sangha (1641–1721), colophon dated 1718 to a set of four ink paintings, Pang Iryŏng Collection.
9. Anonymous (An Yunhaeng?), colophon dated to the cyclical year *kyŏng'o* (1750?) to a set of seven leaves of grass-and-insect paintings, the National Museum, Seoul.
10. Yi Pyŏng'yŏn (1671–1751), colophon to a painting in ink of grapes, Ho-am Art Museum.
11. Cho Kŭmyŏng (1693–1737), *Tonggye manrok* (Collected Writings).
12. Sin Kyŏng (1696–1766), colophon to the ten-panel screen (eight paintings) of grass-and-insect paintings, National Museum, Seoul.

13. Yi Kŭngik (1736–1806), *Yŏllyŏsil Kisul* (Collected Essays).
14. Yun Chŏngsŏp (1791–1870), *Onyujae-jip* (Collected Writings).
15. Kim Sŏnggae, ed., *Tongguk munhŏn* (Documents on Korea), chapter on "Painters," 1804.
16. Sin Sŏggwu (1805–1865), colophon to the eight-leaf *Album of Ink Plum Paintings*, Ewha Woman's University Museum.
17. Yun Chong'ŭi (1805–1886) colophon to a set of six-panel calligraphy by Sin Saimdang, Yulgok Memorial Hall, Kangnŭng.
18. Sin Ŭngjo (1804–1899), colophon dated 1861 to the eight-leaf *Album of Ink Plum Paintings*, Ewha Woman's University Museum.
19. Anonymous, nineteenth century, *Choya chibyo* (A Brief Unoffical History of Korea).
20. O Sech'ang (1864–1953), colophon dated 1946 to the ten-panel screen (eight paintings), National Museum, Seoul.
21. Yi Kwan'gu (1899–1991), colophon dated 1954 to the eight-leaf *Album of Ink Plum Paintings*, Ewha Woman's University Museum.
22. Pak Chaejo (contemporary), colophon dated 1972 to the two-panel *Screen of Landscape Paintings*, National Museum, Seoul.

Of the above twenty-two documents, only the first three were written within a century of Sin Saimdang's lifetime. The rest were written after the time of Song Siyŏl, who was considered the direct heir to Yulgok's school of Neo-Confucian philosophy. Song's illustrious political and scholarly career definitely lent weight to his writings about Sin Saimdang, which in turn had a great impact on the promotion of Saimdang as a painter. To quote from his colophon to Saimdang's *Autumn Grasses and Multitude of Butterflies*: "This painting was done by Mr. Yi [Wŏnsu]'s wife. What is in the painting looks as if created by heaven; no man can surpass [this]. She is fit for being the mother of Master Yulgok."[36]

The colophon indicates that Song Siyŏl came across a painting by Sin Saimdang by chance and wrote the comment that it is only fitting that such a wonderful artist should be the mother of Yulgok. Another important point of this colophon is that this is the earliest document in which Saimdang's grass-and-insect paintings are mentioned. Earlier mentions are only of her landscapes and grape paintings.

Song Siyŏl's long, illustrious political and scholarly career is too complicated to summarize here.[37] During his lifetime, the Chosŏn court was suffering from strife between the factions of the "southerners" (*namin*) and the "westerners" (*sŏin*). Song, who belonged to the latter, naturally suffered many setbacks, including several periods of exile when the former faction was in power. To make the situation worse, around 1683, the westerners' faction was divided into the factions of Young Doctrine (*soron*) and Old Doctrine (*noron*) on the issue of the punishment of the southerners. Song, being the leader of the *noron*, retired from politics when the *soron* faction gained power. In 1689, Song submitted a letter of petition to the king in which he expressed his opposition to the investiture of the crown prince. As a result of his petition, Song Siyŏl was exiled briefly to Cheju Island, but soon was called back to Seoul for questioning. On his way back to Seoul, he was put to death at the instigation of the *sŏin* officials. In 1694, however, when the Western faction regained power at court, Song's titles were posthumously reinstated. In the following year, he was awarded the posthumous title *Munjŏng* and, subsequently, about seventy Confucian academies honoring him were established all over the country. Song's phenomenal resurrection to a position of the highest honor as a Confucian scholar-statesman appears to have been largely responsible for Sin Saimdang's recognition as the preeminently talented female painter in Korean history.

Kwŏn Sangha, the Neo-Confucian scholar-official who wrote the colophon to the set of ink paintings in the Pang Iryŏng Collection, was a direct follower and chief disciple of Song Siyŏl. Kwŏn's respect for Song was such that he adopted as his sobriquet the name Suam, meaning "following Uam" (that is, Song Siyŏl). The politically and intellectually powerful lineage from Yulgok to Song Siyŏl, and then to Kwŏn Sangha, seems directly responsible for the creation of the quasi-mythical aura around Sin Saimdang. Since the eighteenth century, many paintings of grapes, grasses, and insects, or flowers and birds, have been attributed to Sin Saimdang, and works now classified as "folk painting," showing a centralized composition with a simple stalk of flowers and a few insects, have subsequently been assigned to her as well.

However, despite her important position in Korean history, the uneven quality of the works attributed to her makes it difficult to ascertain the true nature of Sin Saimdang as a painter. As a woman living in such a socially restrictive environment, there is no doubt that her training would have been very limited, and perhaps mostly self-directed. Yet if, as some documents attest, she succeeded in acquiring a certain degree of fame as a painter during her own lifetime, the standard of her painting must have been quite remarkable. At the same time, as long as she occupies the formidable position as the mother of Yulgok, it will remain nearly impossible to evaluate her true worth as a painter.

Despite the aura of myth surrounding Sin Saimdang, what seems evident in this survey of works attributed to her is that her ink paintings fall within the general framework of literati painting of her time. This fact is important because only a few paintings of the early Chosŏn period can be dated. Because we know the approximate dates of her activities, the paintings attributed to her that fall within the framework of the period are important as evidence of the stylistic and compositional development of those early Chosŏn ink paintings. Many of her paintings in color, however, seem to be an outgrowth of her embroidery patterns.

Nonetheless, they provide an important link in subject matter and compositional types between Korean and Chinese painting traditions prior to the sixteenth century.

Notes

An earlier version of this chapter appeared in *Oriental Art* 46:1 (2000): 35–47, and is used with permission of *Oriental Art*.

1. There are twelve women artists recorded in O Sech'ang, *Kŭnyŏk sŏhwajing*. Five additional names are found in Kim Yŏng'yun, *Han'guk sŏhwa inmyŏng sasŏ* and in Yu Pongnyŏl, *Han'guk hoehwa taegwan*. This is only about 1 percent of the total number of artists recorded in the biographical dictionaries. By contrast, according to Ellen Johnston Laing, in Yu Jienhua's *Zhongguo meishujia renming cidian* (Shanghai, 1981), approximately 31,200 artists are recorded, of which 1,046—or about 3 percent—are female painters. See Laing, "Women Painters," 81.

2. Sin Saimdang's birthdate, 1504, is adopted from "Sŏnbi Haengjang" ("Biography of My Deceased Mother") by her son, Yulgok Yi I, in *Yulgok Chŏnsŏ*, vol. 4, 300–02. See O Sech'ang, *Kŭnyŏk sŏ-hwajing*, 339, for another birthdate: 1512.

3. With the exception of Chukhyang, all four women are of the *yangban* class. No women painters from families of professional painters were recorded. This is a marked contrast to the situation in China, where several female painters who were daughters of professional painters were recorded. See Marsha Weidner, "Women in the History of Chinese Painting," in Weidner et al., *Views*, 14, and Laing, 31.

4. The Association of Korean Housewives each year selects one model woman as the recipient of the Saimdang Prize.

5. See Yi, *Saimdang*, for comprehensive biographical sketches of Lady Sin and her family members.

6. This purge is known in Korean history as the *kimyo sahwa*.

7. Yi Wŏnsu served as a minor government official late in his life. His last official post was Inspector in the Censorate Board, a position of the sixth rank.

8. During the early Chosŏn period, it was not unusual for a *yangban*-class family to have its married daughter and her husband living at home for several years after their marriage.

9. In Kangnŭng, in commemoration of Saimdang and her son, the Yulgok Memorial Hall was built in 1975. Paintings and calligraphic works of these two celebrated figures are displayed there. The house Yulgok was born in was called Ojukhŏn, or Black Bamboo hall, and was rebuilt on the original site.

10. Quoted in O Sech'ang, *Kŭnyŏk sŏ-hwajing*, 339.

11. Tongyang is an old name for P'yŏngsan.

12. Ŏ Sukkwŏn, *P'aegwan chapki*, quoted in O Sech'ang, *Kŭnyŏk sŏ-hwajing*, 339. Ŏ Sukkwŏn's dates are not known, but he was recorded to have passed the government examination for Chinese language translators in 1541.

13. *Kyujung yoram* (Manual of the Inner Court), attributed to Yi Hwang (1501–70), quoted in *Han'guk yŏsŏng-sa*, 572.

14. See the article on "Injunction," under the Criminal Code, in *Kyŏngguk Taejŏn* (Legal Code of the Chosŏn Dynasty), where it is specified that women of the scholar-official class who go to the mountains and waters for pleasurable gatherings or for the spirit worship will be punished by 100 strokes.

15. As it was unusual for a woman of the early Chosŏn period to be known for her poetry, Hŏ Nansŏrhŏn is also the subject of another essay in this volume entitled "Hŏ Nansŏrhŏn and 'Shakespeare's Sister'" by Professor Kichung Kim. See pp. 78–95.

16. For poetry by Hŏ, Poetry of Hŏ Nansŏrhŏn.

17. On the back of the screen is a colophon, dated 1975, by Pak Chaejo, who owned the paintings before they were sold to the National Museum. In the colophon, Pak recounts the history of the paintings as told to him by Yi Changhŭi, a descendant of Yi Wu, Sin Saimdang's fourth son. According to the story, the paintings were in the possession of Sin Man (1703–1765), a great-grandson of Sin Myŏnggyu (1618–1688), whose mother was the maternal granddaughter of Cho Lin, the eldest son of Maech'ang, Sin Saimdang's daughter. Yi Changhŭi still owns many other paintings attributed to Sin Saimdang.

18. Illustrated as fig. 42 in Yi, *Fragrance, Elegance*, 74.

19. An Kyŏn painted this work for Prince Anp'yŏng (1418–1453), the calligrapher of the early Chosŏn period, and the third son of King Sejong.

20. Kim Allo, *Yŏngch'ŏn Tamjŏk-ki*, 209.

21. The four paintings probably originally formed an album, but now are mounted together in a frame, along with a colophon by Kwŏn Sangha (1641–1721) written in 1718. Kwŏn was a famous Neo-Confucian scholar along the lines of Song Siyŏl (1607–1689), the most prominent scholar of the Yulgok school.

22. As to the present condition of the paintings, the owner explained that, during the Korean War of 1950, the family had placed the paintings in a jar that they buried underground. The silk of the painting became darkened due to excessive moisture in the jar.

23. Illustrated in Ahn Hwi-joon, *Han'guk Hoehwasa*, 105, fig. 39.

24. In a standard biographical dictionary of Korean painters, Yi Chŏng's dates are given as 1541–after 1622. See Yi, "Yi Chŏng," 61–68, for the revised dates given here: 1554–1626.

25. The attribution of this painting of Maech'ang is strengthened by a seal at the lower left corner reading *Tŏksu Yissi*, or the Yi clan of Tŏksu, her family.

26. The paintings are done in ink and light-green on paper. Each leaf measures 54 x 36.7 centimeters. Three colophons written on separate sheets have been attached to the upper and lower edges. The earliest of the three painting is by Sin Sŏggu (1805–1865); the second is by Sin Ungjo (1804–1899); and the third by Yi Kwan'gu (1899–1991). For the contents of these colophons, see Yi Unsang (1982), 178–88.

27. Illustrated in Yi, *Saimdang* figs. 38–42.

28. Recently, there appeared in Kangnŭng, an album of painting in ink of plums allegedly by Kim Sisŭp (1435–?), a famous poet who is also said to have painted two self-portraits. In terms of compositional type, this album painting is very similar to the Ewha Woman's University Museum album attributed to Sin Saimdang.

29. Some are mounted as a small screen, whereas others are separated as single sheets of paintings.

30. See Whitfield, *Fascination*, 50, for a quotation from Guo Roxü's *Duhua jianwenzhi*.

31. The difference between the paintings by Sin Saimdang and Lü Jingfu was pointed out by Kumja Paik Kim in her written comments to me following the symposium. She further pointed out the similar quality of balance and simplicity found in the paintings of Sin Saimdang and in the simple silver-inlaid decor on the bronze *kundika*, and on the incense burners of the Koryŏ period.

32. The present Kangnŭng screen is a ten-panel screen. The eight paintings are mounted on the second through ninth panels. The first panel has a colophon by Chŏng Ho (1648–1736) which is not dated, but datable to 1715 by internal evidence; the tenth panel has a colophon by Yi Ŭnsang dated 1965. Chŏng's colophon was not originally with the paintings, but was found among old documents that had been preserved in a certain Sin Myŏngsŏn's home in Myŏngju, Kangwŏn Province. In the colophon, Chŏng recounts his experience of seeing a screen of grass-and-insect paintings by Sin Saimdang in the Songdam Academy when he visited the place in 1715.

33. This assumption can be strengthened by an eyewitness account of Saimdang's screen of color paintings. In an anonymous colophon to a set of seven grass-and-insect paintings attributed to Saimdang now in the National Museum, Seoul—dated only by the cyclical year *kyŏng'o*—the writer identifies himself as a magistrate of Kangnŭng, who arrived there in the cyclical year *kyŏng'o* and went to the Songdam Academy, where he saw a colored screen, as well as a panel of ink painting by Saimdang. The writer can be identified as An Yunhaeng (born 1692), who began his post as magistrate of Kangnŭng in 1750, the cyclical year *kyŏng'o*. (See Yi Sŏngmi, "Chosŏn sidae yŏryu hwaga yŏn'gu," 129, for the possibility of An Yunhaeng's being the writer of the colophon.) The magistrate expressed his feelings of wonder upon seeing the exquisite screen paintings. The present set of paintings in the Yulgok Memorial Hall would unlikely stimulate such feelings in a viewer.

34. See Yi, *Saimdang*, 347–48, for the details of the line of transmission of this screen. The size of each embroidered panel is 61 x 40 centimeters.

35. When this paper was presented at the symposium, Dr. Kumja Paik Kim pointed out that normally it is the painting, not the embroidery, that has the chance of being more natural. I agree with her in principle. In this case, however, my assumption is that the

paintings I compared with the embroidery might not be original but copies made after the original, or so heavily retouched as to lose the natural or spontaneous quality.

36. This painting is no longer extant. The colophon was recorded in the entry on Sin Saimdang in O Sech'ang, *Kŭnyŏk sŏ-hwajing*, 339.

37. His last official position was as chief of the Privy Council, the first-ranking position. See the entry on Song Siyŏl in *Han'guk Minjok*, vol. 13: 22–25, for his biography.

References

Ahn, Hwijoon. "Yŏnbang tongnyŏn ilsi chosa kyehoedo sogo" (On the Painting of *Yŏnbang tongnyŏn ilsichosa kyehoe*), *Yŏksa hakpo* 65 (March 1975): 117–23.

———. *Han'guk Hoehwasa* (History of Korean Painting). Seoul: Ilchisa, 1980.

Han'guk minjok munhwa taebaekkwa sajŏn (Encyclopedia of Korean People and Culture). Sŏngnam: Academy of Korean Studies, 1991.

Kim Yŏng'yun. *Han'guk sŏhwa inmyŏng sasŏ* (A Biographical Dictionary of Korean Painters and Calligraphers). Seoul: Hanyang Munhwasa, 1959.

Kim Yungjung, ed., *Han'guk yŏsŏng-sa* (A History of Korean Women). Seoul: Ewha Woman's University, 1972.

Laing, Ellen Johnston. "Wives, Daughters and Lovers: Three Ming Dynasty Women Painters." In Marsha Weidner et al., *Views from the Jade Terrace: Chinese Women Artists, 1300–1912*. Indianapolis: Indianapolis Museum of Art, 1989.

———. "Women Painters in Traditional China." In *Flowering in the Shadows: Women in the History of Chinese and Japanese Painting,* edited by Marsha Weidner. Honolulu: University of Hawaii Press, 1990.

O, Hae'in. *Hŏ Nansŏrhŏn sijip* (Poetry of Hŏ Nansŏrhŏn), annotated tr. in Korean. Seoul: Haein Munhwa-sa, 1980.

O Sech'ang. *Kŭnyŏk sŏ-hwajing* (A Biographical Dictionary of Painters and Calligraphers of Korea). Seoul: Kyemyŏng Kurakpu, 1928; Korean tr. from Chinese, Seoul: Shigong-sa, 1998.

Weidner, Marsha S. "Women in the History of Chinese Painting." In Marsha S. Weidner et al., *Views from the Jade Terrace: Chinese Women Artists, 1300–1912*. Indianapolis: Indianapolis Museum of Art, 1989.

———, ed. *Flowering in the Shadows: Women in the History of Chinese and Japanese Painting*. Honolulu: University of Hawaii Press, 1990.

Whitfield, Roderick. *Fascination of Nature: Plants and Insects in Chinese Painting and Ceramics of the Yuan Dynasty (1279–1368)*. Seoul: Yekyŏng, 1993.

Yi I, "Sŏnbi haengjang" (Biography of My Deceased Mother). In *Yulgok Chŏnsŏ* (Complete Writings of Yulgok), vol. 2, translated by the Academy of Korean Studies. Songnan: The Academy of Korean Studies, 1988: 300–302.

Yi Sŏngmi. "Chosŏn sidae yŏryu hwaga yŏn'gu" (A Study on the Women Painters of the Chosŏn Period). *Misul charyo* 51 (1993): 98–149.

———. "Yi Chŏng: The Foremost Bamboo Painter of the Chosŏn Dynasty." *Orientations* 29(1998): 61–68.

———. *Fragrance, Elegance, and Virtue: Korean Women in Traditional Arts and Humanities*. Seoul: Daewŏnsa, 2002.

Yi Ŭnsang. *Saimdang ŭi saeng'ae wa yesul* (The Life and Art of Saimdang), rev. ed. Seoul: Sŏngmun-gak, 1982.

Yu Jien-hua. *Zhongguo meishujia renming cidian* (Biographical Dictionary of Chinese Artists). Shanghai: Renmin Meishu Chubansi, 1981.

Yu Pongnyŏl. *Han'guk hoehwa taegwan* (A Survey of Korean Painting). Seoul: Mun'gyo-wŏn, 1969.

Figure 1. *Landscape*. Attributed to Sin Saimdang. The first panel of the two-panel screen, ink and colors on paper.

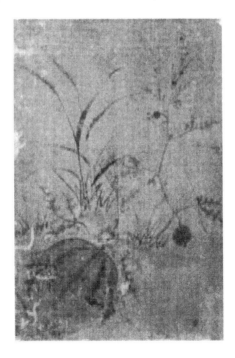

Figure 2. *Watermelon and Plants*. Attributed to Sin Saimdang. The first leaf of a set of four paintings.

Figure 3. *Ink Bamboo.* Attributed to Sin Saimdang. The second leaf of a set of four paintings.

Figure 4. *Ink Bamboo.* Yi Chŏng. Hanging scroll, ink on silk.

Figure 5. The tenth leaf of *Album of Ink Bamboo Paintings.*
Sumun, 1424.

Figure 6. *Bamboo and Sparrows.* Maech'ang. Ink on paper.

Figure 7. *Plum and Moon*. Maech'ang. Ink on paper.

Figure 8. *Plum and Moon*. Ŏ Mongnyong. Hanging scroll, ink on silk.

Figure 9. *Ink Plum.* O Talche. Hanging scroll, ink on silk.

Figure 10b. *Eggplant, Insects and Grasses.* Attributed to Sin Saimdang. The second panel of a ten-fold screen, *"Grasses and Insects."*

Figure 10c. *Cucumber Vines and a Frog.* Attributed to Sin Saimdang. The third panel of a ten-fold screen, *"Grasses and Insects."*

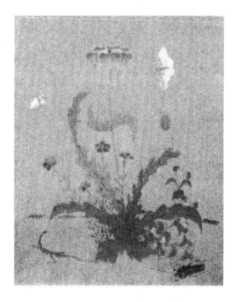

Figure 10d. *Poppy Flower, Morning Glories and Butterflies.* Attributed to Sin Saimdang. The fourth panel of a ten-fold screen, *"Grasses and Insects."*

Figure 11a. *A Cucumber Vine with a Few Stalks of Dianthus.* Attributed to Sin Saimdang. The first panel of a ten-fold screen, *"Grasses and Insects."*

Figure 11d. *Two Eggplant Stalks with Butterflies.* Attributed to Sin Saimdang. The fourth panel of a ten-fold screen, *"Grasses and Insects."*

Figure 12d. *Eggplant Stalks with Butterflies.* Attributed to Sin Saimdang. The fourth panel of a ten-fold screen, *"Grasses and Insects."*

Figure 12f. *Eggplant Stalks with Butterflies.* Attributed to Sin Saimdang. The fourth panel of a ten-fold screen, *"Grasses and Insects."*

4
Hŏ Nansŏrhŏn and "Shakespeare's Sister"

Kichung Kim

How is it that Virginia Woolf, a twentieth-century English writer, when speculating about a totally fictitious woman poet of sixteenth-century England, should shed so much light on the life and work of Hŏ Nansŏrhŏn, a sixteenth-century Korean woman poet? One reason is that not much is known about the life and work of individual women living in the sixteenth century, be it England or Korea. For, as Woolf observes, as soon as we try to find out about the life and work of a woman in sixteenth-century England, we are "held up by the scarcity of facts. One knows nothing detailed, nothing perfectly true and substantial about her. History scarcely mentions her."[1] The same is true of even the best-known sixteenth-century Korean women poets, for beyond the poems they left us, their life and work remain a mystery, even though they contributed significantly to the tradition of Korean poetry.

When Woolf contemplates the literary landscape of sixteenth-century England, what shocks and puzzles her most is "why no woman wrote a word of that extraordinary literature when every other man, it seemed, was capable of song or sonnet."[2] In sixteenth-century England, women of poetic gifts and aspirations found conditions too difficult for them to

78

aspire to, or to write, literature. Even a woman living in the first half of the twentieth century, as Woolf points out, must have "money and a room of one's own if she is to write fiction."[3] In other words, she has to have some leisure, a private space of her own, even a little of her own money—if only for paper, pen, brush, or ink—if she is to produce literature. For the woman living in sixteenth-century England, Woolf writes, in most cases she "could hardly read, could scarcely spell, and was the property of her husband."[4]

Under these conditions, Woolf asks, "what would have happened, had Shakespeare had a wonderfully gifted sister, called Judith."[5] Here is Woolf's own description of what would most likely have happened to "Shakespeare's sister":

> She was as adventurous, as imaginative, as agog to see the world as he [Shakespeare] was. But she was not sent to school. She had no chance of learning grammar and logic, let alone of reading Horace and Virgil. She picked up a book now and then, one of her brother's perhaps, and read a few pages. But then her parents came in and told her to mend the stockings or mind the stew and not moon about with books and papers. They would have spoken sharply but kindly, for they were substantial people who knew the conditions of life for a woman and loved their daughter—indeed, more likely than not she was the apple of her father's eye. Perhaps she scribbled some pages up in an apple loft on the sly, but was careful to hide them or set fire to them. Soon, however, before she was out of her teens, she was to be betrothed to the son of a neighboring wood-stapler. She cried out that marriage was hateful to her, and for that she was severely beaten by her father. Then he ceased to scold her. He begged her instead not to hurt him, not to shame him in this matter of her marriage. He would give her a chain of beads or a fine petticoat, he said; and there were tears in his eyes. How could she disobey him? How could she break his heart? The force of her own gift alone drove her to it. She made up a small parcel of her belongings, let herself down by a rope one summer's night and took the road to London. She was not seventeen. . . . She had the quickest fancy, a gift like her brother's, for the tune of words. Like him, she had a taste for the theatre. She stood at the stage door; she wanted to act, she said. Men laughed in her face. [. . .] At last—for she was very young, oddly like Shakespeare the poet in her face, with the same grey eyes and rounded brows—at last Nick Greene the actor-manager took pity on her; she found herself with child by that gentleman and so—who shall measure the heat and violence of the poet's heart when caught and tangled in a woman's body?—

killed herself one winter's night and lies buried at some crossroads where the omnibuses now stop outside the Elephant and Castle. [6]

Living conditions for women in sixteenth-century Korea—a society rigidly patriarchal and hierarchical—appear to have been similar to those of sixteenth-century English women. Even wellborn Korean women of that time were discouraged and excluded from systematic training in reading and writing, because book learning was considered unnecessary and inappropriate for women. In fact, the absence of learning was considered to promote virtue in women, and, if educated, they were expected *not* to exhibit their learning. Except for *kisaeng* (professional female entertainers who by law belonged to the lowest social class) women were to have no professional or public life, which was the exclusive domain of wellborn men. The Confucian principle of *namjon yŏbi* (literally, the "elevation of men and subjection of women") applied to all areas of social life during the Chosŏn period, and all avenues of professional or public life were closed to women. According to Yi Ik, a respected Sirhak scholar of the eighteenth century, "reading and learning are the domains of men. For a woman it is enough if she knows the Confucian virtues of diligence, frugality, and chastity. If a woman disobeys these virtues, she will bring disgrace to the family." [7] Furthermore, one of the seven rules of proper behavior for a married woman was that "she should not indulge in study or literature because they were considered improper for a woman."[8] In fact, women of marked intelligence and artistic talent were thought to be "ill-fated."[9]

Although literacy was not promoted for women at the time, wellborn women of the sixteenth century, both in England and Korea, appear to have had opportunities to become literate. And a small number of them not only made good use of their educational opportunities but even distinguished themselves by writing significant works—poetry, and prose by wellborn Korean women and mostly translations and devotional works by wellborn English women. Thus, in sixteenth-century Korea, despite all the obstacles placed in the path of a woman's pursuit of learning and literature, a number of women not only became learned but also produced significant works in both *hangŭl* (Korean vernacular alphabet) and *hanmun* (Classical Chinese). Clearly, these were extraordinary, even "odd or eccentric," women, as

Chang Tŏksun has pointed out, who went against the anti-women mores and ideology of their society. Most of these women were privileged by either birth or circumstances: women who had grown up in the household of scholars where they were allowed to learn alongside their brothers; women with learned mothers and grandmothers who were willing to teach them; women who, through their own innate gifts and inclinations, were driven to excel in letters once they gained literacy; and finally those talented *kisaeng* who had to be accomplished in learning and literature because it was their job to entertain wellborn and learned men.[10]

One of the most important of these extraordinary women was Hŏ Nansŏrhŏn (1563–1589), the sister of two prominent literary men of the period, Hŏ Pong and Hŏ Kyun, the latter believed to be the author of *Hong Kiltong chŏn.* Because Hŏ Nansŏrhŏn was from a class far more privileged than that of "Shakespeare's sister," her condition in life must have differed from that of Woolf's "Judith," with privileges and opportunities that "Judith" could only dream of. In other words, there was an enormous class difference between them, which explains, more than anything else, why "Shakespeare's sister" could get nowhere in the London theatrical world despite her innate poetic gifts and burning ambition, while Hŏ Nansŏrhŏn could make herself into a poet in sixteenth-century Korea. She was not only born into one of the elite as well as literary and scholarly families; she also had a loving older brother, himself a poet, who did all he could to draw out and develop her poetic gifts. Her life was therefore far different from that of "Shakespeare's sister," yet in some ways her life seems to have also paralleled that of "Shakespeare's sister." For even though privileged by birth and supported by loving and gifted brothers, she, too, seems to have been unable to overcome, to borrow Woolf's words, the tragedy of a "woman born with a great gift in the sixteenth century."[11] Although Hŏ Nansŏrhŏn's life was lit up with literary accomplishments, it was also darkened by the tragedy of a poetically gifted woman born in the wrong time and the wrong place.

Hŏ Nansŏrhŏn was born into a family of gifted scholar-officials and poets. Her father, Hŏ Yŏp (1517–1580), an official of ministerial rank, had three children by his second wife—Hŏ Pong (1551–1588), Hŏ Nansŏrhŏn (1563–1589), and Hŏ Kyun (1569–1618)—in addition to three children by his first wife. Yet, even in such a family, the father appears to have believed it wrong, as did most Confucian scholars of the time, to encourage his daughter's love of learning and literature.[12] It therefore devolved on her brother Hŏ Pong, twelve years her senior, to actively support his sister's innate poetic gifts, which she seems to have displayed quite early on. Himself a distinguished poet as well as a rising scholar-official, Hŏ Pong not only taught his sister personally but also brought in a close friend of his, Yi Tal—a recognized poet of the day though stigmatized throughout his life for being a secondary son—to teach poetry to his younger sister and younger brother, Hŏ Kyun.

From the poems and letters exchanged between Hŏ Pong and Hŏ Nansŏrhŏn, we can gain a sense of the respect and love the brother and sister had for each other. A quatrain sent to his sister, along with writing brushes, shows the depth of Hŏ Pong's affection and solicitude:

> A companion of my student days sent down from heaven,
> These I send to you at home that you may draw
>   the autumn scene.
> You could draw the moonlight as you look at
>   the pawlownia tree.
> Try drawing insects and fish, too, illuminated by lamplight. [13]

In 1582, a year before he was sent into exile, Hŏ Pong sent his sister a volume of Tu Fu's verse. In an inscription on the back of the volume he recommends that she turn to Tu Fu in her study of poetry:

> This volume of Tu Fu's verses was selected and compiled by Shao Pao. Compared to the edition annotated by Yu, it is short and concise, but it is worth reading. In 1574, when I journeyed to China bearing the king's congratulatory message to the emperor on his birthday, I once stopped in Tong Chuan. There, meeting Wang Zhi Fu, a scholar from Shaanxi Province, we spent nearly a whole day conversing together. He gave me this volume when we parted, and I have kept it like a treasure in my book chest for several years. I now send it to you nicely re-bound so you can peruse it. If you do not reject my heartfelt wish, maybe Tu Fu's voice, which had become faint, will once again flow from my sister's hand. Written by Hagok [Hŏ Pong's pen name] in the spring of 1582.[14]

Two of Hŏ Nansŏrhŏn's most heartfelt poems are expressions of grief over her brother's banishment to Hamgyong Province:

"Sending Hagok Off to Kapsan"

A traveller to Kapsan, a distant place of banishment,
You look harried on your way to Hamgyŏng Province.
The banished official must be another Chia I of Han,
But how could the king be King Huai of Ch'u?
The water laps tranquilly on the autumn riverbanks
And the clouds over the Kwanbuk Pass reflect the setting sun.
Cold wind buffets the geese on the wing,
Sundered in the middle, they cannot hold their formation.

The second poem appears to have been written a short time later:

"For My Brother Hagok"

The candlelight shines low on the dark window,
Fireflies flit across the housetops.
As the night grows late and colder, my care deepens,
And I hear autumn leaves rustle to the ground.
No news has come from your place of banishment,
My mind is never free from worry.
Thinking of a distant temple,
I see a deserted hillside filled with the radiance of the moon.[15]

Hŏ Nansŏrhŏn's 200-odd surviving poems can be divided into three broad groups: 96 of them deal with the world of immortals (Sŏn'gye) and dreams; 90 with real-life situations; and the remaining 27 with empathy, that is, the poet placing herself in the shoes of another person, frequently a poor, abandoned, or lonely woman.[16] Because the poems in the second and third groups are about real people and real-life situations, they could perhaps be grouped together. Broadly speaking, we could say that half of Hŏ Nansŏrhŏn's extant poetry deals with people and situations in the real world, while the other half deals with the world of immortals and dreams.

By one scholar's tabulation, the most frequently recurring words in her poems dealing with real people in the real world are: "tears," "pensiveness," "bitterness," and "sorrow." Another scholar's tabulation goes even further. "The most widely used poetic words are those related to sorrow," she writes, and they are: "weeping, sadness, melancholy, tears, and then there are also those words which are indirectly related to sorrow such as blood, decline, coldness, darkness, emptiness, loneliness, and separation. . . . In her 210 poems such words occur 192 times, thus nearly once in every poem." [17] The dominant theme of half of her poems thus appears to be woman's pain and sorrow. It is for this reason that many Korean scholars have called Hŏ Nansŏrhŏn "the poet of tears."

When we try to look into Hŏ Nansŏrhŏn's life, we are "held up by the scarcity of facts," to borrow Woolf's words, for history is largely silent on her life. Beyond the poems she left us, we have few facts to go on. We are thus reduced to piecing out her life by what we know about the condition of women in sixteenth-century Korea, bits of anecdotal information, and by projecting her poetry onto her life.

From such material from her childhood and teen years, we know that she was considered a poetic prodigy by age seven,[18] and, despite her father's disapproval, her poetic gifts were lovingly nurtured by her older brother, Hŏ Pong, and his friend Yi Tal, a well-known poet of the time. Until her marriage, her life at her natal home had probably been sheltered, privileged, and relatively free as a wellborn daughter surrounded by books, poetically gifted brothers, and the literary friends of her elder brother.

When Hŏ Nansŏrhŏn married cannot be exactly determined; our best guess is that she was betrothed between the ages of fourteen and sixteen. Most likely, even after marriage, she continued to live at her natal home for some years; it was the custom of the times, especially for *yangban* families, for the bridegroom and bride to live at the bride's family home until the birth of their first child.[19] She therefore may have continued to live at her natal home until close to her twentieth year, surrounded by those who loved her and treasured her poetic gifts, where she must have felt free, physically and mentally, to continue writing poetry. Thus, even after she became a wife and a mother, still living at her natal home, she must have continued to write poetry. Although no documentary proof of all this exists as yet, this scenario of her life is essential to our understanding of Hŏ Nansŏrhŏn's poetic achievement. For had she been taken to her husband's family to live immediately after her marriage at age fourteen or sixteen, it is inconceivable that she could have produced the kind or quantity of poems she did.

What did it mean to be born a woman in sixteenth-century Korea? As the well-known creed of *Samjong chi to* (Three Tenets of Obedience) suggests, her life was seen in three stages of submission: as daughter, daughter-in-law and wife, and, finally, mother. For Hŏ Nansŏrhŏn, much more than for most Korean women of her time, the life of submission as daughter-in-law and wife must have been one of the most difficult experiences of her life. And it is not hard to imagine how the condition of her life, especially her life as a poet, must have undergone a drastic change when she had to leave her natal home to live at her husband's. It must have marked her transition from a sheltered, privileged, and relatively free life of a wellborn daughter to that of a confined, burdened, and closely watched life of a daughter-in-law and wife. She was no longer surrounded by those who loved her and treasured her poetic gifts; she was no longer free to explore her own family's books or to converse with her brothers and her brother's gifted friends, such as the poet Yi Tal, her tutor in poetry. Instead she was now surrounded by those who would be scrutinizing her with judgmental watchfulness, especially her poetry-writing, of which her parents-in-law, in particular, would have disapproved. Not only must it have been physically difficult to continue writing poetry; the greater difficulty must have been the mental and psychological contraints she must have felt day in and day out. She was now an outsider: Because she was a woman literally brought in from outside; and because she was a poet, an outlandish thing for a wife to be. She must have remained an outsider because even though she produced a son she failed to raise him to be an heir to her husband.

An exemplary wife and daughter-in-law in sixteenth-century Korea was not only expected but obligated by the mores and morality of that society to submerge herself totally in the domestic, filial, and wifely duties of her parents-in-law's household. According to Confucianism, she was a daughter-in-law before she was a wife. Like Woolf's "Angel in the House" she was expected to be "utterly unselfish"; to excel "in the difficult arts of family life"; to "sacrifice herself daily"; and to be "so constituted that she never had a mind of her own or a wish of her own, but preferred to sympathize always with the minds and wishes of others."[20] Although many gifted women of premodern Korea could and did submerge themselves in the drudgery and obligations of an exemplary daughter-in-law, wife, and mother, it appears Hŏ Nansŏrhŏn could not and would not do so, for she apparently continued to devote herself to the life of poetry even after marriage. In fact, not only did she continue to write poetry, she wrote poetry that was unrestrainedly expressive, outspoken, and self-assertive, poetry that projected into it her own life as a young woman full of needs, hopes, and frustrations as well as the pain-and-sorrow–filled lives of poor, abandoned, and lonely women.[21]

For a wellborn married woman of the times to do what Hŏ Nansŏrhŏn did must have been a clear defiance of the public mores and morality of Chosŏn society, and might even explain the many charges of plagiarism leveled against her by men of her own and later times.[22] And her inability to utterly subordinate her life of poetry to her life as a daughter-in-law, wife, and mother may very well have been one of the reasons for the discord between her and her mother-in-law, because her poetry-writing could only have alienated her mother-in-law. In fact, it is not difficult to imagine the mother-in-law's side. Most likely, her mother-in-law—from a fine family, and if not literary but well schooled in the letters and wifely duties like most wellborn women of the times—must have had to subordinate her own personal interests, desires, and hopes to the work and obligations of her husband's household. And, in turn, she must have expected her daughter-in-law to do the same, because that was the long-accepted pattern of the mother-in-law and daughter-in-law relationship in Korea. Unless she had been extraordinarily understanding, she must have found it difficult to sympathize with or tolerate her daughter-in-law's poetry writing. And add to this Hŏ Nansŏrhŏn's outspokenness and self-assertiveness, how could there have been anything but discord between them? We have Hŏ Kyun's testimony about their troubled relationship. Many years after her death, writing about his sister's unhappiness and death, Hŏ Kyun wrote:

> My late sister was wise and gifted in literature, but she was not accepted by her mother-in-law. And when she also lost her two children, she died with her heart filled with bitterness and sorrow. Whenever I think of her I cannot help but feel the pain and sorrow of her death.[23]

Although we have little documentary evidence on Hŏ Nansŏrhŏn's relationship to her husband, Kim Sŏngnip, nothing in the surviving records indicates he was a poet or appreciative of his wife's superior poetic gifts. On the contrary, what evidence there is suggests he was inferior to his wife in literary gifts: He never advanced beyond the lowest ranks as a government official[24] and Hŏ Kyun makes the following disparaging remark about his literary talents:

There are people in the world who are able to write even though they have no understanding of the underlying meaning of the written text. My brother-in-law Kim Sŏng-nip is one such. When he is asked to read the classics, he can barely read them out loud. And yet when he had to write answers to examination questions, he wrote effectively, scoring high marks several times.[25]

Hŏ Kyun's words could very well have been biased, since they were written many years after his beloved sister's death. And yet combined with Kim Sŏngnip's failure to rise in government service and his rumored literary inferiority to his wife,[26] Hŏ Kyun's words seem evidence enough of Kim Sŏngnip's lack of literary accomplishments. In a world where a wellborn man's accomplishments in learning and letters constituted his principal avenue of success in the world, it would have been difficult for Kim Sŏngnip to have appreciated his wife's superior literary gifts. Few Korean husbands of that time could have. I am reminded of what Margaret Fuller said of a woman of genius yoked to a man of mediocrity:

Woe to such a woman who finds herself linked to such a man in bonds too close. It is the cruelest of errors. He will detest her with all the bitterness of wounded self-love. He will take the whole prejudice of manhood upon himself, and to the utmost of his power imprison and torture her by its imperious rigors.[27]

And this was Fuller speaking of the condition of women in nineteenth-century America.

All serious poetry is autobiographical in some respects, for poetry reflects and represents some aspects of the poet's life. Because we know so little about Hŏ Nansŏrhŏn's personal life, we are tempted to read her life in her poetry. Though perhaps unavoidable, we must nevertheless exercise caution in projecting her poetry too literally onto her life. For one thing, her poems may not always originate in her own life experiences; some of them may originate either in her empathy with another's life or in response to her reading, especially of classical Chinese poetry. It would be a mistake, therefore, to always see in her poems particular aspects of Hŏ Nansŏrhŏn's own life. In fact, the poetic persona of her poems may as often be generic as they are personal, for the experience of her married life was shaped as much by the general condition of the married woman of her times as by her personal circumstances. When she poured out her innermost feelings into poetry, she spoke not only for herself but also for the Korean woman of her age. This is part of the greatness of her poetry.

The following poem, for example, about an orchid beneath the window, is often read biographically, especially since the poet has made explicit her personal identification with the orchid through her pen name (*Nan* of Nansŏrhŏn means orchid):

> The orchid beneath the window swaying in the wind,
> How fragrant are its leaves!
> Once the autumn wind sweeps by,
> Sadly it will wither and fall from the frost.
> Though its beauty will wither away,
> May its fragrance never vanish.
> My mind hurts looking at the flower,
> Tears fall and wet the sleeves of my coat.[28]

As one scholar suggested, it is tempting to read "the autumn wind" with its accompanying frost to refer to the poet's marriage, which brought such unwelcome changes in her life.[29] The freshness and gaiety of her youth blighted by the wind and frost of her married life, we feel the poet struggling to keep alive the core of her creative self in the line, "May its fragrance never vanish." Still, even in this most personal-seeming poem, we see that by speaking her own innermost feelings, Ho Nansŏrhŏn had also given expression to what many wellborn women of her time must have felt about the passing of their youthful beauty and sheltered life, although they themselves had seldom given poetic expression to their sentiments.

The next poem seems equally open to a biographical reading:

> A paulownia tree born on Mt. Yŏgyang,
> It has grown tall over the years in cold wind and rain.
> Luckily discovered by a gifted maker of instruments,
> It was cut and made into a *kŏmun'go.**
> A tune was played on the finished instrument,
> The world has never recognized the music of its sound.
> The "Kwangnŭngsan" tune is played again after a thousand years,
> This ancient tune will be lost forever. [30]
> [*A six-stringed musical instrument]

The first half of the poem delineates, almost step-by-step, Hŏ Nansŏrhŏn's development as a poet. Though born in a society that discouraged its women from pursuing learning and literature, she had the good fortune to have had an older brother (and the poet Yi Tal) nurture her poetic gifts. The second half of the poem focuses on the inevitable disappointment of her poetic career, for she never received the recognition she deserved. As personal as the poem may seem, couldn't it apply also to other unrecognized poets of her times, both male and female?

Because two of the next three poems focus specifically on the unhappiness of a married woman, we wonder whether Hŏ Nansŏrhŏn may have been speaking of her own unhappiness as a married woman:

"Married Woman's Sorrow"

1.
On the silk skirt and silk girdle,
traces of tear stains over tear stains.
Every year when spring grasses sprouted,
I waited for my lord to return.
Holding a *kŏmun'go* by my side,
I play a "South of the River" tune.
The rain scatters the petals of the flowering pear tree,
and the gate is closed shut in broad daylight. [31]

2.
The autumn moon rises over the tower,
the bejewelled folding screen stands empty.
On the frost-covered field of reed grass,
a wild goose alights in the evening dusk.
I play the *kŏmun'go* with all my heart,
still my lord does not come.
On a pond surrounded by a grassy field,
The petals of the lotus fall on the water. [32]

The next poem could apply to a married, as well as to an unmarried, woman:

"Always Thinking of You"

Thinking of you in the morning,
Thinking of you in the evening, too.
Where is that place that I'm thinking of?
The road stretches on endlessly for ten thousand li.
Difficult to reach because of the wind and waves,

> Even the clouds and wild geese cannot keep their promise.
> There's no one I can entrust my letters to,
> My heart is caught in a tangle of threads.[33]

Although the intensity of feelings expressed in these poems tempt us to imagine Hŏ Nansŏrhŏn speaking of her own unhappiness as a married woman, we cannot be certain of that. The poems may originate in her own experience as a married woman, but they may as easily originate in response to her reading of numerous poems on the same theme. What is indisputable, however, is that they express vividly the plight of many married women of Hŏ Nansŏrhŏn's class and times. Though they were bound in body and soul to their husbands, men, on their part, were not equally bound to their wives. Trapped in an unequal relationship, in most marriages only the wife would have suffered from loneliness and futile longing for her husband. How many other gifted women of premodern Korea lived their life of disappointment and heartbreak, never allowing themselves to express their feelings outwardly?

Hŏ Nansŏrhŏn understood what it meant to be isolated, alone, and unappreciated. Was it her own unhappiness as a married woman and a poet that enabled her to place herself so completely in the shoes of women whose lives were filled with pain and sorrow? For example, in a series of four short poems about a poor unmarried seamstress, she is able to evoke the seamstress's life of hunger and bleak isolation with a vividness and poignancy that is utterly compelling. Did she perhaps see in the seamstress another artist as isolated and unappreciated as herself?

"Poor Woman"

1.
In my looks I am not inferior to others.
I excel in sewing and weaving.
Because I have grown up in a poor family,
No reputable match-maker is acquainted with me.

2.
Though cold and hungry, I don't show it in my face.
All day long I weave sitting by the window.
Only my parents feel sorry for me.
How could the neighbors know anything about me?

3.
Late into the night I weave without resting.
The squeaking of the loom sounds cold.

This bolt of woven cloth in the loom,
Whose wedding dress will it make?

4.
Scissors clasped in my hand, I cut out the cloth,
And the chill of the night stiffens all my fingers.
For others I have made the bridal clothes,
Year after year alone in my room.[34]

The most heartbreaking of all her poems is also the most clearly autobiographical, and must have been written some time during the last years of her life:

"Mourning My Children"

Last year I lost my beloved daughter,
This year I lost my beloved son.
Alas, this woeful ground of Kangnŭng!
A pair of mounds stand face-to-face.
The wind blows through the white birch
And the ghostly lights flicker in the woods.
I call to your spirits by burning paper money
And by pouring wine on your mounds.
Will you, the spirits of brother and sister,
Play fondly together each night!
This child growing within me
Dare I hope it will grow safely to full term?
In vain I chant a magic verse of propitiation,
Tears of blood and sorrow swallow up my voice.[35]

This poem requires little commentary for its every line is so palpably steeped in the poet's grief and despair. And yet, perhaps it is necessary to remember that Hŏ Nansŏrhŏn's grief and despair over the loss of her son and daughter must have had a larger, familial, and institutional context, also. Her grief and despair must have come not only from personal sorrow but also from her sense of having failed to fulfill her familial and institutional obligations as a sixteenth-century Korean daughter-in-law and wife. For, by failing to raise an heir to her husband, she had failed her central role as a married woman in that society, and we can easily imagine how drastically her status must have fallen in her husband's household and how great must have been the chill of indifference and hostility of her parents-in-law and husband toward her. In her mid-twenties most likely, suffering frequently from illness,[36] how unbearable must have been her situation in her husband's household! But there is also an objective quality to this most personal of her poems which we must note. As suggested by Yi Sukhi, the poem is enduring in its searing powerfulness precisely because it so palpably objectifies in its unforgettable images the unbearable pain and sorrow suffered by mothers in the loss of their children. That is what makes the poem a great poetic achievement. To borrow Yi Sukhi's words, "It is no easy task to embody in words the mother's sorrow for the loss of her children. It is this which endows permanent life on her poem." [37]

Earlier I mentioned that about one half of Hŏ Nansŏrhŏn's extant poems speak of women's pain and sorrow, whereas the other half pertain to the world of immortals and dreams. One of the key questions about her poetry is, therefore, what the relationship might be between these two halves. I must confess, however, that I don't know how to read these poems dealing with the Sŏn world (the imagined world of Taoist Immortals), because I have not yet been able to gain an adequate understanding of their context, both historical and contemporary. These poems about the Sŏn world have to be read in the larger context of the tradition of Sŏn poetry written in both China and Korea. More important, we must not jump too easily to the conclusion that the Sŏn world meant to Hŏ Nansŏrhŏn and her contemporaries what it might mean to us today, that is, a pure dreamworld without any reality.

The following is just one of nearly one hundred poems she left us on her travels in the Sŏn world:

> I climbed Mt. Pongnae in my dream last night,
> Riding on the back of a dragon reposing in the waves of
> the sea.
> Immortal beings leaning on jade-green canes,
> Welcomed me affectionately on the Lotus Peak.
> Far beneath my feet I saw the East Sea,
> Looking small like wine in a wine glass.
> The phoenix beneath a flowering tree played on the flute,
> And the moonlight shone quietly on a golden water jar. [38]

How small and distant the human world looks, now that she has flown away to her Sŏn world! Could we perhaps compare this world to what religion has been to some people? Hŏ Nansŏrhŏn was not given the recognition she deserved either as a person or a poet in the rigidly patriarchal Confucian society of sixteenth-century Korea because she was a woman, a daughter-in-law, and a wife. She could seek recognition and empowerment only in a radically different world. Could the *Sŏn* world have represented that other world to her? For in order for her to go on living she had to create another world, a more generous world unlike the one she was born into, one where she could be fully accepted and appreciated for her gifts and accomplishments.

Hŏ Nansŏrhŏn died in 1589 of unknown causes at age twenty-seven, one year after her beloved brother Hŏ Pong's death in 1588. As Hŏ Kyun intimated of her death, "when she also lost her two children" on top of all her other woes, did she die "with her heart filled with bitterness and sorrow"?[39] What Virginia Woolf says about the fate of a gifted woman in sixteenth-century England seems also suggestive:

> [A]ny woman born with a great gift in the sixteenth century. [. . .] who had tried to use her gift for poetry would have been so thwarted and hindered by other people, so tortured and pulled asunder by her own contrary instincts, that she must have lost her health and sanity to a certainty. [40]

According to Hŏ Kyun a large number of her manuscript poems were burned at the time of her death per her request.[41] Our good fortune is that enough of her poems survive through Hŏ Kyun's efforts, giving us glimpses into the inner landscape not only of one gifted woman of sixteenth-century Korea but of a countless number of other Korean women of premodern Korea.

Notes

1. Woolf, *A Room of One's Own*, 46.
2. Ibid., 43.
3. Ibid., 4.
4. Ibid., 46.
5. Ibid., 48.
6. Ibid., 49–50.
7. Yung-Chung Kim, *Women of Korea*, 154.
8. Ibid., 157.
9. Ibid., 162.
10. Chang, *Hanguk munhak*, 409.

11. Woolf, *A Room of One's Own*, 51.

12. K. Hŏ, 106; Yongsuk Kim, *Chosŏn yŏryu munhak ŭi yŏngu*, 396.

13. K. Hŏ, *Hŏ Nansŏrhŏn sisŏn*, 91.

14. Ibid., 92; M. Hŏ, *Hŏ Nansŏrhŏn yŏngu*, 46.

15. T. Kim, *Hanguk hansi*, 74–75. Chia I (200–168 B.C.) was an unjustly banished official of Han, and the tradition has it that King Huai of Ch'u (329–299 B.C.)
foolishly banished the loyal minister Ch'u Yuan.

If Hŏ Nansŏrhŏn owed her education and poetic development to Hŏ Bong, her
older brother, it was mainly to her younger brother Hŏ Kyun she owed her poetic
reputation and the dissemination of her poems. When he was magistrate of Kongju
in 1608, twenty years after his sister's death, Hŏ Kyun compiled and published a
volume of more than 200 of her poems in woodblock printing, and it was largely
through this volume that her poetry survived in Korea and her fame spread to China
and Japan.

16. Yongsuk Kim, *Chosŏn yŏryu munhak ŭi yŏn'gu*, 391.

17. Ibid., 394–95; Yi, *Hŏ Nansŏrhŏn siron*, 132.

18. M. Hŏ, *Hŏ Nansŏrhŏn yŏngu*, 25.

19. Deuchler, *The Confucian Transformation of Korea*, 256. I owe much to Mark
Peterson for information on the living arrangements of the wellborn newlyweds in
sixteenth-century Korea.

20. Woolf, "Professions for Women," 236–7.

21. For the outspokenness of her poetry, we can mention her not-so-veiled criticism of King Sŏnjo for banishing her brother Hŏ Pong; the self-assertiveness is
evident in the frequent use of the infrequently used word "I" in many of her poems.
See Cha, "A Study on Feminist Consciousness Appearing in the Works of Hŏ
Nansŏrhŏn," 49–51.

22. Literary men of Hŏ Nansŏrhŏn's and, later, times appear to have found it
difficult to believe a young woman could write superior poetry. See: M. Hŏ, 120–29.

23. Ibid., 26.

24. Ibid.

25. Ibid., 28.

26. Yongsuk Kim, *Chosŏn yŏryu munhak ŭi yŏn'gu*, 401.

27. Kelley, *The Portable Margaret Fuller*, 286.

28. K. Hŏ, *Hŏ Nansŏrhŏn sisŏn*, 16.

29. Yi, *Hŏ Nansŏrhŏn siron*, 139.

30. K. Hŏ, *Hŏ Nansŏrhŏn sisŏn*, 21.

31. Ibid., 68.

32. Ibid., 69.

33. Ibid., 83.

34. Ibid., 37–39.

35. T. Kim, *Hanguk hansi*, 72.

36. M. Kim, *Hŏ Nansŏrhŏn ŭi munhak*, 13.

37. Yi, *Hŏ Nansŏrhŏn siron*, 165.

38. K. Hŏ, *Hŏ Nansŏrhŏn sisŏn*, 19.

39. Ibid., 26.

40. Woolf, *A Room of One's Own*, 51.

41. M. Hŏ, *Hŏ Nansŏrhŏn yŏngu*, 75.

References

Cha, Ok-Deuk. "A Study on Feminist Consciousness Appearing in the Works of Hŏ Nansŏrhŏn," unpublished MA thesis, Ewha Woman's University, 1986.

Chang, Tŏksun, *Hanguk munhak ŭi yŏnwŏn kwa hyŏnjang* (Korean Literature from Its Beginning to the Present). Seoul: Chimmundang, 1986.

Deuchler, Martina. *The Confucian Transformation of Korea: A Study of Society and Ideaology*. Cambridge and London: Harvard University Press, 1992.

Hŏ, Kyŏngjin, *Hŏ Nansŏrhŏn sisŏn* (Selected Poems of Hŏ Nansŏrhŏn). Seoul: P'yŏngminsa, 1987.

Hŏ, Mija. *Hŏ Nansŏrhŏn yŏngu* (A Study of Hŏ Nansŏrhŏn). Seoul: Sŏngsin Women's University Press, 1984.

Kelley, Mary, ed. *The Portable Margaret Fuller*. New York: Penguin Books, 1994.

Kim, Myŏng-hi. *Hŏ Nansŏrhŏn ŭi munhak* (Hŏ Nansŏrhŏn's Literature). Seoul: Chimmundang, 1987.

Kim, Taljin, ed. and tr. *Hanguk hansi* (Hanmun Poetry of Korea). Seoul: Minumsa, 1989.

Kim, Yongsuk. *Chosŏn yŏryu munhak ŭi yŏn'gu* (A Study of Chosŏn Dynasty Women's Literature), revised and expanded. Seoul: Hyejin Publishers, 1990.

Kim, Yung-Chung, ed. with an Introduction, *Women of Korea: A History from Ancient Times to 1945*. Seoul: Ewha Woman's University Press, 1979.

Woolf, Virginia. "Professions for Women." In *The Death of the Moth*. New York: Harcourt, Brace and Company, 1942 edition.

____. *A Room of One's Own*. San Diego and New York: A Harvest/HBJ Book, Harcourt Brace Jovanovich, 1957 edition.

Yi, Sukhi. *Hŏ Nansŏrhŏn siron* (A Study of Hŏ Nansŏrhŏn's Poetry). Seoul: Saemunsa, 1988.

5
Demythologizing Hwang Chini

Kevin O'Rourke

No direct sources of information on Hwang Chini are known to exist; her career can only be pieced together from fragmentary references in a number of sources, all written after the Hideyoshi war, hence some fifty years after Chini actually lived. None of these sources are official records; all belong to the category of *yadam* (an unofficial version of an historical tale), which is a romance genre that is fragmentary and anecdotal. Only three of these sources make direct reference to the poems: Im Pang records the *hansi* (a Korean poem in Chinese) "Farewell to So Yanggok"; Yi Tŏngmu gives "Songdo," which is also a *hansi*; So Yuyŏng has the Pyŏkkyesu *sijo*; and Kim T'aegyŏng gives two *hansi*—"Fond Thoughts of Full Moon Terrace" and "Song to the Half-Moon." Only one direct witness of Chini is quoted: an eighty-year-old man in Yi Tŏkhyŏng's written record, who gives evidence of a fragrance that lasted for days after Chini had been in a room.

A special mystique surrounds this celebrated *kisaeng*-singer-poet of the sixteenth century. Her popular profile depicts her as a member of a despised class, a registered *kisaeng*, who associated freely with aristocrats, scholars, and artists, and gained a reputation for defying the accepted social conventions of the time. She stands today as a symbol of art and the free spirit, a woman who battled the odds to express

96

her individuality. How much of the popular profile of Chini is based on myth? How much on fact? Did she consciously try to subvert the male-dominated institutions of Chosŏn society? So little trustworthy evidence remains, it is virtually impossible to recreate the image of the historical Chini. This lack of historical data ought to ensure that discussions of Chini's social role are based on analysis of her poems rather than on accounts of her life, but the *yadam* accounts, perhaps inevitably, continue to insinuate themselves into evaluations of the poems.

The following are summaries of the principal Hwang Chini–connected documents. Note that the earliest of these documents dates from at least fifty years after Chini's death, and four of them date from the late seventeenth or eighteenth century, raising questions about their reliability. This material is presented here so that the reader may understand the frame on which the Chini myth has been constructed, as is essential for a dispassionate evaluation of the poems.

Document (1): Yu Mongin (1559–1623), Ŏ-u-ya-dam

1. Chini is a famous *kisaeng* in Songdo during the reign of Chungjong (1506–44).
2. Relationship with Sŏ Kyŏngdŏk: her efforts to seduce the venerable scholar before finally admitting defeat. Sŏ Kyŏngdŏk's virtue was beyond reproach.
3. Trip to the Diamond Mountains in the company of Yi Saeng; the trip reputedly took a year, causing confusion in both families. Chini insisted that they travel without a servant. Both wore commoner hemp-and-straw sandals, and she donned a nun's bonnet. They begged for their food in remote temples. On occasion she would sell sexual favors to a monk in return for food, much to the chagrin of Yi Saeng. Once, when faced with severe hunger, she burst in on a *yangban* (nobleman) party, singing and dancing to the enchantment of all. When she had eaten and drunk herself, she requested and received food and drink for her "servant," Yi Saeng.
4. Chini's relationship with the musician Yi Sajong: Chini heard him sing and concluded he must be the famous Seoul singer of that name. She verified her hunch, and insisted on his coming to her house. They made an agreement to live together for six years:

Chini supplied the provisions for the first three years, Yi Sajong, for the latter three. At the end of six years, Chini announced that the time was up and left.

5. Request to be buried not on the mountain but near the open road because she had loved the excitement of an active life.

Document (2): Yi Tŏkhyŏng (1566–1645), Song-do-ki-i

1. The story of Chin Hyŏn'gŭm, Chini's mother. Hyŏn'gŭm was doing her washing beneath a bridge when a handsome young man happened by. There was immediate attraction between the two. Suddenly the young man was gone. That evening, as the sun was going down—the other women had already gone—the young man appeared on the bridge once again. He asked for a drink of water. Hyŏn'gŭm handed him a gourd from which he drank. Handing her back the gourd, he requested that she, too, drink. She did and discovered that the gourd contained a delicious wine. Chini was born from the relationship that developed between them. A delightful fragrance filled the room at the birth of the child.

2. Chini's beauty and skills: her ability as a singer and as a musician. She is called a fairy by the people.

3. The Song Sun episode. Chini came to an official party given by Song Sun. Song Sun was greatly impressed by her beauty. Song Sun's concubine, also a famous kisaeng, was distraught. Servants tried to restrain her but in vain; she ranted and raved to the great embarrassment of Song Sun. Subsequently, Song Sun threw a party in honor of his mother. Again Chini was invited. She arrived in a simple dress and without makeup. By the end of the evening she had captivated everyone in the room. Song Sun did not pretend to notice. He feared a repetition of his concubine's tantrums. However, when everyone was merry, he approached Chini, offered her wine and asked her to sing. Chini's voice was incredible; no kisaeng could match her. Song Sun called her a genius.

4. Ŏm Su, a famous kayagŭm artist, in his seventies at this time, is quoted as saying a voice like Chini's can be heard only in the Land of the Immortals.

5. A Chinese emissary, immensely impressed by Chini's beauty, said she was the most beautiful woman in the world.

6. Chini's character: noble, refined; she disliked shows of display. Even for official parties, she just combed her hair; she did not change her clothes. She did not like dissipation either. She sat down with scholars and artists; but a thousand pieces of gold would not get her to sit with merchants.
7. Chini loved Sŏ Kyŏngdŏk; she studied under his tutelage.
8. When Yi Tŏkhyŏng was a royal inspector, he had occasion to stay in the house of a secretary, Chin Pok, whose eighty-year-old father was related to Chini and had actually met her. The old man described the fragrance that remained for days in a room after Chini left it.
9. Im Che's ritual offering at Chini's grave; he composed his well-known *sijo*.

Document (3): Hŏ Kyun (1569–1618), Sŏng-ong-chi-so-rok

1. The singer, Yi Inbang, pretended to be his own younger brother, but Chini was not deceived.
2. Governor's feast in Naju: Chini sat down with soiled clothes and smudged face, casually cracked a louse before taking the *kŏmun'go* and beginning to sing. Chini was not in the least embarrassed; the other *kisaeng* were horrified.
3. Chini loved Sŏ Kyŏngdŏk for the nobility of his personality. She always brought wine and the *kŏmun'go* on visits to the elderly scholar's hut. Coming away, she would remark on how she had bent to her will a hermit who had meditated for thirty years, but that after all the years Hwadam was as incorruptible as ever.
4. When Chini was dying she asked for *p'ungak* rather than the traditional keening.
5. Chini told Sŏ Kyŏngdŏk that Songdo had three glories: Pag'yŏn Falls, Hwadam, and herself.
6. Songdo was renowned for producing people of genius. Chini was Songdo's most beautiful woman; she has never been forgotten.

Document (4): Im Pang (1640–1724), Su-ch'ŏn-man-rok

1. The romance with So Seyang (Yanggok). So Seyang told his friends that a man who allowed himself to be captivated by a woman was not a man at all. He said he would live with Chini

for a month and leave her without the slightest regret. On the eve of parting, Chini, showing no sign of sadness, composed and sang a *hansi* poem. Captivated by the poem, So Seyang decided he could not leave.
2. The text of the *hansi* "Farewell to So Yanggok."

Document (5): Yi Tŏngmu (1741–1793), Ch'ŏng-bi-rok

1. Chini, a Songdo *kisaeng*, very beautiful and skilled in poetry, said that Pag'yon Falls, Sŏ Kyŏngdŏk and herself were the three glories of Songdo.
2. Chini called at a scholar's house to avoid rain. She was so beautiful that the scholar thought she might be a goblin or the spirit of a fox. So he ignored her and continued his reading. At dawn when the rain had cleared, Chini took the scholar to task, declaring that she was a famous *kisaeng*. The scholar regretted his actions, but it was too late.
3. Text of Chini's *hansi* "Songdo." The document notes that some ascribe the poem to Kwŏn Kyŏp.

Document (6): Sŏ Yuyŏng (1801–1873), Kŭm-gye-p'il-dam

1. Chini was a Songdo *kisaeng*, known throughout the country for her beauty and artistic skills.
2. The Pyŏkkyesu incident. Pyŏkkyesu, a member of the royal family, wanted to meet Chini. On advice from Yi Tal, a poet, he set out on a small donkey behind a boy with a *kŏmun'go*, stopped at the pavilion near Chini's house, drank some wine, played a tune, and set off again on the donkey. Chini followed him and sang her famous Pyŏkkyesu *sijo* at Ch'uijŏk Bridge. The song so captivated Pyŏkkyesu that he fell off his horse. (The record does not say what happened to the donkey.) Chini decided this was no famous man, no man of *p'ungryu*. She went away laughing; Pyŏkkyesu was mortified.

Document (7): Kim T'aegyŏng (1850–1927), Hwang-jin-chŏn

1. Chini was a Songdo *kisaeng* who lived in the reign of Chungjong, the illegitimate daughter of Hwang Chinsa. Her mother's name was Hyŏn'gŭm.

2. The story of Hwang Chinsa and Hyŏn'gŭm meeting under the bridge and the birth of their illegitimate daughter.
3. The fragrance-after-the-birth story.
4. Chini was beautiful and skilled in writing.
5. The story of the boy who sickened and died from unrequited love for Chini. When the bier refused to pass Chini's house, relatives appealed to Chini. Chini put her blouse on the bier and the funeral continued.
6. Chini was so moved by the young man's death that she decided to become a *kisaeng*.
7. Texts of two *hansi* poems: "Fond Thoughts of Full Moon Terrace" and "Song to the Half-Moon."
8. Chini's fame as a poet. She was compared with the great female poets of T'ang and always numbered first in the list of great Korean *kisaeng*.
9. Her last wish was to have her body abandoned on the shore of the stream outside Kodong Gate, where the birds of the air could pick her bones bare, as a warning to all women.
10. Her wishes were carried out. Eventually, a singer gathered up her remains and buried her.
11. Notes that four Chini poems are extant.

Kang Chŏnsŏp's *Hwang Chini yŏn'gu* is a collection of all the important pre-1986 critical articles on Chini.[1] Many of the articles repeat the material in the Chini-related documents; they offer nothing new.

Sim Chaehwan and Pak Ŭlsu, in their *sijo* collections, date Hwang Chini from 1511 to 1541.[2] This is conjecture based on records of Chini's friendship with Sŏ Kyŏngdŏk, So Seyang (Yanggok), and Song Sun, all of whom can be dated precisely. Sŏ Kyŏngdŏk lived from 1489 to 1546; So Seyang from 1486 to 1567; and Song Sun from 1493 to 1583. None of these Confucian worthies mention Chini in their writings, which is not surprising in view of the low esteem in which a *kisaeng* was held in Chosŏn society. However, the fact that these friends never comment on her poems is an indicator of how they viewed her poetry-composition skills.

Pak Yŏngwan, following Kim Yŏngsuk's essay in the Kang Chŏnsŏp volume of 1986, dates Chini from 1502 to 1540.[3] The analysis is based primarily on Yi Tŏkhyŏng's dates. Yi Tŏkhyŏng was born in 1566 and died in 1645. He became governor of Songdo in 1604, at which time the old man in Yi's record who actually met Chini was in his eighties. Thus the old man is surmised to have been born circa 1524. Sŏ Kyŏngdŏk was fifty-eight at the time, and Chini was presumably in her thirties when she first sought him out as a teacher. She would have been some twenty-two years older than the old man of Yi's record, leading to a provisional birthdate for her of 1502. The basis of 1540 as the date of her death is not nearly so clear. Pak contradicts himself by dating her death ahead of Sŏ Kyŏngdŏk's death in 1546, and then going on to say that she wrote "The mountains may be ancient" in tribute to her old teacher upon hearing news of his death.[4]

Curiously, Pyŏkkyesu's name appears in no official record even though he was a member of the royal family. If the dates given for Chini above are accurate, Im Che (1549–1587) could not have known her. Thus his well-known *sijo* written at her grave was a tribute to a legend rather than a personal memory:

> Are you asleep or are you just resting
>   in this mountain valley thick with grass?
> Where is your rose complexion? Is only a skeleton buried here?
> How sad to think
>   there's no one to offer me a cup of wine.

What can we conclude with certainty from the records? We know that Chini was a Songdo *kisaeng* in the reign of Chungjong. In addition to being called Chini ("the true one"), she was sometimes called Chini with a different *chin* character meaning "the rare" or "precious one." She was also called Chin and Chillang. Her *kisaeng* name was Myŏngwŏl ("Bright Moon"). She was said to be very beautiful, a fine musician, and a great singer. She was acquainted with Sŏ Kyŏngdŏk, So Seyang, Yi Saeng, Yi Sajong, Song Sun, and Pyŏkkyesu. The popular tradition is that she was not intimate with Sŏ Kyŏngdŏk, but there is simply no proof one way or the other: She presumably had sexual relationships with So Seyang and Yi Sajong, having agreed to live with the former for thirty days and with the latter for six years, although it is difficult to accept the six-year pact at face value in view of the effect of such an agreement on the life of a working *kisaeng*. The exact nature of her relationship with Yi Saeng is not specified, but the probability is that they were sexually intimate. The trip to the Diamond Mountains was presumably historical, but none of the anecdotal material can be confirmed. Yi Mongin recounts the story of the literati gathering where Chini referred to Yi Saeng as a servant. This was a reversal of status unthinkable in Chosŏn society. As Sŏ Chŏngju points out, Yi Saeng was the son of a prime minister![5] Was Chini's action a prank, an insult, or just a tall story? We have no way of knowing. Finally, there is no indication of an intimate relationship with Song Sun.

Of the two accounts of Chini's birth, the Hwang Chinsa-Hyŏn'gŭm story is older and occurs more often in the records. It is full of fanciful material, such as water becoming wine, fragrance in the room after the birth, and so forth. Hŏ Kyun believes Chini was the daughter of a wandering musician, which seems much more plausible. Kim Chinyŏng points out in a recent study that the two accounts may be poetic versions of the same story: the union of the god of wine with the god of music (Hyŏn'gŭm) in the first account becomes the union of the inexperienced girl (blind to love) with the young gallant in the second account.[6]

The story of the young man who saw Chini in her garden and fell so much in love with her that he sickened and died of his unrequited passion is of very late provenance. Kim T'aegyŏng (1850–1927) records the story, but it lacks corroboration. Also lacking corroboration is the claim in the same document that this experience had such an effect on Chini that she decided to become a *kisaeng*. The explanation that she became a *kisaeng* when marriage negotiations with a *yangban* family broke down is not plausible either. Nor is the argument convincing that she had a personality that disliked the restraints of conventional marriage. Kim Tong'uk suggests that, being lowborn but beautiful and talented, she tended naturally to enter a profession where she was the plaything of the rich and powerful.[7]

The *yadam* accounts affirm that Chini hated pomposity and display and that she never gave her favors to a man who did not appreciate good wine, good music, and good poetry. She sat only with scholars, literati, and artists, never with the philistines of the marketplace. All this seems no more than one would expect from a *kisaeng* with taste.

What are we to make of the two seduction stories, unsuccessful in the case of her teacher, Sŏ Kyŏngdŏk, successful in the case of the monk Chijuk sŏnsa? The popular understanding is that she felt challenged by those who purported to be above the weaknesses of the flesh, taking particular delight in bringing such worthies down to earth. We have no way of establishing the real nature of these relationships. However, whereas the Chini–Sŏ Kyŏngdŏk story warms the heart, the Chini–Chijuk

sŏnsa story brings a shiver. Somehow, it seems out of character for a
gracious woman. The relationship with Sŏ Kyŏngdŏk is made even more
enigmatic by the two *sijo* he wrote supposedly celebrating his love:

> I'm a fool at heart
> and everything I do is foolish.
> It's too much to expect my love to come to this cloudy
>   mountain valley,
> yet at the sound of leaves
> falling in the breeze, I wonder, perhaps, is it she?

> Heart, what is the secret
> of your continuing youth?
> When I grow old, can you avoid growing old, too?
> I fear people
> will laugh at me for following you around.

The fourth and fifth *chang* (line) of the first *sijo* are particularly poignant. The charm of the second *sijo* lies in the adage, "There's no fool
like an old fool."

Sŏ Yuyŏng's account of the Pyŏkkyesu incident is problematic. In the
account Yi Tal supposedly advises Pyŏkkyesu on how to win Chini's
heart. However, scholars today date Yi Tal from 1539 to 1612, which
means he would have been an infant at the time of Chini's death.[8]

Hwang Chini's death, like most of her life, is surrounded in legend.
As she lay dying from a fever of unknown origin, she is said to have
requested that music and dancing accompany her bier rather than the
traditional keening; and she is said to have asked that her body, instead
of being coffined and interred in the usual way, be abandoned on the
sands of a stream outside the city for the magpies to pick her bones. In
her life, she said, she had put a fire in many men's guts, and she wished
to impart a grave warning to all the profligate women of the world.
None of this can be corroborated.

Regret surfaces three times in the *yadam* accounts of Chini's life:
first, at the death of the young man; second, as she comes down the
mountain after seducing the old monk; and third, as she lies waiting for
death. In the case of the old monk the account actually says that she felt
pleased with herself, but that her joy was tempered by a feeling of emptiness. The final bout of regret in the face of death is only recorded in the
Kim T'aegyŏng document, which is very late. None of these stories of

regret are corroborated. They may reflect sentiments of moral rectitude in Chosŏn society.

The *sijo* poets of Hwang Chini's generation lack distinction. Yi Hwang (1501–1570), the great T'oegye, is her most illustrious contemporary, but his fame rests on his scholarship rather than his poetry skills. The *Twelve Songs of Tosan*, renowned though they may be as blueprints of literati lifestyle, are hardly great poems; they are much too deeply weighed down by conceptual Confucian lore. Sŏ Kyŏngdŏk (1489–1546) and Song Sun (1493–1583) wrote *sijo*, but Chinese was the area of their expertise. And Yi Hyŏnbo (1467–1555) hardly ranks among the great *sijo* poets.

The boom in *sijo* writing came in the generation after Chini, notably in the work of Kwŏn Homun (1532–1587) and Chŏng Ch'ŏl (1536–1593), both of whom used the techniques of *Zen hansi* in their *sijo*. They employed a poetic discourse that speaks primarily through images, writing poems that were symbols, that went beyond words and meaning. Theirs is a poetry of sudden intense apprehensions of the nature of the world and of human experience, an approach not articulated in the West until the advent of French Symbolism and Ezra Pound's imagist theories.

Sijo in Chini's age was still in its developing, didactic, moralizing phase, while *hansi* had been in full flower since Koryŏ. When the two traditions met in the work of Kwŏn Homun, Chŏng Ch'ŏl, and the poets of the eighteenth century, *sijo* also flowered. The seeds of this flowering were there from the beginning; the *hansi* influence is evident in the *sijo* of Cho Chun (1346–1405), Maeng Sasŏng (1360–1438), Hwang Hŭi (1363–1452), Prince Wŏlsan (1454–1488), and Yi Hyŏnbo (1467–1555). None of these poets, however, left a significant body of *sijo*. It is in the work of Kwŏn Homun, Chŏng Ch'ŏl, and their successors that we see the full blooming of the *sijo* tradition.

Hwang Chini is usually credited with six *sijo* poems. "The mountains may be ancient" is recorded in Kim Sujang's *Haedong kayo* (1755); four *sijo* are listed in Kim Ch'ŏnt'aek's *Ch'ŏnggu yŏng'ŏn* (1728): "Long Winter Night," "When was I faithless?" "Blue Stream, do not boast," and the anonymously listed "What have I done?" "Blue mountains are my love" is listed as a Chini poem in Kim Kyohŏn's *Taedong p'unga* (1908), but there are serious doubts about the authenticity of the ascription. "Long Winter Night," Chini's best-known *sijo*, is sometimes accredited to Kim Sanghŏn (1570–1652).[9] Thus, of the six poems traditionally ascribed to Chini, there are doubts about three. Since the earliest extant textual record dates from 1728, almost 200 years after Chini's death, such doubts are inevitable.

Sijo can be sung to a *kagokch'ang* or a *sijoch'ang*.[10] The *kagokch'ang* is much older than the *sijoch'ang*; the latter was not invented until sometime in the nineteenth century. Almost all extant *sijo* were written to be sung to the *kagokch'ang*. It has five sung *chang* and two musical interludes, *chung-yŏ-ŭm* and *tae-yŏ-ŭm*. The music is complex, is difficult to play, and demands a professional singer and a large number of players. The *sijoch'ang* is much less complex, requiring only a singer and a drum accompaniment, but it did not emerge until the *sijo* genre was in decline in the nineteenth century. The translations in this essay follow the five-*chang* structure of the *kagokch'ang*. *Ch'ang* refers to the music, *chang* refers to the text line. The translations have a five-*chang* (line) format. The third *chang* is usually long. The fourth *chang*, the twist, is ideally three syllables; the translations, however, while approximating this principle, do not adhere rigidly to it.

The commentators, for the most part, take the ascription of Chini's poems at face value and are unanimous in extolling her skill as a *sijo* poet. Cho Unjae, quoting the T. S. Eliot dictum, "The great poet, in writing himself, writes his time," says she is Korea's greatest poet.[11] Chini wrote about herself and her time, he says, in poems characterized by delicacy, wounded pride, loneliness, love, and generosity of spirit. He goes on to note Chini's qualities as a technical innovator: She breaks free from the rigid 3, 4 count to a more fluid 2, 3 or 2, 4 count; she uses the run-on effect in "What have I done?" and she shows flexibility in using a 6– or 7–syllable phrase in place of the more usual five-syllable first foot of the fifth *chang*. Kim Chinyŏng reveals flexibility of imagination, love of the natural landscape, self-awareness, and compression in his list of the qualities of Chini's poems.[12] Although Cho Unjae's claim that Chini is Korea's greatest poet is patently excessive, most commentators concede the general qualities enumerated by Cho and Kim. The fact remains, however, that six poems are not sufficient samples for definitive judgments, the more so when three of them are problematic in terms of ascription. It is a flimsy basis upon which to build a poetry world.

The commentators consistently appraise Chini's poems within the Chini myth rather than on internal criteria. They use the poems to embellish a preconceived idea of Chini as a noble-minded, gracious, artistic lady.[13] This is to accept the *yadam* accounts at face value and to glamorize what was a very inglorious profession. Kathleen McCarthy paints a vivid picture of *kisaeng* life in early Chosŏn, showing how the institution was under fire throughout the dynasty, and how it was tolerated at best, because in providing sex for lusty bureaucrats it also protected *yangban* daughters. She also paints a vivid picture of these bureaucrats indulging in the pleasures of *kisaeng* dalliance.[14] Not much of this activity was related to poetry.

Hŏ Kyun's claim that Chini demonstrated masculine qualities has been very influential in critical comment. It is a concept of dubious merit, capable of a host of interpretations, pejorative as well as affirmative. It says little for Korean women that the sixteenth century's greatest woman poet achieved that greatness because she had the heart of a man! The commentators interpret this masculinity in terms of liberality of spirit and decisiveness, implying presumably that women in general, and *kisaeng*, in particular, lacked these qualities. They then proceed to find these qualities in the poems, particularly in the "What have I done?" *sijo.*[15]

Chini's *sijo* and *hansi* differ from the work of other *kisaeng* poets in that they transcend the rather limited range of regret for lost love or unrequited love that is typical of *kisaeng* poetry. Hŏ Yŏngja, reflecting Hŏ Kyun's masculine point of view, says Chini's poems reveal a great strength of character, that Chini is always in control of her emotions.[16] She does not explain, however, why such control guarantees good poetry. The point of view seems solidly Confucian.

Yi Sinbok goes a step further: He claims that in transcending the limited range of most *kisaeng* poetry, Chini achieved a poetry of "*mŏt.*"[17] This claim is even more problematic. *Mŏt* is a quality of elegance greatly admired by contemporary critics. This *han'gŭl* term has been a subject of discussion in Korean academic circles only since the publication of Sin Sŏkcho's "Mŏtsŏl" in the March 1941 issue of *Munjang.*

Kim Chonggil tells us in *The Darling Buds of May* that *mŏt* is a phonetically corrupt form of *mat* (taste), and that the word first appeared as late as the second half of the nineteenth century. He tells how Professor Kim Hŭnggyu found the phrase *matto morŭgo* in a *p'ansori* version of the classical Korean novel *Hŭngbu chŏn,* written presumably in the latter half of the nineteenth century. This phrase means "without knowing taste," but, in the context here, it is used in the sense of "unwittingly" or carelessly," the present-day version of which is *mŏtto morŭgo.* This may be one of the most recent cases in which the word "*mat*"was also used in the sense of *mŏt.* The word *mŏtchige,* the adverbial form of *mŏt,* occurs in an An Minyŏng *sijo* contained in his collection, *Kŭmok ch'ŏngbu,* edited in the 1870s. Thus, Professor Kim believes that the word *mŏt* began to be used in the second half of the nineteenth century, together with words like *mŏtchaengi* or *motchida.*[18]

For many contemporary commentators, *mŏt* is a defining concept of Korean sensibility. They explain it in terms of the ability to break out of the emotional mold, to eschew the conventional response, and at the same time to preserve due harmony.[19] To cultivate a culture of *mŏt* in the twentieth century is one thing. It is something else to hang the aesthetic response of a sixteenth-century woman on a *han'gŭl* word, used only since the latter half of the nineteenth century, when the whole world knows that *han'gŭl* was not held in high repute in intellectual Korea until the surge of nationalism that marked the end of the Enlightenment period. In fact, the word *han'gŭl* itself was not coined until the twentieth century. *Ŏnmun* (vulgar writing), an obviously deleterious expression, was the term in common use. And *sijo* are written in *ŏnmun*!

The commentators try to give some historical depth to the concept of *mŏt* by linking it with the Chinese term *p'ungryu,* but the link is tenuous. Silla *p'ungryu* is a version of Chinese *fengliu,* which, according to Kim Chonggil, originally meant "social morale" but came to mean a "carefree, detached style of life"; it was masculine and associated with lute, poetry, wine, and female entertainer. *Fengliu* reached its full development during the T'ang dynasty and subsequently found its way into Korea as *p'ungryu* and into Japan as *miyabi.*

Sŏ Chŏngju explains the *p'ungryu* concept in "*P'ungryu* Discrimination":

> The Silla poet, Ch'oe Ch'iwŏn, said that *p'ungryu,* as first understood in this country was a fine amalgam of Buddhism, Taoism, and Confucianism. Ch'oe Namsŏn, who passed away some years ago, claimed that the old Korean term *pu-ru,* meaning the light of heaven, was matched to the Chinese characters *p'ung* and *ryu* [wind and flow].[20]

P'ungryu then is a concept with strong religious overtones: It is the light of heaven in a man's inner being.

When the commentators speak of Chini's "poetry of *mŏt,*" they are trying to establish her as a *p'ungryugaek.* They believe her liberal lifestyle and her delight in wine, love, and song warrant the appellation. This is applying the *yadam* account of Chini after the event in an effort to make her the first female *p'ungryugaek* in history. Chini was an entertainer, lowborn but allowed to mingle with the highborn, not on terms of equality but as a plaything. There is no way around this unbridgeable status gap. To say Chini was a *p'ungryugaek* is to give her parity with the men she served. This was unthinkable in Chosŏn dynasty Korea.

"Long Winter Night" is one of the finest examples of the *sijo* genre:

> I'll cut a piece from the side
> of this interminable winter night
> and wind it in coils beneath these bedcovers, warm
>   and fragrant as the spring breeze,
> coil by coil
> to unwind it the night my lover returns.

This poem is built around a marvelous central image in which eternal night, cold and loveless, is changed into an eternity of warmth and love. The personification in the first and second *chang*, which allows the speaker to cut the abstract night, gives the poem a fresh immediacy, imparting visually the feel of the length and misery of that interminable night. The "spring breeze" image in the third *chang*, with all its East Asian intimations of warmth and fragrance (suggested rather than spelled out in the original), changes the mood to warmth and joy, followed in the fourth and fifth *chang* by the eternal prolongation, coil by coil, of the delights of love. The cutting, coiling, and uncoiling process gives the poem a striking unity that is strengthened by a series of contrasts that are implied rather than stated: winter–spring, cold–warmth, sorrow–joy, love absent–love present, coil–uncoil, eternal–transitory. The last pair, eternal–transitory, is perhaps the key to the poem; their force derives from the conceit they express: Love is not eternal; it is definitely of this world.

No Korean poet had written anything like this since the halcyon days of "Manjŏn ch'un" (Spring Pervades the Pavilion), a Koryŏ *kayo* (song) (author and date unknown) that is recorded in *Akchang kasa*.

> The bed I make is bamboo leaves:
> I spread them on the ice.
> Though my love and I should freeze unto death,
> slowly, slowly, pass this night
> in love's enduring gentleness.

Both poems work out of the contrast between hot and cold; both poems celebrate passion. The Koryŏ poem is filled with the passion that is characteristic of the love songs of the day. Chosŏn, however, was a different time. When Hŏ Kyun (1569–1618) compiled the poems of his sister, Hŏ Nansŏrhŏn (1563–1589), some of the best were put into a supplement because they were regarded as risqué. Passion was not tolerated in the poetry of Chosŏn; great literati like T'oegye regarded it as vulgar. In Eliot's terms, Chosŏn society experienced a sort of dissociation of sensibility; passion was banished.

In Chini's "Long Winter Night," we see a return to the passion of Koryŏ, which makes it a landmark in the resurgence of Korean lyric poetry. Perhaps only a *kisaeng* could have written it. And it goes without saying that T'oegye would have disapproved. The content of the poem goes a long way to discounting any claim to authorship by Yi Sanghŏn. The evidence available at the moment accepts the poem as authentically Chini's. One final point: Note the beauty of the Korean in "Long Winter Night"; the poem flows like a stream, and it has a lovely pattern of repetitions—*sŏrisŏri, kubikubi,* and so on.[21]

We have already seen that the ascription of "What have I done?" is doubtful:

> What have I done?
> Did I not know I'd miss him so?
> Had I bid him stay, would he have gone?
> But I did it;
> I sent him away and I can't tell you how I miss him.

The poem is quite different from Chini's other poems: It uses no image, and it employs a discursive technique new in *sijo* poetry, and not found in any other Chini poem. On the other hand, the self-mocking, ironic tone of the poem is found not only in other Chini *sijo* but also in her *hansi.* If, on this basis, we accept the ascription as authentic, Chini's claim to fame as a *sijo* innovator receives another boost. *Kisaeng* poetry traditionally took the point of view of the woman pining for a lover who does not come, or lamenting her fate in being abandoned by some heartless paramour. Here the speaker has taken the initiative in ending the relationship, and she asks some fundamental questions about the psychology of love and freedom. Hŏ Yŏngja remarks on the strength and resilience of the speaker, qualities, she says, that differentiate Chini's *sijo* from the mainstream of *kisaeng* poetry.[22] Note the Hŏ Kyun influence again. Ch'oe Tongho's conclusion that this *sijo* is the portrait of a tragic woman hardly seems tenable; such an interpretation misses the frustrated, humorous, self-deprecating, and ironic element that accounts in large part for the poem's charm.[23] The poem is unusual in that the third *chang* is not end-stopped; the run-on, however, is not attempted in the English translation. How the run-on would have affected performance in the five-*chang kagokch'ang* is unclear. One further point of interest is that the *che* of the third *chang* in the original can mean "I," "you," or perhaps both.

Loneliness is a dominant emotion in Chini's *sijo*:

> When was I faithless,
> when did I ever deceive my love?
> The dark moonless night runs late and still
>   there's not a sign of him.
> Leaves falling
> in the autumn breeze, what can I do?

This poem may strike the reader as being right from the heart of the tradition of *kisaeng* poetry, yet it is subtly different. The speaker be-moans not so much the faithlessness of the lover as her fate in being a victim of her own emotions. There is no despair here; rather the speaker seems to say mockingly to herself: *fool, fool!* in that characteristic Chini ironic mode. Her dilemma is heightened by the intimations of mortality inherent in the imagery of the falling autumn leaves.

Then there is the celebrated Pyŏkkyesu *sijo*. Blue Stream is a pun on the gentleman's name and Bright Moon is Chini's *kisaeng* name:

> Blue Stream, do not boast
> of swift passage through green mountains,
> for having once reached the sea the return trip
>   assumes real difficulty.
> Bright Moon fills
> the empty mountain; why not rest on your journey here?

The poem is clever and satirical in its use of the pun. The pun may be a lesser form of wit in Western languages, but in Chinese it shows not only wit but a virtuoso poetic sense. The Korean commentators are in-variably unstinting in their praise. This *sijo* shows a different aspect of Chini. She is not on duty here as *kwan'gi*, or official provincial *kisaeng*. Yet she sets out to seduce Pyŏkkyesu because he represents a challenge. This is her idea of fun. Although her actions in the poem are less than commendable, the satirical, mocking mode she employs in offering her-self here was new in *sijo* writing.

Chini's *sijo* in praise of Sŏ Kyŏngdŏk again employs the overworked image of the river of no return, though in a slightly different way to the Pyŏkkyesu *sijo*:

> The mountains may be ancient,
> not so the waters.
> Water flowing day and night, how can it grow old?
> A great man
> is like that water; he goes and does not return.

The final Hwang Chini *sijo*, much quoted and translated though it may be, seems to resist translation into English. This is due perhaps to the quality of the central images, which appear cliché-ridden to the modern reader.

> Blue mountains are my heart;
> green waters are my love's love.
> Though green waters flow away, can blue
>   mountains change?
> Unable to forget
> blue mountains, green waters weep as they go their way.

Korean commentators admire this poem greatly; they make much of the flowing water and blue mountain images in terms of the waxing and waning of love. The reference is to the *Analects* 6.2 (translation from Wylie): "The Master said, the Wise man delights in water, the Good man delights in mountains. For the Wise move; but the Good stay still. The Wise are happy; but the Good secure." The speaker in Chini's poem seems to say that though man and woman bring all their wisdom and goodness to the love relationship, the nature of love itself is ephemeral. The poem does seem to postulate a contrast between a woman's love and a man's, but such a contrast can hardly be set up as a general prin-ciple in human relations.

"Long Winter Night" and the Pyŏkkyesu *sijo* certainly challenge the prevailing standards of male orthodoxy in Chosŏn society. The challenge of "Long Winter Night" is indirect: It subsists in the way Chini uses her images. Reading it as simply a poetry text, one feels no challenge; it is a love poem wherein the speaker delights in the pros-pect of reunion with the lover. It is only against the background of the censorship imposed on Koryŏ love songs by the Chosŏn court that the challenge becomes clear. This must have been a daring poem in its time. The challenge of the Pyŏkkyesu *sijo* was a little more direct, but the playful tone of the poem must have softened the impact. "What have I done?" and "When was I faithless?" suggest new attitudes to love and loneliness that challenge the stereotypical *kisaeng* approach; the former inflicts the loneliness by ending the relationship; the latter addresses the loneliness of waiting for a lover who is not coming. "Blue mountains and green waters" seems to be a paradoxical statement of the inevitability of parting and of the abiding nature of love. "The mountains may be ancient" is simply a poem in praise of a great man.

What is constant in the poems, however, is a speaker who knows her own mind. She is aware of love's delights and inconstancies, and of her own foolishness in the grip of her emotions. She prepares a memorable homecoming party for one lover, sends another lover away, mocks a third as she offers the lure of seduction, and scolds herself for waiting for a fourth who is not coming. Thus, far from being a tragic heroine, she sees humor in her romantic situation, and makes fun of herself and others; all this was new in *sijo* poetry.

Chini's generation of *hansi* poets was not particularly distinguished either. Kim Sisŭp, one of the best *hansi* poets of the previous generation died in 1493; Ch'oe Susŏng (1487–1521), an excellent *hansi* poet, died before Chini was twenty. Song Sun (1493–1583) was also a fine *hansi* poet. However, in general terms, there was a noticeable slackening in the flow of good *hansi* poetry in Chini's generation. The next group of distinguished *hansi* poets, Yi Tal (1539–1612), Paek Kwanghun (1537–1582) and Ch'oe Kyŏngch'ang (1539–1583), did not appear until the generation after Chini. Sin Saimdang (1512–1559) was a contemporary, but not nearly as fine a poet. Yi Okpong (?–1592), an accomplished woman *hansi* poet, may have been a contemporary, but her dates make it more likely that she belonged to the next generation.

Hwang Chini's *hansi* were recorded in a number of literary records and poetry collections in addition to the *yadam* sources already pointed out:

Tongguk sihwa hŭisŏng, compiled by Hong Chungin
Taedong sisŏn, compiled by Chang Chiyŏn
Haedong sisŏn, compiled by Yi Kyuyŏng
Yŏktae yŏryu hansi munsŏn, compiled by Kim Chiyŏng

Eight *hansi* poems are extant. There are some differences in the versions of the poems, but nothing major. In the translations, the version deemed to give the better poem has been chosen. The poems are in a variety of styles: five-syllable quatrain, five-syllable *yulsi* (regulated verse), seven-syllable quatrain, and seven-syllable *yulsi*.[24] Yi Kawŏn casts doubt on the ascription of "Song to the Half-Moon"[25]; most commentators, however, accept it.

There are a number of references in classical documents to Chini's *hansi*. Kim Manjung (1637–1692) sets up a double standard when he notes in *Sŏp'o manp'il* that Chini's poems are inferior in quality but are passed on because they are the work of a woman.[26] It is a general comment, without explanation or illustration, but presumably the charge of inferiority is based on failures in the technical features of Chinese poetry. Hong Manjong (1643–1725), on the other hand, praises Chini in *Sohwa sip'yŏng*. However, he gives no details. He merely notes the lack of women poets in the Chosŏn era, and goes on to say that two women poets, Chini from Songdo and Kyesaeng from Puan, have emerged recently to rival the literati. Among the *yadam* accounts, Yi Tŏngmu notes that Chini was a skilled poet, and Kim T'aegyŏng praises her poetry and compares her to two great Chinese poetesses. Significantly, he concludes that Chini's name is synonymous with *myŏnggi* ("great *kisaeng*"); he does not say "great poet."[27]

Contemporary critical comment on Chini's *hansi* is meager. Critics are content to feature accounts of Chini's beauty, spiced with tales of gallants from Seoul, confident of their abilities to resist any woman, who inevitably succumbed to Chini's charms. None of this tells us anything about the poems. A number of the leading commentators treat Chini's *sijo* and *hansi* together, but none of them gives a formal appraisal of the *hansi* in terms of the techniques of Chinese poetry, rhyme, antithesis, parallelism, and so forth. At most they say whether the poems are *yulsi* (regulated verse) or *chŏlgu* (quatrain)—the two divisions of modern style (*sinch'esi*)—and give the number of characters per line. Pak Yŏngwan provides the fullest account. He refers constantly to the four-fold structure of modern style: theme (*ki*), development (*sŭng*), twist or anti-theme (*chŏn*), and conclusion (*kyŏl*), but his appraisal, too, is in general terms, and usually falls within the Chini myth.[28] The presumption is that Chini learned the striking use of the image from the earlier Korean poetry traditions, *hansi* and Koryŏ *kayo*. Take this simple quatrain, "Song to the Half-Moon." The poem treats the age-old Chingnyŏ-

Kyŏnu theme—once a year the magpies make a bridge to facilitate the
meeting of lovers (Altair and Vega):

> Who cut Kullyun jade
> into a comb for Chingnyŏ's hair?
> Now that Kyŏnu has gone,
> it hangs fretful in the blue sky.

The half-moon and comb images express the complex emotions of the
lovers: The joy of meeting is in the beauty of the jade comb; the sorrow
of parting is in the abandoning of the jade comb in the sky. The comb
image appears also in the Koryŏ *kayo* "Tongdong," wherein the girl throws
the comb in the hope that her lover will follow her and pick it up.

> Sixth month, full moon.
> I follow a while
> the comb cast from the cliff,
> in the hope my love will look back.
> *Ah, ah tong-dong-da-ri.*

The hope that the lover will pick up the comb accounts for some of the
tension in Chini's poem, too. The comb may be seen as a symbol of a
woman's fate and perhaps also as a symbol of Chini's *kisaeng* status—
ornament or plaything in a man's world.[29] Commentators point out that
Chini's poem closely resembles a composition of So Seyang.

"Farewell to So Yanggok," written by Chini for So Seyang when the
month was up and it was time to part, is a delightful poem:

> Paulownia leaves fall in the moonlight;
> wild chrysanthemums yellow in the frost.
> The pavilion reaches within a foot of heaven;
> drunk, we've supped a thousand cups.
> The flowing water is shivery as the *kŏmun'go*;
> plum fragrance suffuses the *p'iri* pipe.
> In the morning we part,
> but our love will be as long as the blue waves.

Who could resist this? The season is beautifully rendered in the pau-
lownia and wild chrysanthemums, the latter being particularly effective
in depicting the ephemeral nature of love. According to the *yadam* account, Chini showed no mark of sadness in singing her poem, but So

Seyang was overcome. He had to admit ruefully that he was no man and had to beg her to let him stay. The commentators treat the poem as an account of love inevitably coming to a tragic conclusion. Chini is seen once again as the strong, in-control, masculine type, whereas So Seyang is portrayed as weak. The commentators conveniently forget the *yadam* account, which points to challenge rather than passion as being at the center of the encounter. So Seyang boasts he can control his feelings, and, by implication, control any woman; Chini proves him wrong. Irony is the key here. A month's dalliance can hardly be considered tantamount to love. Chini is manipulating rather than allowing herself to be manipulated. The challenge to Chosŏn society's male orthodoxy is apparent, but it is a laughing challenge.

The images reach out to the senses; scene, sounds, scents, sensations, season, mood. The final tongue-in-cheek couplet drives home the nail. Could we be so stupid, she asks, as to end a beautiful affair? The poem is five-character *yulsi* with end rhyme in the even lines. The first three couplets all show parallelism; the second and third, where parallelism is mandatory, are particularly striking.

> pavilion – high – heaven – one – foot
> people – drunk – wine – thousand – cup
> flowing – water – like – *kŏmun'go* – cold
> plum – blossom – enter – pipe – fragrant

The last line offers all sorts of intriguing possibilities to the translator in terms of weighting the interpretation toward plum or pipe fragrance.

Chini's other poem of parting, "Parting from Kim Kyŏngwŏn," while typical of *kisaeng* poetry in its fear of losing the beloved, nevertheless shows a woman with a firm grip on reality:

> We are an ideal couple bound through the generations;
> each heart knows the living and dying of the other.
> I won't renege on the flower pledge we made in Yangju;
> my only fear is that like Du Mu-zhi you'll go away.

By all accounts, Du Mu-zhi was a handsome man. *Kisaeng* poetry traditionally was not so self-assured.

"Dream of Fond Lovers" mingles dream and reality. Centered on a conceit, the poem is whimsical and clever:

Fond lovers' assignations are predicated entirely on dreams,
but when boy visits girl, girl has gone to visit boy.
My wish is that in all our future dreams
we set out at the same time and meet along the way.

"Small White-Pine Boat" has a strong central image; the boat presumably represents Chini herself:

That small white-pine boat afloat on the water,
how many years has it been tied to blue waves?
When men to come ask who crossed first, tell them:
a great lord, one skilled in letters and arms.

Note again how self-assured the speaker is. Presumably she is answering a question from guests at a *kisaeng* party: "Who was your first lover?"
Her humorous answer is, of course, a putdown to the present company;
a man more noble than anyone here is the implication.
"Songdo" is filled with nostalgia for the glories of the Koryŏ dynasty.

The old dynasty tints the snow;
the bell coldly tolls the voice of that ancient land.
Anguished, I stand alone on south pavilion,
the castle ruin fragrant with evening mist.

The speaker stands on the pavilion, haunted by the sadness of the bell, smelling the sweet fragrance of the ruin, transported inwardly to Songdo's glory days. The sentiment, for the most part, is in the images of bell, castle, and fragrance; the appeal is to sight, sound, and smell. The only direct statement of emotion is in the word "anguished."
In "Fond Thoughts of Full Moon Terrace" the speaker is again reflecting on the glories of Koryŏ.

Desolate the old temple beside the palace stream;
sunset on the towering trees makes men sad.
Misty twilight's chill is what remains of the monk's dream;
the good times have shattered against the pagoda top.
The golden phoenix has fled; only sparrows come and go.
Cattle and goats graze where azaleas flourished.
Remember the glory days of Pine Ridge Mountain;
who could have known that spring would feel like fall?

Again the emotion is in the images: the temple and palace reflected in the stream; the setting sun; the towering trees, relics of former glory; the twilight chill in the monk's dream; the shattering of Koryŏ's greatness against the pagoda; the flight of the phoenix (the king); wild grass where azaleas flourished. The final couplet is brilliant: It presents the summit of Koryŏ's achievement in the single image of "the glory days of Pine Ridge Mountain" and tempers Koryŏ's greatness with the reflection that today spring has the chill of autumn. The best *hansi* poems invariably end with this kind of moral assessment. It is an assessment that comes from the heart rather than the head.

Chini's name is invariably linked with "Pag'yŏn Falls," one of the boasts of Songdo. It seems particularly appropriate that she should have written a poem on the theme. Here is Chini's "Pag'yŏn Falls":

> A streaming jet spews out of rock valley;
> a hundred feet of booming water forms a dragon pool.
> The tumbling spume is like the Milky Way;
> a white rainbow forms across the angry spill.
> The thunder of cascading water floods the village;
> shattered jade dusts the air.
> You folks at play, don't say Lu Shan is best;
> don't you know Crystal Sky crowns the East Coast?

This may have been the inspiration for Chŏng Ch'ŏl's waterfall in "Kwandong pyŏlgok." The poems echo each other in the power and noise of the description, the dragon image, the white rainbow, Chŏng Ch'ŏl's snow, and Chini's jade. And, of course, the comparison between Lu Shan and the Diamond Mountains is further common ground between the two poems. Chŏng Ch'ŏl writes:

> I see a silver-white rainbow and a jade-tailed dragon.
> Coiling, swirling, the spew explodes for miles around;
> thunder in the ear, snow in the eye.

Later, when he climbs Buddha's Terrace, he makes the comparison with Lu Shan:

> A thousand feet of sheer cliff stand in the air.
> Slowly I count the strands of the Milky Way;
> warp and woof, it hangs there on the loom.
> Twelve strands the book says. To me, there are more.
> Had Li Bai the chance to talk it out,
> he'd never have claimed Lu Shan was lovelier than here.

The challenge to male supremacy in Chosŏn society is evident in a few of Chini's *hansi*, notably "Farewell to So Yanggok" and "Small

White Boat." To those who make the case that "Farewell to So Yanggok" shows great composure tinged with sadness and a real sense of beauty and romance, it must also be pointed out that at the heart of the poem Chini holds the hapless So Yanggok to ransom. She plays cat and mouse with her victim. Conquering male pride is at stake here, not prolonging love. "Small White Boat" can also be seen as a putdown to male arrogance. The rest of the *hansi* are either love poems, poems looking back nostalgically to the glory of Koryŏ, or descriptive poems. "Song to the Half-Moon" is a poem of the sorrow of separation, with echoes going back to "Tongdong." "Dream of Fond Lovers" is whimsical, a lesser poem. The second of the two Songdo poems is particularly moving, with its strong feelings carried convincingly by the imagery. "Pag'yŏn Falls" looks with awe at beauty and power in nature. One scholar has linked the poem with *mŏt* and *p'ungryu*,[30] and another links it to a sensibility that has masculine strength.[31] The arguments are not really persuasive.

Chini's *hansi,* as a group, present a woman of refined sensibility, in control of her emotions, with a keen sense of beauty, a strong sense of self-worth, a sharp sense of history, and a mischievous sense of humour. Once again, eight poems make up a slight scaffolding to hold the tower of greatness. Nevertheless, these poems reveal a poet with a refined sensibility, the ability to craft a poem, and the skill to use irony to telling effect. In sum, despite the misgivings of Kim Manjung, it can be fairly claimed that Hwang Chini rivaled the best literati poets of her time. This should surely be word enough of praise.

In this essay, I've tried to separate the historical Hwang Chini from the mythical Hwang Chini in the belief that this demythologizing process is necessary for a proper evaluation of the poems. The mythical Chini lives on in every Korean's heart, a proud, defiant, individual woman, who always insisted on the best and who usually managed to get it. Her legend will survive in Korea as long as the need persists for "characters" or "artists" to inject a little poetry into our lives. The poems, however, do not require the legend. They stand independent of it, a monument to the artistic skills of an exceptional woman.

Notes

1. Kang et al., *Hwang Chini yŏn'gu*, 1986.
2. Sim, *Sijo chŏnjip*, 1984. Pak Ŭlsu, *Han'guk sijo taesajŏn*, 1991.
3. Pak, *Hwang chini munhak yŏn'gu*, 12–15.

4. Ibid., 14.
5. Kang et al., *Hwang Chini yŏn'gu*, 76.
6. Kim, *Yŏsŏng munhwa ŭi saeroun shigak*, 163.
7. Kang et al., *Hwang Chini yŏn'gu*, 58.
8. Hŏ, *Yi Tal shisŏn*, 125.
9. Sim, *Sijo chŏnjip*, 230.
10. Cho, *Kagokch'angsa ŭi kungmunhakchŏk ponjil*, 19–77.
11. Kang et al., *Hwang Chini yŏn'gu*, 156.
12. Kim, *Yŏsŏng munhwa ŭi saeroun shigak,* 170–77.
13. See Chang's essay "Hanguk ŭi Sap'o Hwang Chini," 15–33.
14. MacCarthy, *Kisaeng*, 4–14.
15. See Ch'oe Tongho, "Hwang Chini shi ŭi yangmyŏngsŏnggwa hyŏndaejŏk pyŏnyong" (Duality and Modern Transfiguration in the Poems of Hwang Chini), in Kang et al., *Hwang Chini yŏn'gu*, 124.
16. Kang et al., *Hwang Chini yŏn'gu*, 13.
17. Ibid., 88–92.
18. Kim, *The Darling Buds of May*, 201–17.
19. Kang et al., *Hwang Chini yŏn'gu*, 89.
20. Excerpt from Sŏ Chŏngju, *Collected Poems*, 570.
21. See Cho Unjae, "Hwang Chini shiwa hangukshi ŭi chŏnt'ong" (Hwang Chini's Poetry and the Korean Poetry Tradition), in Kang et al., *Hwang Chini yŏn'gu*, 150.
22. Kang et al., *Hwang Chini yŏn'gu*, 11.
23. Ibid., 125.
24. For texts and sources, see Ibid., 189–92.
25. Ibid., 52.
26. Pak, *Hwang Chini munhak yŏn'gu*, 37.
27. For the references to classical documents see Ibid., 37–39.
28. Ibid., 37–51.
29. Kang et al., *Hwang Chini yŏn'gu*, 126.
30. Ibid., 90.
31. Song, *Chousen-shi*, 138.

References

Yadam Sources

Yu Mongin (1559–1623): *Ou yadam.*
Yi Tŏkhyŏng (1566–1645): *Songdo kii.*
Hŏ Kyun (1569–1618): *Song'ong chisorok.*
Im Pang (1640–1724): *Such'on manrok.*
Yi Tŏngmu (1741–93): *Ch'ŏngbirok.*
Sŏ Yuyŏng (1801–73): *Kŭmgye p'ildam.*
Kim T'aegyŏng (1850–1927): *Hwangjin chŏn.*

Classical Sources

Kim, Manjung. *Sŏp'o manp'il* (Sopo's Miscellany), kwŏnha 116, tr. and annot. Hong In'gyun. Seoul: Ilchisa, 1987.
Hong Manjong. *Sohwa ship'yŏng* (Essays on Korean Poetry in Chinese), kwŏnha 97.

Contemporary Sources

Chang Tŏksun, "Hanguk ŭi Sap'o Hwang Chini" (Korea's Sappho: Hwang Chini), in Kang, et al.

Cho, Kyuik. *Kagokch'angsaŭi kungmunhakchŏk ponjil* (The Essence of the *Kagokch'ang* Song Lyric in the Korean Literature Tradition). Seoul: Chimmundang, 1994.

Hŏ Kyŏngjin. *Yi Tal shisŏn* (Selected Poems of Yi Tal). Seoul: P'yŏngminsa, 1989.

Kang, Chŏnsŏp, et al. *Hwang Chini yŏn'gu* (Hwang Chini Studies). Seoul: Changhaksa, 1986.

Kim, Chinyŏng. *Yŏsŏng munhwa ŭi saeroun shigak* (New Angle on Female Culture). Seoul: Kyŏnghee Inmunhak Research Center, 1999.

Kim, Chonggil. *The Darling Buds of May*. Seoul: Korea UP, 1991.

MacCarthy, Kathleen. *"Kisaeng* in the Koryŏ Period." Ph.D. diss., Harvard University, 1991.

O'Rourke, Kevin. *The Sijo Tradition*. Seoul: Jungeumsa, 1987.

———. *The Book of Korean Sijo*. Cambridge: Harvard University Press, 2002.

Pak, Ŭlsu. *Han'guk sijo taesajŏn* (Comprehensive Dictionary of Korean *Sijo*). Seoul: Asea Munhwasa, 1991.

Pak, Yŏngwan. *"Hwang Chini munhak yŏn'gu"* (Hwang Chini Literary Study). Ph.D. diss., Ch'ungnam University, 1995.

Sim, Chaewan. *Sijo chŏnjip* (Collected *Sijo*). Seoul: Ilchogak, 1984.

Sŏ Chŏngju, *Collected Poems*. Seoul: Mineumsa, 1983.

Song, Ryurcha. *Chousen-shi no onna-tachi* (Women in the History of Chosŏn). Tokyo: Chikuma Shobo, Korean translation Nexus, 1998.

6
Private Memory and Public History

The Memoirs of Lady Hyegyŏng and Testimonial Literature

JaHyun Kim Haboush

The memoirs of Lady Hyegyŏng (1735–1815), known in Korean as *Hanjungnok* (Records Written in Silence), or *Hanjung mallok* (Memoirs Written in Silence), are viewed as both a literary masterpiece and an invaluable historical document. Lady Hyegyŏng was the wife of Crown Prince Sado who, at age twenty-seven, was executed by his father, King Yŏngjo. The Sado incident, even by the standards of ruthlessness and cruelty associated with royal houses, was quite a gruesome affair. One hot day in July 1762, King Yŏngjo ordered his son to enter a rice chest of about four feet square, which was then sealed. There, in the chest, Prince Sado died eight days later. This incident, the only publicly known filicide in the 500-year Chosŏn dynasty, cast a terrible pall over those who were involved in and had lived with the tragic act. Most conspicuous among them were his father, King Yŏngjo, whose long and brilliant reign was deeply compromised by this inhumane filicide; Sado's son, King Chŏngjo, whose reign surpassed even that of his grandfather in brilliance and accomplishment, and yet who, all his life, battled the shame and grief his father's tragic death had left behind; and other ministers and tutors, some who would take their own lives or suffer political upheavals on account of their relationships to Prince Sado.[1]

As his wife, Lady Hyegyŏng was profoundly affected by the prince's death and its repercussions. Nonetheless, as was the custom for a woman in Chosŏn Korea, she was to be mostly hidden from public view. Had it not been for her memoirs, Lady Hyegyŏng, like countless other women whose husbands, fathers, or sons were involved in political incidents, would have been dimly perceived as someone who suffered silently behind the scenes, with only the barest of biographical facts known about her. Breaking that long silence, however, Lady Hyegyŏng wrote four sets of memoirs in which she narrates, not only her own life, but also the Prince Sado affair from her perspective, and renders judgment on all concerned.

Narration is not only a mode of expression but also one of empowerment. Until recently, in most societies women did not narrate their own lives, not to mention the lives of others. Autobiographies by women were few, and those written tended to be private and domestic. In Europe or Japan, for example, women's autobiographies were confined to the interior or domestic aspect of their lives. That a woman would narrate a royal filicide, the most public of incidents that can only be described as the ultimate in male power rivalry, makes Lady Hyegyŏng's memoirs unique in autobiographical literature. Moreover, Prince Sado reigns supreme in the tragic domain of the popular imagination in contemporary Korea, a supremacy attributable to Lady Hyegyŏng's memoirs.

How did Lady Hyegyŏng accomplish this? When she wrote her memoirs, there existed neither an accepted tradition nor a well-defined genre of a written memoir by women. In this essay, I will place the memoirs of Lady Hyegyŏng in the context of Chosŏn Korean testimonial narratives that, in turn, developed out of dual linguistic traditions—classical Chinese and Korean. I will also speculate on the cultural significance of this genre.

From the time the Korean alphabet of *hangŭl* was devised in the mid-fifteenth century and then up to the early twentieth century, the written culture of Korea consisted of writings in classical Chinese and vernacular writings in Korean. Classical Chinese functioned something like a sacral or universal language of East Asia, similar to Latin in Europe. Educated men in East Asia, that is, in China, Japan, Korea and Vietnam, felt themselves to be members of a civilization rooted and conducted in classical Chinese. Starting from the seventeenth century, the output of vernacular writing increased vastly both in volume and in variety. But its popularity did not diminish the prestige of the classical Chinese tradition, and Korea enjoyed a diglossic effervescence in written culture.

Scholars often describe this diglossia as based on dichotomous traditions. In this framework, discourse in Chinese was conducted by men, and was canonical (Confucian), public, universal, and hegemonic. Discourse in Korean was practiced by women, and it was local, private, domestic, and subversive. On closer examination, however, the relationship between the two traditions was much more complex. Men began to write in Korean as well as in Chinese. Also, substantial interplay occurred between the two: Each tradition influenced, appropriated, and challenged the other. Thus, the intertextuality of a text written in one language often transcended the limits of that language and extended to the other.

What do we find in testimonial narratives in the diglossic culture? By "testimonial narratives" I mean those genres of writing in which one testifies to the innocence and honor of the self or of someone else who had been close to the narrator and also was accused of wrongdoing. This genre was made up of various modes of writing, but the best-known testimonial narratives written in classical Chinese are petitions that were presented to the throne in the form of memorials. The petitioning memorials usually follow an established format—for example, the writer attests to the innocence of the subject and details the suffering and pain the subject had to bear because of slanders and wrongs done to him or her, concluding with a plea for justice.

What should be remembered about these petition-memorials is that one was allowed to send them only for oneself or someone in the following categories: for one's father, one's husband, one's older brother, and, if a slave, for one's master.[2] These petition-memorials are interesting because they straddled the boundaries between public and private spaces. That the writing is a legal petition seeking justice from the throne marks it definitely as public in nature. It would be accurate to call these historical documents. At the same time, the petition-memorials were invariably written in a personal and subjective mode full of emotion and protest—that is, in a personal mode reserved for autobiographies and memoirs. In other words, the manner in which the form and content meet in testimonial narratives blurs the boundaries between history and autobiography, genres that remained polar opposites most of the time.[3]

If you examine the conventions of history and autobiography, it is not difficult to see why the genres should remain separate. Historiography was arguably the most sacrosanct of literary genres. In the Confucian tradition, historiography was viewed as a central means of upholding the vision of the moral order. History had transcendent value; it was seen as expressing a cosmic moral pattern. But this moral pattern was not measured on an individual scale; individuals did not always receive just treatment. The cosmic realm and the individual realm did not always coincide. Faith that justice will ultimately prevail in human history did not mean that each individual received justice.

This discrepancy led to the second function of history—to mete out moral judgment on the individual, thereby posthumously rendering the justice that fate did not. The Confucian worldview did not offer a clear conception of an autonomous world beyond this life. Instead, it stressed a close relationship between the living and the dead, placing responsibility upon the living for the welfare and memory of the dead. This meant that historical remembrance was the only form of immortality a Confucian could hope for. Under the circumstances, historical judgment carried immense significance. Moreover, historical judgment on the dead had direct bearing on their living descendants. This was based on a view of the present as morally determined by the past, and descendants determined by the morality of their ancestors. It is easy to understand that writing history could become an act zealously guarded by the highest authority.

The prestige of history writing, however, rested on the belief that it was an objective rendering of truth, an impartial record of human phenomena. This meant that even remotely personal observations should be scrupulously avoided.[4] In Korea, as in China, the government had an elaborate apparatus for keeping records. The king, for example, was attended in all his public functions by historians who recorded his every word. Each bureau kept an exhaustive record. Out of these records, "official histories" were compiled by committees. To justify the claim of impartiality and objectivity, these histories were usually composed by a mix of high officials and scholars.[5] These official histories were classified as "authoritative" or "legitimate histories" (*chŏng sa*). All the official histories were written in classical Chinese, and they were written right up to the end of the Chosŏn dynasty in 1910. In contrast, histories and accounts written by single authors, especially memoirs and autobiographies, were viewed as "private" reminiscences. A distinction between these two kinds of writing was rigidly maintained. In this context, petition-memorials, because they were at once personal and political, private and public, can be seen as anomalies. But as the relationship of the petitioner to the petitioned was rigidly defined and as the petition-memorials had to follow a narrowly prescribed format, the petition memorials had to be written within the limits imposed by legal procedures.

The testimonial narratives written in vernacular Korean, however, were not subjected to the same constraints. Unlike their classical Chinese counterparts, they were not legal documents. Thus, there was a far greater range in who the petitioned was, in what form the testimony was written, and to whom it was addressed. Written in Korean, the memoirs of Lady Hyegyŏng challenged the official historiography on a most sensitive and grave matter touching on dynastic legitimacy— King Yŏngjo's filicide.

In this chapter, I concentrate on two issues: (1) to present her memoirs as private narratives that contested official history and to try to identify what were the cultural imperatives for writing them and the cultural context in which they were written; and (2) the related question of genres—the different genres in which the four separate memoirs were written, their intertextuality with male genres of writing, and their relationship to one another, especially the relationship of autobiography to historiography.

The incident of Prince Sado is among those events treated evasively and cryptically in the official historiography. The incident clearly touched on the legitimacy of the Yi royal house. For one thing, the character and virtue of the principal actors involved were called into question. The filicide did not reflect well on the royal house. But it happened, and the best way to deal with it was to say as little as possible. The *Yŏngjo sillok*, the Annals of Yŏngjo's reign, for instance, includes the barest of chronology. At fourteen, Sado was appointed prince-regent and took part in governing along with his father. Although Sado was extremely intelligent as a child, he grew negligent of his studies, which brought his father disappointment and anger. At some point, something apparently went terribly wrong. Prince Sado went mad. He grew violent, and he began to kill people. Finally he posed a threat to the whole court; hence Yŏngjo's final decision to eliminate him. Moreover, the *Yŏngjo sillok* presents the whole Sado affair—Sado's insanity, and his subsequent execution—as a tragedy, the reasons for which were beyond human understanding. In this way, both the father and the son were exempted from responsibility.

The second reason the incident touched on the legitimacy of the royal house was more immediate. Prince Sado's son by Lady Hyegyŏng was the remaining heir to the throne. He succeeded his grandfather and ruled as King Chŏngjo. By Chosŏn law and custom, a criminal's son was not allowed to hold public office, much less occupy the throne. In fact, the bizarre method employed in killing Sado was an attempt to avoid the appearance of a criminal execution. Chosŏn custom forbade shedding royal blood. The accepted form of execution was a cup of poison, but this definitively would have signified criminal execution. So the only way for Sado to die was for him to commit suicide. Yŏngjo repeatedly urged his son to kill himself, and Sado attempted to strangle himself, but each time, his tutors untied him. So this method was not practicable. With the rice chest, it was different. Yŏngjo ordered Sado to get into it. Sado jumped in; Yŏngjo closed the cover and sealed it. Then, no one save the king himself could unseal the chest. Perhaps, according to the narrowest interpretation of the letter of the law, this was not considered an execution.

Yŏngjo was still uncomfortable to leave the matter as it stood. Two years after Sado's death, Yŏngjo made Chŏngjo a posthumously adopted son of Prince Hyojang, Prince Sado's deceased older brother. This measure legally severed Chŏngjo from Prince Sado. It meant that Chŏngjo was not in any legal sense the son of someone who might be called a criminal. Now the line of succession from Yŏngjo to Chŏngjo went through Prince Hyojang, making Prince Sado a nonentity. When Chŏngjo ascended the throne, he could not offer his parents the honors due to the parents of the king, such as the posthumous title of king and queen or places in the royal temple, for example. Along with her husband, Lady Hyegyŏng lost her place of honor as the legal mother of the king; thus, she could not become the queen dowager. From Chŏngjo's point of view, this was a reminder of his father's tragic death and the precariousness of his own legitimacy. Chŏngjo was nine years old when Prince Sado died.

All throughout his reign, Chŏngjo displayed uncommon devotion to his father's memory. He had his father reinterred and built a grand tomb along with a new city that surrounded the site. He made frequent visits to the tomb in regal pomp, and commissioned official paintings of many of the royal processions to his father's tomb.[6] As devoted as he was to his father's memory, Chŏngjo did not seem to have been able to accept his father's insanity. (We don't need Michel Foucault to know that mental illness was not very well understood in many societies.) In whatever way he felt about his father's madness, Chŏngjo did not want the details of Sado's sick behavior to be transmitted to history. So, in 1776, several months before Yŏngjo died, Chŏngjo petitioned for his grandfather's permission to erase all the entries pertaining to Sado in the *Sŭngjŏnwŏn ilgi* (Records of the Royal Secretariat). This was the day-to-day entry of what took place in the royal court, and because Sado had been a regent, he had a court. So, the records of Sado as prince-regent were all but erased, save the barest minimum of formalities. In this way, silence reigned in the official historiography on the Sado affair.

Enter Lady Hyegyŏng. Seizing the narration, she narrates the filicide; she reintroduces Sado's psychotic conduct and presents a clear cause-and-effect account of Sado's madness. By constructing a world of comprehensible human psychology in which human actions are explainable, she challenges the official historiographical presentation of Sado's erratic behavior as mysterious and unknowable.

Lady Hyegyŏng, however, does not discuss the filicide until the last of her four memoirs. She gradually builds up to it. She had to overcome great cultural inhibitions on self-narration. And, in her last memoir, she had to transcend the reluctance to discuss the deficiencies and erratic behavior of her husband and her father-in-law. Only by examining all of her four memoirs, is it possible to see how each of them relates intertextually to male narratives in classical Chinese; how she taps cultural resources to construct persuasive testimonial narratives; how she reconciles her beliefs with her experiences; and how she transforms her pain and sorrow into writing.

The four memoirs were written from 1795 to 1805. Their structure is quite intriguing. They were neither conceived nor composed as a single work. They were written on separate occasions for specific audiences in defense of specific causes and individuals. Despite their separateness, the memoirs constitute a certain integral whole. It is noticeable that they move from the personal to the public. The first three memoirs describe at length the emotional turmoil and political repercussions of the Sado incident, yet the incident itself is referred to only cryptically. So, when this story is narrated in the last memoir, it functions almost as the solution in a detective story in that it answers many questions that arise but are left unanswered in the course of reading the first three.

From the beginning, Lady Hyegyŏng was keenly aware that narration was a mode of empowerment. She did not have a ready-made form available to her, and so she appropriated for each memoir a genre from classical Chinese prose that had been used almost exclusively by men, and used it for her own purpose. As the memoirs move from the personal to the public, so do the genres in which the memoirs are written, from autobiography to historiography.

The first memoir, written around the time when Lady Hyegyŏng had just reached her sixtieth birthday in 1795, was addressed to her nephew, the heir of her natal family. It is in the form of a family injunction; to write something for one's children has been a rather common practice in many cultures. But in Korea, family injunctions tended, as a rule, to be purely instructional; they were brief and not written in a personal voice. They read like books of mottoes, consisting of short instructions such as "be diligent, be frugal," and so forth. Lady Hyegyŏng's first memoir, written in 1795, departs from this model. It contains advice and exhortations to the younger generation, but its main body is a self-narration followed by a postscript devoted to short remembrances of members of her family. It begins with her remembered childhood; a description of childhood is rare in any literature dating from this period.

Lady Hyegyŏng was born in Seoul in 1735 as the daughter of Hong Ponghan of the illustrious P'ungsan Hong family, and Madame Yi of an equally illustrious family. She had one older and three younger brothers, and one younger sister (the two youngest born after her departure to the palace) and grew up as the only daughter, apparently the favorite of her parents. She presents her childhood as a perfectly happy one—loving parents, bright and affectionate siblings, prosperous and harmonious relations, although her family was not wealthy.

This almost Edenic childhood abruptly came to an end. In 1743, the royal house sent out an edict announcing that it was seeking a bride for the crown prince and that *yangban* families—aristocratic-scholar families—were to submit the names of their eligible daughters. This was in accordance with the custom known as three-step selection, which was used in choosing spouses for royal children; this was done when the children were about eight or nine, although the nuptials would not take place until they were about age fifteen. The custom was designed to familiarize outsiders to court life. Hyegyŏng's father sent in her name. The first presentation took place in October, and Hyegyŏng, nine years old, went into the palace for the first time. With the remembering eye of a curious child, she captures vivid impressions of the royal family and palace, providing a unique record of the process of selecting the spouse of a royal child.

Her account of the presentation of the candidates sounds a little like a beauty pageant of today. The king and the queen were present, evaluating each girl. The royal child, for whom the selection was being made—in this case, Prince Sado—was not allowed to be present. By the second presentation, it was obvious that Lady Hyegyŏng had been chosen. For instance, when she returned home, her palanquin was carried by palace servants. This was the first instance of the palace taking possession of Hyegyŏng's life. A messenger carrying the formal message accompanied, and Hyegyŏng's parents received the message with due respect. Her relationship to her parents and relatives changed. She says, "From that day, my parents changed their form of address to me; now they spoke to me exclusively in respectful language." (One should note that the Korean language has several levels of honorifics, and parents use the informal form to children, while children use the formal form to parents.) But she was designated as crown princess consort. So the change in form of address was a sign that her public status preceded her private relationship.

Hyegyŏng also turns a longing gaze toward the house that she was leaving behind. She recounts a touching scene of her mother making a skirt for her: "Just after the second presentation, her mother burst into tears and said, 'I never got to dress you in pretty clothes. In the palace you won't be able to wear ordinary clothes. I had better make something pretty for you now, just as I always wanted to.' Grieving all the while, my mother made me a skirt of double red silk and made me wear it before the final presentation. I wept, and I wore it." Because she left her childhood home, she probably idealized her youth. Her remembrance of it is always accompanied by a sense of loss. In fact, her childhood that ended abruptly becomes a metaphor for everything that ends before it runs its natural course and for unfulfilled promises. This sense of unrequitedness defines sadness for her.

After the final presentation, Hyegyŏng was housed at the bridal pavilion, a detached building outside the palace wall, until the wedding ceremony that was held two months later, in February 1744. Her parents also stayed at this pavilion; this arrangement was a concession on the part of the royal family to Korean custom, in which the wedding ceremony takes place at the bride's house. The first part of the wedding ceremony took place at the bridal pavilion, and was followed by the grand ceremony, later the same day, at the palace. On the following day, a ceremony of bowing took place in which the new bride bowed to the king. Afterward, accompanied by her mother, Hyegyŏng paid respect to the ladies of older generations. She settled into her residence, a house within the Crown Prince Residence. Then it came time for her mother to leave. Hyegyŏng was presented to the Royal Ancestral Temple, and her life as the crown princess consort began.

Life at court was governed by ritual and ceremony, of which the most important was the ancestral ceremony. Hyegyŏng was expected to perform her part, but mostly in domestic ritual. There were four people of the older generations that she had to serve. Yŏngjo, Queen Chŏngsŏng, and Queen Dowager Inwŏn, Yŏngjo's stepmother—who are referred to as the Three Majesties—and Lady Sŏnhŭi, Sado's mother. Yŏngjo and Chŏngsŏng were estranged from one another, and it was Lady Sŏnhŭi who, despite her lower status, was the king's favorite companion. In any case, Hyegyŏng was expected to pay respect to Queen Dowager Inwŏn and Queen Chŏngsŏng on every fifth day and to Lady Sŏnhŭi on every third day. She says, "At that time palace regulations were strictly observed. One could not visit the Queen or the Queen Dowager in anything but formal robes, nor could one go if it was too late. Lest I oversleep the greeting hour [that is, dawn], I could not sleep comfortably. I repeatedly emphasized to my nurse the importance of waking for the visiting hour." Hyegyŏng brought her nurse and several maidservants with her to the palace, and they helped her to do her duty. There were also a number of princesses, Prince Sado's sisters, most of whom were born of Lady Sŏnhŭi. She seems to have gotten along with them, although it required a certain tact on her part.

Hyegyŏng appears to have adjusted to the rigors of palace life quite well. For example, she says that she never once missed visiting her elders. Things did seem to be going well for her. Early in 1749, Prince Sado and Hyegyŏng, both fourteen years of age, took their nuptials. In 1750, she gave birth to a son. Although this son died two years later, another was born in 1752 to the immense joy and relief of the royal elders and her parents. This son would later become King Chŏngjo. She repeatedly says that he was the brightest, best, and most handsome of living beings. Though this was obviously the statement of a loving mother, judging by what he accomplished, he must have been an exceptional child. Two daughters followed, Princess Ch'ŏng'yŏn in 1754 and Princess Ch'ŏngsŏn in 1756. Prince Sado, soon after he turned fourteen, was

appointed prince-regent and given heavy governing duties. Her natal
family did well. Soon after her wedding, her father passed the civil service examination and, under royal patronage, moved into a position of
power; he would eventually become prime minister. Her brothers excelled in their studies, and her parents had another daughter; Hyegyŏng
was overjoyed at the birth.

At some point, however, the tone of Hyegyŏng's memoir becomes
perceptibly dark and anguished. First, her mother died in 1755. Her royal
in-laws extended their sympathy to her at this loss but, when she persisted in her grief, they chided her, saying that her mourning for her
mother violated the sartorial codes of the court. Ordinarily, married
women mourned for their mothers for a year; her mourning for her mother
was seen as a private matter, and Hyegyŏng laments that it had to be
shortened. Then, in 1757, Queen Chŏngsŏng and Queen Dowager Inwŏn
both passed away within a month of each other. As women married into
the royal family as legal consorts, the three ladies seem to have developed a sense of affinity and sympathy across generations, and Hyegyŏng
expresses a sense of loss and loneliness at their passing.

Her anguish, however profound and mysterious, is not something that
can be explained by the deaths of elders. Sometime around 1756, she
begins to refer cryptically to Prince Sado's illness. She says things like,
"The deep worry, which burned in my heart like a flame, grew worse,
and I really lost my desire to live." Again, "I would rather not discuss
the depths of my disquiet and nervousness during this period." Also about
her father: "He was profoundly troubled by the state of things at court.
We spent our days in deep gloom. Things grew even harder. I longed for
oblivion." Then, in 1762, she says, "Things grew still worse. My desire
to do away with myself, and thus to attain a blissful ignorance, became
ever so strong." Then finally, "On the thirteenth day, Heaven and Earth
clashed and the sun and the moon turned black." This was the day Prince
Sado was put into the rice chest. The memoir of 1795 does not say more
on the topic; indeed she does not narrate the event until her last memoir,
written ten years later.

Valuable though the memoir of 1795 is in its description of her childhood and her life at court, it was written as an apologia for herself and
her father in the defense of their choices to live on after Prince Sado's
death. It is not that widows were expected to follow their husbands to
death in Chosŏn Korea, but this was a special case. Prince Sado had
been put to death by his father, and to be indebted for life to the king

who had killed her husband would have carried compromising implications. But, on the other hand, had she chosen to die, it would have implied a protest against the royal decision, or it might have deepened the suggestion that Prince Sado had been guilty. Neither would have furthered her son's legitimacy.

Lady Hyegyŏng presents this as an ultimate example in the conflict between the demands imposed by her different roles. Wifely duty and maternal duty claimed her with almost equal force, but each required an opposite course; one demanded the taking of her own life while the other demanded living on in shame. Lady Hyegyŏng presents her decision to live as a decision to choose the most public of her duties, in this case, the course that benefited dynastic security. This coincided with her maternal duty. That this obligation had a prior claim does not obliterate the fact that she failed to discharge her wifely duty to follow her husband. That was of course the cause of her shame. She says: "Wishing to repay the throne and to protect the Grand heir, I gave up the idea of killing myself. Nevertheless, how can I ever forget, even to the last moment of my consciousness, the shame of not having known the proper end and my regret over my long and slow life." At the same time, she implies that it was also her ultimate sacrifice born of her devotion to the public cause. In fact, the choice between personal honor and public cause is a familiar theme in her narration. She defends the rest of her family in the same manner—that the choices they made also required deep compromises of personal honor, but they did so for public cause. She, in fact, presents her narrative as an "elaborate drama of honor," a drama of her class and milieu.

The last three memoirs were written after the death of her son Chŏngjo and are addressed to King Sunjo, her grandson who ascended the throne as a minor and thus began his reign under a queen dowager's regency. These memoirs are more public, each one becoming a little more so than the previous. The second memoir, written in 1801, is a defense of her younger brother, Hong Nagim, who was executed in the first major persecution of Catholics. The charges against Hong Nagim were unsubstantiated and seem, in all likelihood, to have been unfounded.[7] Lady Hyegyŏng attributes the outcome entirely to an acrimonious interfamilial feud. In any case, this is written in a form resembling a petition-memorial. Lady Hyegyŏng's memoir of 1801 privatizes a mode of writing that had been reserved exclusively for public discourse. Availing herself of her position as the grandmother of the king, she appropriates this genre and uses it for testimony in Korean.

The memoir of 1802, the third, presents a moving portrayal of Chŏngjo as a son obsessed with restoring honor to his ill-fated father. Lady Hyegyŏng recounts that in his unrequited obsession, Chŏngjo drew up a plan in which he would fulfill his dream of restoring honor to his father and the dishonored members of his maternal family. He died before he could enact his plan. Recounting Chŏngjo's filial devotion, she appeals to Sunjo. In this way, Lady Hyegyŏng privatizes the genre of biography as well as its subject. This memoir is the biography of a filial son, rather than that of a king who was, in fact, one of the most brilliant rulers of Chosŏn dynasty. And it is written by the mother of this filial son and addressed in turn to his son upon whom filiality presumably weighed just as heavily.

The Memoir of 1805 presents the incident of Prince Sado. With Lady Hyegyŏng's claim that it recounts a truthful history of the royal filicide of the crown prince, it enters into the realm of historiography. But, in several crucial ways, her narrative differs from conventional historiography. This memoir is addressed to her grandson. Befitting its public subject matter, she speaks to him as a senior member of the royal family to a royal descendant. Also, her narrative is a first-person eyewitness account based on her own private memory. In fact, the authenticity and value of her account lay precisely on her claim that she alone witnessed the event and she alone knew the truth. And she professes that the reason for writing was her sense of duty that she transmit to Sunjo this knowledge about his ancestors. In other words, she wants to establish "public history" with her private memory. In so doing, she eschews the customary indirection in describing the failings of the king or the royal family. It is as if she believed that the only redemption for them and the other players involved in the incident lay in her portrayal of them in their full human complexity and imperfection, causing and enduring pain.

Indeed it is a remarkable story. As each player fulfills his or her sorrowful destiny, terror and sadness become unbearable. The psychological persuasiveness of her memoirs comes from Princess Hyegyŏng's keen observation, apparently related to her status as outsider, someone born and raised outside the palace. And she uses her keen outsider's gaze in commenting on the rigors of court ritual and on the causes of the deepening conflict between father and son.

She narrates the story of father-son conflict in two modes. In one mode, she evokes the cosmic realm—ultimately human motives, and human emotions are mysterious and beyond human comprehension. Using this mode she discusses the reasons for Yŏngjo's harshness toward his own son, sometimes despite himself. She acknowledges that he had his own demons to fight, but she leaves these strange impulses unexplained. Most of the time, however, she narrates in the realm of human comprehensibility.

When Sado was born, Yŏngjo was overjoyed. He had been without an heir since the death of his first son, Prince Hyojang, in 1728, a year marked by another disaster. A rebellion was exploding in the south, and though it was soon pacified, Yŏngjo never forgot the terror of thinking that he might have lost his mantle. He redoubled his effort to bring prosperity to the country. He was also anxious to secure his successor.

Usually the heir was formally invested as crown prince when he became about seven or eight. In his desire to cement dynastic security, Yŏngjo appointed Sado as crown prince when he was only fourteen months old, and installed him in the Crown Prince Residence complete with tutors and military guards. Chŏsŭng Pavilion, Sado's residence, was far from the residences of Yŏngjo and Lady Sŏnhŭi. Although the prince's removal occurred before she entered the palace, Hyegyŏng presents this distance as the seed of trouble. Though both the father and the mother visited their son daily, whether it was cold or hot, she believes that it could not have been the same as bringing him up in their own establishment, seeing him morning and evening and guiding him constantly. As the son grew older, they spent less and less time with him. Away from parental view, the prince spent most of his time in the company of eunuchs and ladies-in-waiting, hearing gossip and tales of scandal. The distance created a psychological barrier between father and son. Prince Sado began to fear his father, while Yŏngjo, who had placed so much hope in his late-begotten son, began to feel apprehensive over his development.

Princess Hyegyŏng also points out their differing personalities. Hyegyŏng says Yŏngjo was articulate, bright, benevolent, and kind. He was penetrating in observation and quick of comprehension. Prince Sado, on the other hand, was reticent, slow, and deliberate of movement. She cites as an example that when Yŏngjo asked him the most ordinary questions, the prince answered very slowly and hesitantly. It was not that he did not have opinions or views but he was just too worried that his answer might be wrong or foolish. This tried Yŏngjo's patience.

This is how Hyegyŏng found them when she entered the palace. She says that she was struck by the strictness of life at court. Laws were severe and rituals elaborate, with no allowance for private sentiment. She was fearful of making mistakes. What surprised her, however, was that Prince Sado too seemed to feel awe. He was only nine, but he did not dare to sit in front of his father except in a prostrate position just as the officials did. He referred to himself as "your servant." From the beginning, she sensed that something was amiss. The prince never finished his morning toilet on time. She says that on those days when they were supposed to visit the elders, she was ready and on time, but she had to wait for him for quite a while. She thought it peculiar and wondered whether he was somehow ill. Then he grew terribly afraid of thunder. When it thundered, he lay on the ground on his face, his hands covering his ears.

Yŏngjo began to humiliate his son in front of people. He would test him in front of a large crowd and, when the prince answered incorrectly, he ridiculed him. Prince Sado's appointment as prince regent created additional conflict. In the complex politics of the time, factional animosities ran deep. Yŏngjo was hoping that Sado would be able to alleviate some of the pressures he felt, but fearful of paternal disapproval, Sado was ineffectual. Infuriated, Yŏngjo faulted Sado for incompetence. If, however, Sado were to make a decision, then he would scold him for making decisions without consulting him. Sado's performance grew even more ineffectual. Hyegyŏng says that there was no way Sado could please his father.

Hyegyŏng says that at some point, Sado began to react to his father. Yŏngjo wrongly accused him of drinking—this was in the midst of prohibition against alchohol—and Sado began to drink. Yŏngjo scolded him for his unkempt attire. Sado developed what Hyegyŏng refers to as "clothing phobia"—difficulty or inability to get dressed. In order to get dressed, he destroyed many sets of clothing, and he often physically hurt those who helped him dress. This symptom grew worse. Hyegyŏng talks about having to have tens of sets of clothing on hand.

Space is an important metaphor in Hyegyŏng's narration of Sado's deterioration. The Yi royal family did not casually venture outside the palace wall. Royal visits to Yi ancestral tombs were one of the few common outings. Since coming of age, Sado wished to be included in the entourage, but at the last minute Yŏngjo always struck his name. Once, at the ministers' urging, Yŏngjo finally included Sado. But when the entourage stopped on the way because of rain, faulting the prince's improper headgear, the king ordered him to return to the palace. When he came back, soaked with rain and white with fury, Sado said to his mother and wife, "It's becoming harder and harder for me to live." Then, through his sister's mediation, he received royal permission to go to Onyang, a hot spring, south of Seoul. Hyegyŏng says that Sado was badly off. It seems that, outside the palace wall, he became instantly better. He played the role of a concerned future ruler effectively, earning praise from the population on the way. Jubilant, he sent letters of greeting to his family. Once back in the palace, however, he retreated into his world of insanity.

In spring 1761, Sado began to leave the palace in disguise. Going outside of the palace walls without prior arrangement was strictly forbidden. This was probably for security reasons, but also because the royal house did not want its members to make demands on the population. The first time, he went to P'yŏngyang, the present capital of North Korea, returning after several weeks. We do not know what Sado did on this trip, but there are intimations that he behaved rather badly. He picked up a couple of *kisaeng* (women entertainers) and some male cronies, and brought them with him to Seoul. He routinely left the court's environs in disguise, and, with several attendants, he prowled the environs of the city. Inside the palace, he avoided staying in his official quarters. He dug an underground space in which he built a house with three small rooms, just like the inside of a grave, spending many hours inside this subterranean chamber.

Sado also grew violent. From 1757 on, he began to kill people. The first was the eunuch on duty. He came in with the bloody, severed head and showed it to Hyegyŏng and some ladies-in-waiting. As the court watched in shock, horror, and dismay, Sado descended into destructive violence. Most of those he killed were in service at his residence. Many ladies-in-waiting, including his favorite concubine, were hurt. Hyegyŏng says that she feared for her life and her son's. This state of terror continued until Lady Sŏnhŭi, Sado's mother—alarmed by a rumor indicating that Sado had attempted patricide—urged Yŏngjo to protect the safety of the dynasty by carrying out the final act (of execution). Sado was placed in the rice chest in July 1762. He died eight days later, on a day of torrential rain and thunder.

In narrating Sado's deterioration and breakdown, Hyegyŏng implies that his transgressions were caused by mental illness and that this was directly attributable to a profound sense of rejection and injury by his father.

In this sense, she is intent on constructing a plea for Sado. She does not condone his transgressions, but she implies that even his transgressions were testimony to the depth of his suffering. The underlying theme is that he lost his battle to meet his father's demands not because he did not want to comply but because he desired so intensely to live up to his father's expectations. Constant paternal disapproval was too great to bear. As for Yŏngjo, she is less forgiving. She felt he was simply too harsh to his son. Completely departing from the official historiographical view, she presents her opinion that Yŏngjo's cruelty was responsible for Sado's madness. But she offers sympathy for his pain in the end, when, to restore order, he had to put his son to death. She thus offers a historian's compassion and consolation to all. But her historical vision was that of a private person, vastly different from the one presented in the official historiography. Thus, in the last memoir, there is a curious exchange between the public and the private. The history of a ruler and his heir is recounted as the story of a father and son by the son's wife. Here is an extreme case of the privatization of an impersonal and public genre. At the same time, it exteriorizes and historicizes her private memory as public history.

What is the cultural meaning of the memoirs of Lady Hyegyŏng's progression in genres from autobiography to historiography? In studies of Western autobiography it has been posited that a sense of the discrete self is a precondition for writing autobiography.[8] Women autobiographers are seen a little differently. The female sense of self is viewed as more relational, defined by its relationships to the persons surrounding the self, and autobiographies by women show this. Their autobiographies talk not only of themselves but frequently at great length of persons around them. Sometimes women autobiographers, like Margaret Cavendish, Duchess of Newcastle of seventeenth-century England, appended short autobiographies to long biographies of their husbands.[9] In Lady Hyegyŏng's case, the sense of a relational self seems to be very strong. Even in the first memoir—which is the only piece among the four that is in accordance with the definition that Philippe Lejeune calls the "autobiographical pact," in which the writer, the narrator, and the protagonist are the same person,[10]—a great deal of attention is devoted to defending her father and her family. Writing the last memoir, in which she narrates her husband's madness and death, was her way of asking her husband's forgiveness for not following him to death. Because she did not follow him, she should at least record his suffering as accurately as possible so that he would be judged fairly by history.

At the same time, through the act of writing, the author desires to recompose and discover herself. By writing her memoirs, Lady Hyegyŏng was engaged in a quest for an understanding that would explain the vagaries of human fate and the haphazardness of the moral order. In the first memoir, the narrative probed her doubt and disillusion over the discrepancy between her beliefs and her experiences. She grew up believing in a correspondence between the moral order and human affairs; however, this was constantly challenged. Her life was repeatedly visited by difficulties and tragedies. Why did such terrible things happen to her? Did Heaven hate her? She even suspected that she was the cause of her own fate. She felt deeply guilt-ridden, especially about her husband and her father. She says: "Thus I sinned against conjugal duty and deserted filial obligations. I lay awake at night, guilty over the decline of my family. Sometimes I felt as though fire was burning inside of me, and on those occasions, my bedding became so hot that I rose and pounded the walls in utter misery. Indeed, for how many years was I unable to fall asleep in peace!" Then, her grandson, a long-awaited heir to the throne, was born on her birthday. She took his birth as a sign that Heaven affirmed her worth. A tentative conciliation was struck between her belief and life.

The second memoir was written in a much more aggrieved spirit, in a spirit that Heaven dealt her more blows than she deserved. Her son had suddenly died in his prime, at the age of forty-nine. Because her grandson was in minority, a queen dowager regency was enacted. Queen Chŏngsun, Yŏngjo's second wife, became regent, and so her family, the archrival of Lady Hyegyŏng's family, came into power. Soon, her brother was executed. The memoir is born of a sense of betrayal by fate, a sense that she should take matters into her own hands in the limited time left to her. In the last memoir, she somewhat resolves the conflict between belief and experience. She does not claim any greater understanding of the mystery of the workings of Heaven than she did when she wrote the first memoir. But, rather than displaying a sense of outrage or betrayal, here she seems to acquiesce to the idea that Heaven must have its own way of operating even if it cannot be discerned. Lady Hyegyŏng acknowledges that if the workings of each sphere—the personal, the social, the human, and the cosmic—are quite complicated separately, the relationship between them is even more complex. She does not deny that there is a correlation between them, but she concedes that, ultimately, these forces are mysterious and not immediately apparent. So, though she validates the moral order, she does not demand its transparency in individual lives. In the same vein, she upholds the primacy of the social order. Individual considerations, no matter how compelling, must be subservient to the public cause. This view is accompanied by full sympathy for the human condition and respect for individual endeavors, regardless of results. So, she offers sympathy to all of those who, in 1762, voluntarily or involuntarily, had to do what it took to uphold the social order. This cost each a great deal. While it meant different things to different people, it caused all of them deep pain. She describes all of their pain and struggle, including her own, and she offers them a historian's consolation. As she transforms pain and sorrow into writing, the boundaries between autobiography and historiography, a discrete sense of self and a relational sense of self are almost completely blurred.

Notes

The author would like to acknowledge that the argument presented in this chapter follows that of her introduction to Hyegyŏnggung Hong Ssi, *The Memoirs of Lady Hyegyŏng: The Autobiographical Writings of a Crown Princess of Eighteenth-Century Korea*, edited and translated by JaHyun Kim Haboush. Berkeley and Los Angeles: University of California, 1996. Copyright © 1996 by the Regents of the University of California; used with permission.

1. See Haboush, *The Memoirs of Lady Hyegyŏng*.
2. Han, Sanggwŏn, *Chosŏn hugi sahoe wa sowŏn chedo*, 13–35.
3. For a discussion of petition-memorials, see Haboush, "Gender and the Politics of Language in Korea."
4. Wu, *The Confucian's Progress*, 3–12.
5. For a discussion of the process of compiling the *sillok*, see McCune, "The Yi Dynasty Annals of Korea," 57–82.
6. One set of Chŏngjo's processional paintings to Sado's tomb was auctioned at Christie's Auction House several years ago, selling for about $600,000.
7. Dallet, *L'histoire de l'église de Corée, Tome* 1, 145.
8. Gusdorf, "Conditions and Limits of Autobiography," 29–30.
9. Mason, "The Other Voice," 210–212.
10. Lejeune, *On Autobiography*, 3–30.

References

Dallet, Charles. *L'histoire de l'église de Corée*, 2 vols. Paris: n.p., 1874.
Gusdorf, Georges. "Conditions and Limits of Autobiography" In *Autobiography: Essays Theoretical and Critical*, edited by James Olney. Princeton, NJ: Princeton University Press, 1980.

Haboush, JaHyun Kim, ed. and trans. *The Memoirs of Lady Hyegyŏng: The Autobiographical Writings of a Crown Princess of Eighteenth-Century Korea.* Berkeley and Los Angeles: University of California Press, 1996.

———. "Gender and the Politics of Language in Korea." In *Rethinking Confucianism: Past and Present in China, Japan, Korea, and Vietnam,* edited by John B. Duncan, Benjamin A. Elman, and Herman Ooms. Los Angeles: Asian Pacific Monographic Series, UCLA, 2002.

Han, Sanggwŏn. *Chosŏn hugi sahoe wa sowŏn chedo.* Seoul: Ilchogak, 1996.

Lejeune, Philippe. *On Autobiography.* Minneapolis: University of Minnesota Press, 1988.

Mason, Mary G. "The Other Voice: Autobiographies of Women Writers." In *Autobiography: Essays Theoretical and Critical,* edited by James Olney. Princeton: Princeton University Press, 1980.

McCune, G.M. "The Yi Dynasty Annals of Korea." *Transactions of the Korea Branch of the Royal Asiatic Society* 18 (1929).

Wu, Pei-yi. *The Confucian's Progress: Autobiographical Writings in Traditional China.* Princeton, NJ: Princeton University Press, 1990.

7
Kyubang Kasa

Women's Writings from the Late Chosŏn

Sonja Häußler

The literary genre of *kasa*—a lyric poem in the vernacular—was adopted by *yangban* (elite class) women of the later half of the Chosŏn dynasty as their favored way for expressing their specific thoughts and feelings. *Kasa* are long poems with a set rhythmic pattern extended over an indefinite number of verses, ranging from two dozen lines to more than 1,000. All verses of a *kasa* are composed of two half-lines made up of two phrases of either three and four syllables or four and four syllables. Having no stanzaic division, *kasa*'s relatively free form and the way it lends itself to description and realistic exposition renders the poet's inner world as well as the outer conditions of her life in a broader scope than the rigidly structured *sijo*, the other popular poetic form in the vernacular of the Chosŏn dynasty. For these reasons *kasa* became the preferred form for women and the common people to express themselves in poetic language in the eighteenth and nineteenth centuries.[1]

Kasa written by women came to be called *kyubang kasa*, *kyujung kado*, or *naebang kasa*, all meaning "songs of the inner chambers." People in the countryside simply call them *kasa* or *turumari*; the latter term refers to the *turumari* (scroll) on which they were written and then handed down through generations. Such a scroll usually had a length of five meters, bearing just one poem. However, some extended up to forty meters, including not only several pieces of *kyubang kasa*, but also didactic texts in prose form or even *sosŏl* literature as well.

Most authors of *kyubang kasa* are unknown; most were proba' 'v wives of Confucian scholars who lived in retirement in the countryside. The anonymity of the women who wrote the *kasa* can partly be attributed to the fact that a woman was not given her own first name in those times. As a young girl, she was provided with only a nickname that she gave up when she married; after marriage one referred to her as so-and-so's wife or so-and-so's mother, or the person from such-and-such place. The absence of the author's name could also be attributed to the standards of feminine modesty prevalent at that time. A woman would rarely reveal her authorship of a literary work, even if it were possible. In addition, it was not necessary to state who the author was because a *kasa* was composed for a specific individual, usually a close relative, who knew from whom she received the poem. The authors of many anonymous *kyubang kasa* can be identified through interviews with today's owners of the manuscripts.[2] From field research we have learned that they know their family's history thoroughly, and that they have a great deal to say about the *kasas*: who wrote or copied them, how the respective families acquired the *kasa* scrolls, and how they were preserved and used.[3]

If a poem were composed collectively, and many *kasa* were, naturally there would be no indication that any particular person was the author. Instead of information about an author, information about the person who copied the text was occasionally added in an epilogue to a poem.

Without exaggeration, one can say that *kyubang kasa* turned into a mass phenomenon among *yangban* women near the end of the Chosŏn dynasty. Still-extant texts number in the tens of thousands as the latest estimate by Kwŏn Yŏngch'ŏl, the leading scholar on *kyubang kasa*, shows.[4] Kwŏn Yŏngch'ŏl himself has collected about 6,000 poems, and those were mainly written in the Yŏngnam area.[5] That is to say, we are faced with a striking amount of poems in a relatively short time of circulation and, apparently, a relatively small area of circulation. Compared with the tiny number of *sijo* composed by female authors, *kyubang kasa* are transmitted to us in an overwhelming quantity.

Nearly 92 of the 4,000 surviving *sijo* can be ascribed to women and only about half a dozen of that number are attributed to *yangban* women; the rest are the work of *kisaeng*.[6] The difference between the number of *sijo* written by women and the number of *kasa* by women authors shows that women preferred *kasa*. Most women did not have the amount of necessary leisure time in order to learn the refined, rigidly structured form of the *sijo*. Women preferred the more utilitarian character of the *kyubang kasa*, as can be seen from their subjects. Another reason the *kasa* was more attractive is that *sijo* presents the perspective of a single poet and therefore cannot be duplicated, whereas *kyubang kasa* are well known for having many variants of the same poems.

The estimated number of *kyubang kasa* bears no comparison to the number of poems by men, especially those written in Chinese. The collected writings of the most productive of the male poets would include several thousand poems by a single author! More than 2,000 poems by Yi Kyubo (1168–1241) and Kim Sisŭp (1435–1493), for instance, are preserved, although both men lived many centuries ago.

But poetry by women was produced in very different circumstances from those in which male poets did their writing. In Neo-Confucian society, women were assigned domestic functions. Tradition demanded from them that they fulfill four roles in the house: spinning, needling, cooking, and child care. They were not expected to have literary ambitions. As Yi Ik (1682–1764), one of the Sirhak scholars, declared in his *Sŏngho sasŏl* (Collected Essays of Sŏngho): "Reading and learning are the domains of men. For a woman it is enough if she knows the Confucian virtues of diligence, frugality, and chastity. If a woman disobeys these virtues, she will bring disgrace to the family."[7] And the *Kyujung yoram* (Manual of the Inner Rooms)[8] stated: "The names of their country and ancestors are enough for women to learn. Writing prose or poetry is the specialty of *kisaeng* (professional female entertainers); it is not a desirable subject to teach women of a learned family."[9]

The pattern for that restraint placed upon women in the literary field was set by Cheng Yi (1033–1107), the most authoritative Chinese Neo-Confucian, next to Zhu Xi (1130–1200). Of his mother, he wrote: "She loved literature but did not write compositions. In her view it was very wrong the way some women let their writings or calligraphy circulate. Her lifetime output of poetry did not amount to more than thirty pieces, none of which has been preserved."[10]

Commending his mother for limiting the number of literary works she produced, Cheng Yi also praised the modesty she displayed in not exposing her poems to the outside world. This was the ideal set by Neo-Confucian ideology, but practice usually differs from a set ideal in one way or another. *Kyubang kasa* are evidence that women, even in strongly Confucianized *yangban* households, were not willing to submit fully to the propagated ideal of women keeping their literary talent under wraps. As daughters, mothers, or sisters of zealous scholars, they felt the urge to emulate the male members of their family in striving for literary creativity, at least in the field of *han'gŭl* literature! Under the pressure of Neo-Confucianism, however, their literary products did not surmount the walls of the secluded women's quarters in *yangban* houses. Circulating in handwritten form, they were the exclusive property and the object of pride of women, which answers the question of why we have no published works until the twentieth century when scholars started to collect and analyze them.

In general, the reign of King Yŏngjo (r. 1725–76) is considered to be the time when women began to pick up the *kasa* genre, previously dominated by men. Among the hitherto discovered poems there are only a few where time, place, and purpose of composition are known. The earliest of those dates is the eighteenth year of King Chŏngjo, that is, 1794 according to the Christian calendar. [11]

It was in that very same year that the *Ssangbyŏk ka* (A Pair of Jade Discs) was written by Madam Yi of the Yŏn'an Yi clan in Hahoe on the occasion of her son's successful passing of the civil service examination. The poem's title comes from the fact that Madam Yi's son Yu T'aejwa had passed his examination that year, along with Yu's cousin Yu Sangjo, who was the same age and with whom he had prepared for the examination. That's why Madam Yi called the two cousins "a pair of jade discs," using a widely known Chinese metaphor for talented brothers. In her poem, Madam Yi expresses her joy over the two men returning home as successful exam candidates, as well as her gratitude for the royal benevolence that allowed them to take and pass that exam and her pride in the family's membership in the scholar Yu Sŏngnyong's clan to which they belonged. But apparently this is not the earliest *kyubang kasa* at all. One contemporary scholar has concluded that, from the quality of the paper on which they were written and the language of some of the other *kyubang kasa* unearthed so far, some *kasa* must have been written by women even earlier. Yet no exact dates for those earlier texts have as yet been determined. [12]

Among contemporary Korean scholars there is a consensus that the prototypes of *kyubang kasa* were didactic poems, like *Kyenyŏ ka* and *Kyonyŏ sa,* concerned with the promotion of Confucian ideals for women.

These admonitory and instructive poems are assumed by contemporary Korean scholars to have emerged before *kasa* that had other purposes were written. Congratulations and blessings, as in the *Ssangbyŏk ka,* presumably are a later development. Thus, the origin of *kyubang kasa* is estimated to be about half a century before the *Ssangbyŏk ka,* in the first decades of the eighteenth century.[13] This period coincides with the heyday of men's *kasa* (*yangban kasa*) and the rise of narrative literature (*sosŏl*), two genre that influenced the form and style of *kyubang kasa* considerably. ·

As has already been mentioned above, the overwhelming majority of *kyubang kasa* has been found in the Yŏngnam area.[14] In the last decades some scholars have concentrated their search for *kyubang kasa* on other regions of the Korean Peninsula where a few such poems have also surfaced.[15] Unfortunately, unlike the reports on the Yŏngnam area, those on other regions do not provide any indication of exactly how many poems have been discovered. Therefore, no numerical comparison can be made.

Field research on that subject since 1955 shows that *kyubang kasa* were produced for the most part in the Yŏngnam area. Within that area, most of the *kyubang kasa* were found to have been produced in Yongnam's northern section, embracing the province of North Kyŏngsang.[16] Three great regions of dissemination were identified—the regions around Andong, Kyŏngju, and Sŏngju—and the number of poems discovered therein showing a ratio of 5 (Andong) : 3 (Kyŏngju) : 2 (Sŏngju).[17] From the number and the subjects of the poems as well as the cultural features of the region, a contemporary Korean scholar concluded that Andong is the area where *kyubang kasa* originated.[18]

A song from Andong called *Andong chach'ŏng* (Crimson and Blue) dates from the Koryŏ dynasty. This poem in the *kayo* genre is reported to have been composed by an unknown Koryŏ woman. Though the text itself has been lost, a brief note about the content of this poem as well as the reason for its composition are found in the *Koryŏ sa* (History of Koryŏ) and in the *Chŭngbo munhŏn pigo*. It contains the warning that once a woman has lost her chastity, she must suffer all sorts of humiliation and insults. Like a colored thread whose strands are unpure, mixed crimson and blue, she will be despised and thought of as "dirty." In its admonition for women to watch their conduct and to guard their bodies, the poem's subject matter resembles the *Kyenyŏ ka* and other *kyubang kasa* from later centuries. What is remarkable in this connection is the report that the Andong chach'ŏng has been used as court music during the Chosŏn dynasty.[19]

Whatever influence that song may or may not have had on the genesis of *kyubang kasa*, it is clear that by the time of *kyubang kasa*'s emergence that Andong had already developed a long tradition of promoting woman's virtue. For centuries, Andong figured prominently in the development of Neo-Confucianism in Korea, both in its philosophical and its cultural aspects. (Even now it is known as the most conservative area of Korea, where traditional Confucian culture is preserved most perfectly.)

Andong is especially well-known for being the homeland of Yi Hwang (1501–1570), the leading Korean Neo-Confucian philosopher who followed Zhu Xi in his interpretation of the primacy of principle (*li*) over material force (*ch'i*) as well as in his concepts of social order. Regarding the family as the basis and micro-model of society as a whole, Yi Hwang was very much concerned with transplanting Zhu Xi's ideal family structure into Korean society and with encouraging Confucian ideals of filial piety, feminine chastity, and wifely obedience. His emphasis on moral questions was carried on by his disciples, many of whom also had settled down in the Andong county or in the adjacent territories.

Gradually nests of Confucian scholars spread here and there, centering around the numerous newly opened *sŏwŏn* (private academies). From the middle of the Chosŏn dynasty, whole villages with only one *yangban* family living in them developed: The descendants of Yu Sŏngnyong (1542–1607), for instance, settled down in Hahoe village; those of Kim Sŏngil (1538–1593) settled in Kŭmgye. And the Yean district (now Tosan) nearly became the exclusive home of Yi Hwang's descendants, with only one family from a different lineage, the offspring of Yi Hyŏnbo (1467–1555), living there.

This tendency toward single-clan or *yangban*-only villages (*tongjok purak*), naturally stimulated by the desire to be close to educational institutions, increased as factional strife intensified. Large numbers of *yangban* barred from office on account of their affiliation with a defeated faction retired to private life in their native region and dedicated their energy to teaching and studying. The followers of Yi Hwang had all belonged to the eastern faction, which later split into the northern and the southern factions. After a fierce struggle with the westerners at the end of the seventeenth century, the southern faction was eliminated from the political arena with many of its followers taking refuge in the Yŏngnam area.[20]

Although the kings who ascended the throne after this factional fragmentation, Yŏngjo (1725–1776) and Chŏngjo (1777–1800), pursued a policy of impartiality, this policy had little consequences for the ousted southern faction.

According to research, these events seem to have had a direct impact on the dissemination of the *kyubang kasa*. All poems that were written (or copied) before the end of the Chosŏn dynasty are attributed to families affiliated with the southerners. Due to the hostility between the southern and the western factions, the women of these factions had scarcely any contact with each other. No marriage ties were arranged between the two factions. And because the traditional gatherings and outings of women—being occasions of producing and exchanging poems—were limited to the members of a single clan, hardly any poems were introduced to the westerners. Therefore, only by the end of the Chosŏn dynasty were these restrictions weakened concerning marriage between enemy factions; only then the tradition of *kyubang kasa* was able to pass into the hands of westerners.[21]

Further investigation into and collection of *kyubang kasa* (especially in regions other than Yŏngnam) will show whether this regional and factional characteristic, observed by Professor KwŏnYŏngch'ŏl, is irrefutable or not. If future research will confirm his thesis, it would be an additional tessera in the picture of Korean *yangban* women's restricted life and their limited range of literary production.

The subject matter of *kyubang kasa* is directly related to the conditions under which women lived after Neo-Confucianism began to play a stronger role in Korean society. The change from uxurilocal to virilocal residence, in particular, brought deep changes in women's position. In earlier times, a husband residing with his wife in her parents' household was the preferred pattern in Korea, but in the later part of the Chosŏn dynasty the woman's transfer to her in-laws' house had become the general custom. Thus, marriage was the most crucial moment in a woman's life. Moving to her husband's house, she was confronted with the total change of all the conditions affecting her daily life. She had to leave the most beloved people on her side—her parents, siblings and friends—whom she would see only rarely now. In her new residence she had to accustom herself to another system of relationships wherein she would rank as the last link in the chain for a long time. New habits and customs and an unfamiliar landscape awaited her.[22]

For that critical change in her life a woman needed moral and psychological support. Careful preparations for her role as a wife started early in her childhood, with oral instructions from her parents and the study of such ethical classics as *Naehun* (Instructions for Women), *Yŏllyŏ chŏn* (Five Biographies of Faithful Women), *Yŏch'ik* (Rules of Conduct for Women) and others. But, as the burden she would have to bear was immense, the concern her parents showed for her did not stop with marriage. It only took another form, namely that of personally written advice and encouraging words she could take with her to her new residence. In a moment of weakness, or perhaps when she had the rare leisure moment, she could find spiritual edification in reading what her mother or grandmother (or, occasionally, her father or grandfather) had written for her. Touching the scroll and looking at the calligraphy of her loved ones, she would be with them in her thoughts.

This, apparently, was the premise on which the early *kyubang kasa* promoting Confucian virtues arose. Those classifiable as didactic are by far the greatest in number. Numerous titles have been handed down, and of each title numerous emulations and copies exist. The most prominent are the *Kyenyŏ ka*, *Kyŏnggye ka*, *Kyohun ka*, and *Kyujung haengsil ka*, all of which could be translated as Song of Admonitions. The main ideas and the general framework of these songs follow Zhu Xi's *Minor Learning* (Xiaoxue, Kor. Sohak) and his *Family Precepts of Master Zhu* (Zhu zi jia xun, Kor. Chuja kahun).[23]

In their complete form, the *Songs of Admonitions* contain a long commentary of precepts a married woman was obliged to observe: how to serve her parents-in-law, how to prepare the ancestral offerings, how to dress and how to cook, how to serve guests, how to deal with the brothers- and sisters-in-law, how to support harmony in the family, how to raise children, how to employ servants and how to manage the household economy. Conspicuous is the overemphasis on the moral qualities a woman was required to display. In correspondence with the Confucian tradition, a woman's diligence, modesty and obedience ranked first among the obligations listed in every *kasa*. Take the following *Kyujung haengsil ka*, for example:

My child, it is difficult to get experienced in woman's conduct.
One woman is intelligent, another is obedient.
When the ten thousand things were born, who would not have been lucky,
Being born as a human being and not as an animal?

Man and woman live segregated; the propriety of that segregation is
  shining.
Man is outside, woman is inside.
Learn each and every thing related to woman's work.
A family's rise and fall depend on the wives they marry.
If you observe your in-laws carefully, neighbors will applaud.
Inquire if a meal suits them and prepare the dishes they prefer.
Dress neatly, show a bright smile on your face.
Be careful about every step you make.
Don't draw a long face, even on impulse.
As the ancients have said, married life is hard.
Three years be deaf and three years be dumb.
Because every house has its own experiences, listen to your in-laws'
  instructions.
In every situation worry about getting a reprimand.
If you try to excuse your actions after being scolded, it sounds like prattle
  in your in-laws' ears.
Don't do anything for which your parents will be stigmatized because of
  their married daughter.
Offerings for ancestors and service for guests will be guided by your
  parents-in-law.
On long winter nights, on short summer nights,
Don't think about your body's pain, take care not to sleep too deeply.
If you serve your in-laws faithfully, your progeny will prosper.
If a guest comes to your house, don't judge whether he is a distant or a
  close relative.
Receive him without making any fuss.
Guests have long ears. Don't think about food rations.
Serve them all you have in your house. . . .[24]

Typical indications of the didactic character of that poem are the many
hanmun phrases, along with the quotations from Chinese and Korean
classics it is filled with.

However, not all didactic poems sound as dry as a Confucian textbook. One of the more heartrending is the *Kyŏnyŏ ka*. It was composed
by a father who had to raise his four children alone after the early death
of his wife. Burdened with financial troubles, he did not even have the
time to have been fully aware that his youngest daughter had left for her
husband's house. Now, he wrote, he realized that his daughter's parting
had been much more difficult for her than for him and he expressed his
guilt. He feels sorry that he had not done all he could to support her
morally in that moment. This poem has a highly lyrical beginning:

Unnoticed, already a month has passed since you have left.
Would you forget your heedless father forever?
The love of parents' thinking of their child is so sweet.
Stepping out the door, my eyes turn to that place.
Sinking into contemplation, I recall you even more. . . .

Having squandered all my property, I suffer hardship in age.
And you, innocent children, have to suffer with me.
Of four siblings, you are the youngest.
A parent's love for the youngest lies in the nature of man.
If one can do as he pleases, he dresses and feeds her well,
And gives her the best instructions, when he marries her off. [25]

After a long personal introduction in which the father reminisces about his daughter and explains his troubled situation, he then proceeds with the typical admonitions. As with the author of the *Kyujung haengsil ka*, he, too, is concerned with the family's reputation and how much it depends on a woman's correct conduct. Using her elder sisters as examples, he insists that even a woman deficient in training can achieve perfect conduct if she listens to her in-laws.

A personal note is found in the *Poksŏn hwaŭm ka* (Song of Blessing, Virtue, Calamity, and Indecency). Here, the admonitions are based on a mother's own dramatic story of raising her husband's household from poverty to affluence mostly through her own intelligence and hard work. The mother's instruction is underpinned by an interpolated, contrasting story of another woman, Koettong Ŏmi. Though it is an admonitory *kasa* in purpose and content, the poem stands out because of its artfully constructed real-life depiction. It speaks of women's endurance and spiritual power that enables them to overcome all kinds of hardships they had to suffer in those times.[26]

A later development, perhaps, is the appearance of didactic poems written, not for adult women, but for young girls. One such *kasa* is found in Ch'un-ch'ŏn in the house of the Kohŭng Yu family. It was written by Yu Chunggyo (1832–1893), a disciple of the Neo-Confucian scholar Yi Hangno (1792–1868). The text makes clear that it was composed in 1887 when Yu's granddaughter, to whom he dedicated the poem, was only six years old. This *Yŏson hunsa ko* (Instructions to the Granddaughter) is a detailed narration of all those obligations a girl has to observe during a day. Starting with getting up and washing in the morning, it meticulously, almost minute by minute, reports what to do and what to learn from sunrise till evening. The *kasa*'s form itself indicates a later development. It is very irregular; besides using the typical four-syllable form, some phrases even ranged between three and seven syllables.[27]

A main subject of *kyubang kasa* directly related to married life was a woman's lament over parting from her parents, siblings and friends. With strong voices, women expressed their pain at leaving the people they felt closest to. Being aware that parting from their home meant parting from their youth as well, desperate words were said about the passing time and their lot as females. In the *Sŏkpyŏl ka* (Song of Painful Parting), for example, a bride starts with the following laments:

> My friends, who will marry, listen to my song of painful parting.
> In the world, is there anything more sorrowful than parting?
> Of partings, the most bitter kind is forced parting.
> No matter how great one's parents' benefits, after parting nothing is left.
> No matter how exceptional friends' affection, after parting all is forgotten.
> How can our feelings enjoyed over twenty years be cut off one morning?
> Though we all have been born of our parents' flesh and blood
> And equally grown up under our parents' wings, woman's and man's
>   position is entirely different.
> Neither hearing nor seeing, being locked deep in the inner quarters,
> I was absorbed without a break in making clothes and preparing food.
> In this way the years slipped past, like running water, and, suddenly, I
>   arrived at the age of sixteen.
> Under such circumstances how could I become a mature person as
>   stipulated in the ancient laws?
> Those heedless men, becoming adults, enjoy a fine life.
> But women have all kinds of trouble.[28]

This poem is highly complex, composed of various scenes reflecting a bride's unhappy situation in a moving manner. Dealing with the unequal treatment between a man and woman, the bride recalls the immense work she had to do in preparation for her wedding (*sinhaeng*). While the groom could enjoy that time by looking forward to the feast, a bride had to prepare innumerable gifts for her parents-in-law, including cloth, wine, and special foods. All year round having no relaxation even on feast days, she is busy with embroidering coin pouches, and sewing wristbands, socks, and clothes for her in-laws. ("Hansik, Tano, Ch'usŏk and New Year's Day passed unnoticed, dim like in a dream.") With the day drawing nearer of her entering the groom's house, she must hurry. Besides having to race against time, she frets about another problem, too: How can she make the clothes that will fit her in-laws if she has never even seen them? If they come out the wrong size, perhaps the whole village will poke fun at her. However, finally her work has come to an end—she thought. Opening one cabinet, she realizes that there is still some cloth to sew. When can she do it? There she breaks down: She remembers that she has sewn her fingers to the bone while quilting the spring and autumn clothes. While sewing the winter and summer clothes, she has lost all energy in her arms. At that moment she decides to stop working!

> I went to the room across the way and closed the door.
> Putting on a quilt, I lay down desolately.
> Though I asked, all was silent; though I called out for somebody, there was
>   no answer.
> But then, once more thinking about what would happen, if I, before dying,
> Would lose my fitness for work, I grasped: No, it just won't work.

This *Iri haesŏ ani toenda* (No, it just won't work) comes out so faintly, so listlessly, that it reveals more about the woman's desperate situation than would an outcry. Nobody will help her do the housework. In this moment of weakness there is nobody to respond to her call. She can only rely on herself, mobilizing all her inner power. The poem proceeds as follows:

> That moment I sprang to my feet. I opened this door and that door,
> Looking in this cabinet and that cabinet.
> Hey, you tape measure, where have you gone? Let's cut out the upper- and
>   the underclothes!
> Having found the gooses and the scissors, I threw them hither and thither.
> Having chosen a small needle, a large needle, I thread this twine and that
>   twine.
> Green cloth and red cloth, make them fit that arm! . . .

Her work goes on . . .

Having gone through such hardship, relying on her own experience, the bride advises her unmarried friends to enjoy their lives before it is too late: "If you do not play and relax in childhood, you will regret it in your adulthood."

The *chat'an ka*—as the category of poems concentrating on women's laments of their fate is generally called—comprise a great variety of subjects. One type of *chat'an ka* deals with longing for one's relatives and friends, the impatient waiting for the day when they can meet again. Others deal with longing for one's husband who stays far away because of his duties. We hear of the solitude and pain of neglected wives, the grief of childless women, and the ill fate of widows.[29]

In the *Yi ssi hoesim kok* (Lady Yi's Song of Longing), a descendant of Yi Hwang expresses her yearning for the relatives she has lost. When she was three years old her father died, and at seventeen she lost her husband whom she had married only one year before. Widowed at such an early age, her only comfort were her parents-in-law and her mother toward whom she turned all her affection. But her parents-in-law died when she was thirty-eight, and now, eight years later, her mother followed them, too. To console herself, she writes a poem in which she recalls various stations of her life. Trying to find some support in nature, she looks out through her window. But her insecurity intensifies as she recognizes that the universe mercilessly rushes on its own way, regardless of the pain human beings feel. Lying under the earth, none of her loved ones could come back to this world, to be with her again. As she observes nature bursting with vitality, she wonders how there can be such a discrepancy between the actual state of nature and her inner mood.

> The moon that had risen above the east mountain, for whom had he shone?
> The sun that is climbing over the western mountain, where do you hasten?
> The world restless revolves around and the fleeting years run like water.
> Who can catch the running time? Yesterday a tragedy happened, suddenly.
> Today there are green shades and fragrant plants, the scenery is balmy.
> The weather, too, is mild and on the riverside all kinds of flowers are
>   blooming.
> Blossoms and leaves are growing closely.[30]

A completely different kind of *kyubang kasa* is the group of *hwajŏn ka* (Songs of Enjoying Flowers). In number, they rank second only to the admonitory poems. They pertain to women's outings in the wilderness in the third month of the lunar calendar. With spring came warm sunshine, fragrant breezes, and flowers of all kinds and shapes bloomed, and women of all ages visited places of scenic beauty to spend a day in mirth and revelry. On this glorious day they gathered azalea flowers and made *hwajŏn* (flower cakes), frying in sesame oil the dough of glutinous rice powder in small round flat shapes, along with flower petals. They ate and drank wine, sang flower songs and enjoyed the beautiful landscape.

The custom of making flower cakes and enjoying a spring day in nature in full bloom can be traced back to the Koryŏ dynasty.[31] However, its origin may lie in an even more remote past. The original meaning and function of this custom in later times still remain an object of further study. At this moment nothing more can be said than that these spring outings initially functioned as a ritual means to guarantee the continuity of life.[32]

The season alone chosen for these outings could testify in support of the hypothesis: spring = rebirth of nature. In this context, the joint action of women (= symbols of fertility) collecting and eating flower cakes (= signs of awakening nature) could be interpreted as efforts to reinforce the creative, prolific forces of spring. Another hint to the meaning and function of the hwajŏn custom is provided by the fact that women of all ages, old and young, took part in these gatherings, thus demonstrating the continuation of generations in their respective community and, in a broader sense, in the society and the cosmos as a whole. Most likely, these spring outings also were of considerable significance for strengthening the spirit and the solidarity of those who participated in them. In the study of this custom, the *kyubang kasa* composed on such occasions could be particularly useful. An allusion to the stability of life that is actually achieved (and that should be prolonged by ritual means) usually is given in the poems, either in the beginning or somewhere else. The *T'aep'yŏng hwajŏn ka*, for instance, begins with the following phrase:

> In the time of Great Peace, in the Village of Peace,
> We play the Game of Great Peace.[33]

However, the ritual aspects of the *hwajŏn ka* (Songs of Enjoying Flowers) and the custom to which they are related represent a special subject that should be left for further research. At a quick glance, one can say that these songs deal with the women's admiration of beautiful, awakened nature, their joy about their ramblings in mountains and valleys or boating on the rivers. At the same time the women usually expressed their regret that they could enjoy this free life in nature only for one day a year. Highly individualistic picturesque depictions of the landscape are at times found when the women speak about conquering this valley or that mountain. More often, however, the description of nature follows a standard model that is filled with elements of the native landscape. If nature is rendered in such manner, the poem opens an outlook onto eternity. Consider, for example, a *kasa* of women from Hahoe who spent their annual flower picnic on *P'alsŏndae* (Eight Fairies Rock):

> Under the clear Nŭngp'adae, the fishes and dragon are immersed.
> The bright color of the Lotus Cliff is quite black with age /is venerable/.
> Human affairs changed,
> But the mountains and water are as before . . .
> Climbing up Lotus Cliff,
> /I/ look around at the mountains and waters.
> It is the most beautiful place under heaven;
> Shall we ever see this kind of landscape again?
> The clear and clean Naktong River flows day and night,
> Like the spirit /nature/ of a hero.
> The high and lofty Flower Mountain is constant for ever,
> Like the integrity of a virtuous man.
> The splendid Lotus Cliff, high in the sky,
> Wards off the northerly wind and cold snow.[34]

An essential element of the *hwajŏn ka* was the description of the various preparations for the picnic (the call to join the outing, selection of the day and place, for example). The report about the event itself normally contained more or less detailed information about the women's activities—their gathering of azaleas, exchanging of poems, and enjoying the picnic fare. At times, an account of the women's conversations is provided, of course dealing with their hard lives. Even on such a blessed day as the spring outing was, they could not escape from their gloomy thoughts. Therefore, though different in purpose of composition from the hitherto discussed types of *kyubang kasa*, a lot of *hwajŏn ka* reflect women's discontent with their lot as females. A powerful illustration of the reality of the grief the women had to live in provides the *hwajŏn ka* containing the tragic story of Tendong Ŏmi.[35]

Nevertheless, despite women's underprivileged social position, sometimes a note of self-confidence sounds in the poems. Passages critical of *musimhan namja* (heedless, neglectful men), who are contrasted with the way women manage all the household affairs, as we have seen in the *Sŏkpyŏl ka*, are found in many of the poems. At least in moral aspects, this might indicate that the women felt themselves superior to men because their sense of responsibility for family matters and their ability to overcome all kind of difficulties and trouble was much greater than men's. Occasionally, however, we find women even challenging men's traditionally claimed supremacy in the literary field.

In the *T'aep'yŏng hwajŏn ka* (Song of Enjoying Flowers in the Time of Great Peace), the women mock men's laziness and ignorance. Though men have much more time to study, they fail to excel in literature because of their lack of interest.

Hey you, men, listen to our words.
You were born as men, we were born as women.
The difference between men and women is clear; each has his special work.
Only having done women's work
We, women, could look through our ancestor's library.
Until now, we had only known by hearing that he excelled in writing.
We did not know how brilliant he was, but after having studied his literary
    works,
We suddenly understood how magnificent he was.
How can you decline studying having such an ancestor?
Though we are only women, if we try our literary talents,
Would be there some Qu Yuans with literary skills of ten thousand
    antiquities among us?
Though Li Bai and Du Fu, too, were distinguished for their literary skills,
We, too, are distinguished. Will be there such poets among us?[36]

The women's triumphal mood, of course, cannot last long, for they grasp that their aim at excellence is a vain effort. Unlike men's endeavours, theirs will not be rewarded in public life. They can demonstrate their literary skills only on their outings in spring:

What a pity, what a pity! Our brilliant talent! What a pity!
No matter how talented we may be, of what use is it?
It's useless, it's useless. Woman's fervor is useless!
We cannot gain merit and fame. Perhaps we shall go
    sightseeing to mountains and rivers?

As time passed, the range of subjects rendered in the *kyubang kasa* widened significantly. From congratulations, blessings, and letters of thanks to prayers (Buddhist and Shamanistic) and funeral odes, women covered nearly all aspects essential in daily life. In the course of their work, they adapted other literary genres for the *kasa* composition, such as *sosŏl* (prose writings), *chemun* (funeral orations), *naegan* (private letters) and *minyo* (folk songs). Travel notes and poetic versions of novels also appeared.

No longer did women confine themselves to the description of their private lives but they sought to emulate their husbands in turning their attention to historical subjects as well. They wrote poems on Chinese and Korean history, thus penetrating the eagerly protected domain of the men: There were the *Ch'ohan ka* (Song about Chu and Han) dealing with the struggle between Chu and Han from 206 to 203 B.C., and the *Yŏktae ka* (Song of Successive Dynasties) depicting the main historical events from Chinese antiquity to the end of the Ming dynasty. Among the poems on Korean history we find the *Hanyang ka* (Song of the Metropolis), the *Chosŏn kŏn'guk ka* (Song of Establishing the Chosŏn State) and *Haedong manhwa* (A Talk about the Land in the East of the Sea).

The *Song of the Metropolis* tells about the 500 years of Hanyang, praising all the kings in succession who had governed that capital of the Chosŏn dynasty. *Song of the Metropolis* has two male counterparts, one written by an anonymous author (dated 1844) and one by Kim Hojik (1874–1953).[37] In contrast to the *kasa* of the male poets, the *kyubang kasa* did not limit the narration to kings, but extended it to their queens as well. Thus the woman's *Song of the Metropolis* followed the general character of the *kyubang kasa* in dealing with female matters and encouraging feminine virtues. The tone of this song, too, can be clearly defined as a woman's; it is smoother and reveals the rhetoric typical of the *kyubang kasa*.

Later on, contemporary political topics joined the long list of *kyubang kasa*'s subject matter: There are poems related to the Enlightenment movement at the end of the Chosŏn dynasty, and still later such poems as the *Tongnip ka* (Song of Independence) and the *Haebang ka* (Song of Liberation).

These subjects indicate slow, but steady, changes in the position of women. As women moved into the modern era, their vision extended to the outside world and to the politics of their homeland. Along with their increasing participation in the political life of their country, we witness an extension of the scope of subjects and topics in the *kyubang kasa*.

Since 1945 this genre, however, has steadily declined. In the past few decades it has been maintained only by elderly women who have learned the skill of composing such poems from their mothers or aunts.[38]

A remarkable feature of *kyubang kasa* is the attention to daily life, which provides invaluable material for cultural anthropologists. There are multifarious descriptions of the work done in homes and fields, of customs (especially those related to ancestor worship and child care) and popular games. Not only do they provide a vivid picture of the circumstances under which upper-class women in the later Chosŏn dynasty lived, more important, they are a mirror of the feelings and thoughts of those women, providing authentic sources for analyzing their intellectual and psychological states. Among the numerous texts that have been found are, of course, many repetitive poems following established literary patterns and lacking in poetic vigor and individuality. In a cultural environment wherein almost every *yangban* woman who took pride in herself tried to write her own *kasa*, the poetic quality naturally suffered in many a case. Yet, in the vast ocean of *kyubang kasa* a considerable number of truly poetic verses have been written in which one feels the women's hearts beating with exceptional power. If one, without bias, comes to this form of poetry—accepting the fact that most *kyubang kasa* were dedicated to female subjects—one can discover poems so touching and fascinating as any *kasa* written by a man has ever approached.

Notes

The author is grateful to Professor Don Baker of the University of British Columbia for his most generous editorial help in improving an earlier verion of this chapter.

1. For detailed information about the *kasa* genre see Peter H. Lee, *Korean Literature: Topics and Themes* (Tucson: University of Arizona Press, 1965), 51–63.

2. Yi Tongyŏng, *Kasa munhak non'go* (Essays on *Kasa* Literature) (Seoul: Hyŏngsŏl ch'ulp'ansa, 1977), 70–102.

3. Ibid, 70–102.

4. Kwŏn Yŏngch'ŏl, *Kyubang kasa kangnon* (Discussion of *Kyubang Kasa*) (Seoul: Hyŏngsŏl ch'ulp'ansa, 1986), 3.

5. The poems collected by Prof. Kwŏn are printed in Kwŏn Yŏngch'ŏl, ed., *Kasa munhak taegye* (An Encyclopedia of *Kasa*) vol. 1, *Kyubang kasa* (Sŏngnam: Han'guk chŏngsin munhwa yŏn'guwŏn, 1979).

6. Kim Kichung, *An Introduction to Classical Korean Literature: From Hyangga to P'ansori* (Armonk, NY: M.E. Sharpe, 1996), 111; Hwang Chaegun, *Han'guk kojŏn yŏryu si yŏn'gu* (A Study of Classical Korean Poetry by Women) (Seoul: Chimmundang, 1985), 55–59.

7. Kim Yung-Chung, ed. and trans., *Women of Korea: A History from Ancient Times to 1945* (Seoul: Ewha Woman's University Press, 1979), 154.

8. This work is traditionally attributed to the greatest Korean Neo-Confucian philosopher Yi Hwang, but there are doubts about his authorship. As Martina Deuchler has indicated, the *Kyujung yoram* cannot be found in Yi Hwang's *Collected Works*. Using this opportunity, I would like to give my thanks to Martina Deuchler for her comments and suggestions on an earlier version of my paper.

9. Yu Anjin, "Child Education in Traditional Korean Society," *Korea Journal* 21(May 1981): 27.

10. Patricia B. Buckley Ebrey, *The Inner Quarters: Marriage and the Lives of Chinese Women in the Sung Period* (Berkeley and Los Angeles: University of California Press 1993), 124.

11. Kwŏn Yŏngch'ŏl, *Kyubang kasa yŏn'gu* (A Study of *Kyubang Kasa*) (Seoul: I-u ch'ulp'ansa, 1980), 70–71.

12. Ibid.

13. Han'guk chŏngsin munhwa yŏn'gu wŏn, ed., *Han'guk minjok munhwa taebaekkwa sajŏn* (Encyclopedia of Korean National Culture), vol. 4 (Seoul: Samhwa, 1996), 57.

14. Besides the results of Kwŏn Yŏngch'ŏl the following works (to mention but a few) reveal the concentration of *kyubang kasa* in the Yŏngnam area: Kim Sayŏp, *Yijo sidae-ŭi kayo yŏn'gu* (A Study of Songs of the Yi Dynasty) (Seoul: Taeyang ch'ulp'ansa, 1956), 344; Yi Chongsuk, "Naebang *kasa* yŏn'gu" (A Study of *Naebang Kasa*), vol. 1, in *Han'guk munhwa yŏn'guwŏn nonch'ong* (Series of Articles of the Korean Cultural Institute) (Seoul: Ehwa University, 1970), vol. 15, 55–59; Yi, *Kasa munhak non'go*, 70–102; Cho Tongil, *Han'guk munhak t'ongsa* (A Comprehensive History of Korean Literature), 2d ed. (Seoul: Chisik sanŏpsa, 1989), vol. 3, 333; *Han'guk munhak taesajŏn* (Encyclopedia of Korean Literature), ed. by Koryŏ ch'ulp'ansa (Taegu: Taesin munhwasa, 1992), 751; Yi Hongjik, *Han'guksa taesajŏn* (Encyclopedia of Korean History) (Seoul: Kyoyuk tosŏ, 1992), 396.

15. See Sa Chae-dong, "Naebang *kasa* yŏn'gu sŏsŏl" (Introduction in the Study of *Naebang Kasa*), *Han'guk ŏmunhak* (Korean Philology) 2 (1964): 127–41; Chŏng Chaeho, *Han'guk kasa munhak non* (Theory of Korean *Kasa* Literature) (Seoul: Chimmundang, 1982), 204–15; Pak Hyosun, "Honam chibang-ŭi yŏryu *kasa* yŏn'gu" (A Study of Women's *Kasa* in the Honam Area), in *Kasa munhak yŏn'gu* (A Study of *Kasa* Literature), ed. by Kug'ŏ kungmun hakhoe (Seoul: Chŏng'ŭmsa, 1979), 157–76. The latter article, however, has a tendentious, partial overtone running through the description, provoking the thought that it was written in an effort to claim the cultural importance of the Honam area. Besides, several *kyubang kasa* were discovered thanks to Professors Cho Chongŏp, Kim Chunyŏng and Kang Chŏnsŏp.

16. Kwŏn Yŏngch'ŏl, *Kyubang kasa yŏn'gu*, 19–22, 52–92.

17. *Han'guk minjok munhwa*, vol. 4, 56.

18. The area of dissemination in the Andong county Professor Kwŏn describes as an ellipse with Andong city as its center, Imha and Ch'ŏnjŏn in the east, Tosan in the northeast, Hahoe in the west, and Kŭmgye in the northwest. His attempts to define the initial area of *kyubang kasa* still more narrowly resulted in outlining Tosan or Hahoe as the possible area of origin. Kwŏn Yŏngch'ŏl, *Kyubang kasa yŏn'gu*, 91–92. The fact that Kwŏn Yŏngch'ŏl himself comes from Andong raises some doubts about the impartiality of his investigations and calls for further careful examination of the poems' regional background, especially for more fieldwork on collecting material. This question was particularly raised by Prof. Kim Kichung in his discussion of the present paper at the HMS Colloquium in the Korean Humanities at the George Washington University, Oct. 24–25, 1998. However, it is a fact that Kwŏn's research of the origin and circulation of the *kyubang kasa*, based on an exact analysis of a great number of collected texts, cannot yet be challenged by equally convincing, precise data concerning other regions on the Korean Peninsula.

19. *Han'guk minjok munhwa*, vol. 14, 448; *Tusan segye taebaekkwa sajŏn* (Doosan World Encyclopedia), ed. Tusan tonga paekkwa sajŏn yŏn'guso, vol. 17 (Seoul: Doosan-Donga, 1996), 582.

20. Han Woo-keun, *The History of Korea*, trans. Lee Kyung-shik, ed. Grafton K. Mintz (Seoul: Eul-yoo, 1986), 302–4.

21. Kwŏn, *Kyubang kasa yŏn'gu*, 21–22, 88. The same opinion is held by Pak Hyosun and Kim Haksŏng. See Pak, *Honam chibang-ŭi yŏryu*, 162, and *Han'guk minjok munhwa*, vol. 2, 237.

22. The importance of a (pleasing) landscape's effect on a person's state of mind should not be ignored. In traditional society, it also functioned as a means of mental comfort. Kim Sung-Kyun, "Winding River Village: Poetics of a Korean Landscape" (Ph.D. thesis,University of Pennsylvania, 1988), 107–8.

23. Kwŏn, *Kyubang kasa yŏn'gu*, 260.

24. *Kasa chip* (Collection of *Kasa*), ed. Hyŏn Chongho with a popularized version in modern Korean (*yunsaek*) by Yun Sŏkpŏm and Pak Hyŏngyun, *Chosŏn kojŏn munhak sŏnjip* (Collection of Selected Works of Classical Korean Literature), vol. 4 (P'yŏngyang: Mun'ye ch'ulp'ansa, 1985), 615–16.

25. *Kasa chip*, 515–16. Unfortunately, the translation of the poem can give only a suggestion of its meaning without its literary flavor. In particular, the special choice of sounds cannot be rendered in the English translation.

26. See the detailed discussion of that poem by Kim Kichung, *An Introduction*, 127–29.

27. Chŏng, *Han'guk kasa munhak*, 204–15.

28. This and the following excerpt from the poem are from *Kasa chip*, 527–31.

29. See also Kim Kichung, *An Introduction to*, 132–36.

30. Kwŏn, *Kyubang kasa yon'gu*, 153.

31. *Han'guk minjok munhwa*, vol. 25, 337. This encyclopedia gives a photo of a flower cake made of chrysanthemum in autumn. On each cake there are put on five or six petals, thus resembling the shape of sunbeams.

32. *Kalendarniye obychai i obryady narod of vostochnoy Azii, godovoy tsykl* (Annual Customs and Rituals of the People in East Asia, the Year's Cycle), ed. R. S. Dzharylgasinova and M.V. Kryukov (Moscow: Nauka, 1989), 132.

33. Kwŏn, *Kyubang kasa yŏn'gu*, 127.

34. The English translation of the poem is from Kim Sung-Kyun, Winding River Village, 59.

35. See Kim Kichung, *An Introduction*, 129–31.

36. Kwŏn, *Kyubang kasa yŏn'gu*, 127–28.

37. Lee, *Korean Literature*, 60; Yi, *Kasa munhak non'go*, 237–49.

38. Cho Aeyŏng, "Naebang *kasa-ŭi ŭiŭi*" (The Meaning of *Naebang Kasa*), in *Yŏsŏng-kwa munhak* (Women and Literature), ed. by Kim Haesŏng et al. (Seoul: Taegwang munhwasa, 1985), 45; Pak, *Honam chibang-ŭi yŏryu*, 161.

References

Cho, Aeyŏng, "Naebang *kasa-ŭi ŭiŭi*" (The Meaning of *Naebang Kasa*). In *Yŏsŏng-kwa munhak* (Women and Literature), ed. Haesŏng Kim et al. Seoul: Taegwang munhwasa, 1985.

Cho, Tongil, *Han'guk munhak t'ongsa* (A Comprehensive History of Korean Literature), 2nd ed. Seoul: Chisik sanŏpsa, 1989.

Chŏng, Chae-ho, *Han'guk kasa munhak non* (Theory of Korean *Kasa* Literature). Seoul: Chimmundang, 1982.

Ebrey, Patricia Buckley, *The Inner Quarters, Marriage and the Lives of Chinese Women in the Sung Period.* Berkeley and Los Angeles: University of California Press, 1993.

Han, Woo-keun, *The History of Korea.* Kyung-shik Lee. tr., Grafton K. Mintz, ed. Seoul: Eul-yoo, 1986.

Han'guk minjok munhwa taebaekkwa sajŏn (Encyclopedia of Korean National Culture), ed. Han'guk chŏngsin munhwa yŏn'gu wŏn. Seoul: Samhwa, 1996.

Han'guk munhak taesajŏn (Encyclopedia of Korean Literature), ed. Koryŏ ch'ulp'ansa. Taegu: Taesin munhwasa, 1992.

Hwang, Chaegun, *Han'guk kojŏn yŏryu si yŏn'gu* (A Study of Classical Korean Poetry by Women). Seoul: Chimmundang, 1985.

Kalendarniye obychai i obryady narodof vostochnoy Azii, godovoy tsykl (Annual Customs and Rituals of the People in East Asia, the Year's Cycle). Moscow: Nauka, 1989.'

Kasa chip (Collection of *Kasa*), ed. Chongho Hyŏn with a popularized version in modern Korean (*yunsaek*) by Sŏkpŏm Yun and Hyŏngyun Pak. *Chosŏn kojŏn munhak sŏnjip* (Collection of Selected Works of Classical Korean Literature). P'yŏngyang: Mun'ye ch'ulp'ansa, 1985.

Kim, Kichung, *An Introduction to Classical Korean Literature: From Hyangga to P'ansori.* Armonk, New York: M.E. Sharpe, 1996.

Kim, Sayŏp, *Yijo sidae-ŭi kayo yŏn'gu* (A Study of Songs of the Yi Dynasty). Seoul: Taeyang ch'ulp'ansa, 1956.

Kim, Sung-Kyun, *Winding River Village: Poetics of a Korean Landscape.* Ph.D. dissertation, University of Pennsylvania, 1988.

Kim, Yung-Chung, ed. and tr., *Women of Korea: A History from Ancient Times to 1945.* Seoul: Ewha Woman's University Press, 1979.

Kwŏn, Yŏngch'ŏl, *Kyubang kasa kangnon* (Discussion of *Kyubang Kasa*). Seoul: Hyŏngsŏl ch'ulp'ansa, 1986.

————, *Kyubang kasa yŏn'gu* (A Study of *Kyubang Kasa*). Seoul: I-u ch'ulp'ansa, 1980.

————, ed., *Kasa munhak taegye* (An Encyclopedia of *Kasa*). Vol. I, *Kyubang kasa.* Sŏngnam: Han'guk chŏngsin munhwa yŏn'guwŏn, 1979.

Lee, Peter H., *Korean Literature: Topics and Themes.* Tucson: University of Arizona Press, 1965.

Pak, Hyosun, "Honam chibang-ŭi yŏryu *kasa* yŏn'gu" (A Study of Women's *Kasa* in the Honam Area). In *Kasa munhak yŏn'gu* (A Study of *Kasa* Literature), ed. Kug'ŏ kungmun hakhoe. Seoul: Chŏng'ŭmsa, 1979.

Sa, Chaedong, "Naebang *kasa* yŏn'gu sŏsŏl" (Introduction in the Study of *Naebang Kasa*). In *Han'guk ŏmunhak* (Korean Philology), vol. 2, 1964.

Tusan segye taebaekkwa sajŏn (Doosan World Encyclopedia). Seoul: Doosan-Donga, 1996.

Yi, Chongsuk, "Naebang *kasa* yŏn'gu" (A Study of *Naebang Kasa*) (1), *Han'guk munhwa yŏn'guwŏn nonch'ong* (Series of Articles of the Korean Cultural Institute), vol. 15. Seoul: Ehwa Woman's University Press, 1970.

Yi, Hongjik, *Han'guksa taesajŏn* (Encyclopedia of Korean History). Seoul: Kyoyuk tosŏ, 1992.

Yi, Tong-yŏng, *Kasa munhak non'go* (Essays on Kasa Literature). Seoul: Hyŏngsŏl ch'ulp'ansa, 1977.

Yu, Anjin, "Child Education in Traditional Korean Society." *Korea Journal* 21:5 (May 1981).

8
A Celebration of Life

Patchwork and Embroidered *Pojagi*
by Unknown Korean Women

Kumja Paik Kim

Because *pojagi*, Korean wrapping cloths, were such an integral part of everyday life among all classes of people in Korea during the Chosŏn dynasty (1392–1910) and until the 1950s, scarcely any attention was paid to these functional and ever-present objects for many centuries, and their unusual beauty remained unnoticed. It was not until the late 1960s—when Mr. Huh Dong-hwa, the director of the Museum of Korean Embroidery, first recognized an esthetic value in these wrapping cloths and began to collect them—that their striking beauty captured people's attention. Since the 1980s many exhibitions have been organized in Korea, Japan, Europe, and the United States to showcase the stunning beauty of *pojagi* made by Korean women.[1]

Although *pojagi* had probably been in use from the Three Kingdoms period (57 B.C.E.–668 C.E.), most extant examples date from the late Chosŏn dynasty, except for a few *pojagi*, such as the one covering the table used by the illustrious Buddhist priest, Taegak Kuksa, Ŭich'ŏn (1055–1101).[2] The earliest extant Chosŏn-dynasty *pojagi* are the seven wrapping cloths made in 1415 by Lady Yi to wrap and cover Buddhist sutras that her husband, Yu Kŏn, had copied. Three out of these seven

163

are wrapping cloths embroidered with designs of lotuses and other flowers, Tang scrolls, grasses, reeds, clouds, and cranes. (They are now in the collection of the Chŏnju Provincial Museum.[3]) Another early wrapping cloth that survives, in the collection of the Museum of Korean Embroidery in Seoul, is believed to have been used in 1681 on the occasion of the wedding of Princess Myŏng'an (1665–87)—daughter of King Hyŏnjong (r. 1659–74)—to O T'aeje.[4]

Pojagi were used for wrapping purposes, as well as for covering, storing, and carrying objects; they were used for objects small and large, ordinary and precious. *Pojagi* served a variety of functions, from covering a food table, to draping a Confucian or Buddhist altar, or wrapping a sacred text. Lady Hyegyŏng wrote in her memoirs that when she returned home from the palace after having been selected as the wife of the crown prince, Sado, not only was she brought through the gate reserved for men and received by her parents attired in ceremonial robes, but she also noticed the table covered with "a red cloth," as was done on special occasions.[5] Covering a table or an altar signified the importance of the occasion as wrapping an object represented an individual's concern for that which was being wrapped, as well as respect for its recipient. There was an unspoken folk belief that, by wrapping an object, *pok* (good fortune) could be enclosed or captured within a *pojagi*.[6] Special events such as betrothals and weddings, therefore, required a whole set of new *pojagi*.

Pojagi are generally square; on rare occasions, however, they are made in rectangular shapes. Depending upon their use, *pojagi* came in varying sizes ranging from one *p'ok* (about 35 cm) to ten *p'ok*. The *pojagi* used for wrapping a personal ornament was small, measuring approximately one *p'ok* square. In contrast, the *pojagi* used for wrapping bedding was usually ten times wider on each side. Silk, cotton, ramie, and hemp were popularly used to make wrapping cloths, in colors ranging from red, purple, blue, green, yellow, and pink to dark blue, white, and black. The construction and embellishment of *pojagi* were also diverse. Some were lined, others unlined; some were padded or quilted, while others were decorated with painting, paper-thin gold sheets, embroidery, and patchwork.

Wrapping cloths can be divided first into two large groups, *kung po* (*kung* = palace + *po*, short for *pojagi*) made for the court and *min po* (*min* = people) made for common people. Although both types served similar functions, *kung po* were different from *min po* in several ways.

Kung po were made for specific purposes; they were usually made of luxurious fabrics; they were also always from a single piece of cloth, either lined, unlined, padded with cotton, quilted, or painted; and they were made by court women and needlework artisans belonging to the Sangŭiwŏn (Office of Royal Costumes) and the Cheyonggam (Office of Royal Necessities). Although their works were unsigned, the names of artisans from these offices who were responsible for producing wrapping cloths for the court on various occasions have survived in Chosŏn dynasty court records. Also, painted wrapping cloths used only at the palace were decorated by court painters (*hwawŏn*) belonging to the Bureau of Painting (Tohwasŏ) at the court,[7] placing *kung po*—wrapping cloths for the palace—outside the scope of this chapter, which focuses on the patchwork and embroidered *pojagi* by unknown artists.

The custom of making and using *pojagi* began at court where, in accordance with strict rules of etiquette, every object had to be properly wrapped. Not only are 133 *kung po* still preserved in the Royal Museum at the Tŏksugung Palace, but references to *pojagi* can frequently be found in Chosŏn dynasty records, such as *Chosŏn wangjo sillok* (Veritable Records of the Chosŏn Dynasty); *Karye togam ŭigwe* (Records of the Superintendencies of the Royal Wedding Ceremonies); *Kungjung palgi* (Inventory Lists of Objects Used in the Palace); *Sangbang chŏngnye* (Regulations on Royal Costumes and Objects) and others.[8] Records mentioning *pojagi* in *Chosŏn wangjo sillok* include one that quotes the concerns of King Sejong (r. 1418–50) about painting dragons and phoenixes accurately on *pojagi* according to established conventions, and another containing the comments of King Sŏnjo (r. 1567–1608) on wrapping cloths painted with motifs in gold.[9]

That an enormous number of *pojagi* were in constant demand at the court can be seen in *Sangbang chŏngnye* (Regulations on Royal Costumes and Objects), a three-volume work written in 1750, listing in detail all the items that had to be presented to the king and queen, and the crown prince and princess on their birthdays, as well as on on New Year's Day, on the fifteenth day of the eighth lunar month, and on other special days. This book not only enumerates the clothing, headgear, and footwear required for different occasions—together with stipulations regarding the colors, fabrics, thread, and other materials for their manufacture—but also shows that for each of these items a total of 225 wrapping cloths had to be made ranging in size from one to eight *p'ok* on each side.[10] The royal wedding in 1882 of the crown prince who became King Sunjong (r. 1907–10) required 1,000 plain and 650 painted *pojagi*.[11]

Just as *pojagi* had become an integral part in the life at court where the rules of proper conduct had to be strictly adhered to, they also played an indispensable role in the daily life of ordinary people, who used a variety of wrapping cloths every day. Unlike the *kung po* made for specific purposes, *min po*—wrapping cloths made by and for ordinary people—often served more than a single purpose. Also, unlike *kung po,* which were always made of a single piece of cloth, *min po* were most frequently made by patching together small fragments of fabric, hence the name *chogak po* (*chogak* = small pieces), or patchwork wrapping cloths. Another type are those with embroidered decorations called *su po* (*su* = embroidery), which incorporated abstract design motifs and expressive color combinations without any concern for realism. Because Korean *chogak po* and *su po* brim with creativity and originality, and can be viewed as strong works of art from an esthetic point of view, they merit our special attention.

As mentioned earlier, the names of the palace needlework artisans who produced *pojagi* for the palace have been kept in the *Karye togam üigwe* (Records of the Superintendencies of Royal Wedding Ceremonies). On the other hand, the patchwork and embroidered *pojagi* for ordinary people were made, without exception, by unknown women. In a rigidly Confucian era, when women were taught to follow the Three Tenets of Obedience and discouraged from engaging in any form of intellectual pursuit, unknown women artists of the Chosŏn dynasty poured their creative energies into many stunning works reflecting their own individual sense of harmony and beauty.

Judging from the number of surviving examples of *pojagi*, the *chogak po*, or patchwork wrapping cloths, were clearly favored by their makers over other forms of *pojagi*. I also believe that they reflect most accurately the world of Korean women of the Chosŏn dynasty. Korean women, taught from an early age to be patient and frugal, would save even the smallest scraps of silk, cotton, or ramie cloth when they designed, cut, and sewed their family members' clothes. And then, when they found some quiet time, they brought out these colorful remnants and spread them on the floor of their room. They would separate these small pieces into different groups according to their weight—heavy silk pieces, light gauze-like silk pieces, or ramie pieces. They would then cut them into appropriate shapes such as squares, rectangles, triangles, and trapezoids, and match these forms, their colors, and weight, until they felt that everything looked just right (plates 1, 2; plates follow page 170).

Though the initial process of laying out forms and colors provided an opportunity for Chosŏn dynasty women to test their own esthetic sensibilities and discover their innate creative talents, the actual sewing must have been akin to sutra copying, or painting multiple images of Buddhas or Bodhisattvas. The extraordinary trouble many makers of *pojagi* went through to connect small pieces is noteworthy (plates 3, 4). It is as if they wanted to multiply the necessary stitches myriad times over. Instead of sewing two pieces from the back in a straight line, which would have been the quickest and easiest way, the majority of makers of *pojagi* used countless short horizontal stitches to connect two pieces. They made no effort to hide their stitches. Also on the back, rather than using the easiest way, which would have been to have the thread cross over, they made their needle come up from the same side, thus conforming to their virtue of frugality, since the length of thread necessary to cross over would have been slightly longer than to move immediately next to the previous stitch on the same side. As both the copiers of Buddhist sutras and the painters of Buddhist images believed that each character and each image of the Buddha brought them additional merit and placed the Pure Land of the Buddha Amitabha ever closer to their reach, the makers of the patchwork wrapping cloths must similarly have believed that blessings and good fortune (*pok*) accumulated with each added stitch and piece.

During the Chosŏn dynasty, among the objects a bride customarily took with her to her new home were dozens of *pojagi* that had been made by the mother of the bride. Unlike the sutra copiers or painters of the Buddha images, however, whose activities were meant to benefit themselves and their sponsors, the good wishes of the makers of patchwork wrapping cloths were aimed at the recipients of their works. The sincere prayers and wishes of the mothers, grandmothers, and aunts who pieced together the patchwork wrapping cloths were directed to the happiness of their sons, daughters, grandchildren, nieces, and nephews. Many Chosŏn patchwork wrapping cloths were never used, perhaps indicating that their recipients knew them to be the tangible signs of affection and good wishes of the makers and wanted to keep and remember their love and blessings forever. These patchwork wrapping cloths brought by a bride to her new home represented her fine upbringing and womanly virtues held significant by her natal family, thus winning her respect from her husband's family.[12] Because not a single *kung po* made with a patchwork design has so far surfaced or been recorded, we can assume that wrapping cloths made from small remnants had no place in the palace.

Most frequently, patchwork wrapping cloths were made to cover the food table and therefore are called *sang po*.[13] During premodern times they were used not only to keep food warm, but also to protect food from flies and other insects (plates 5, 6). *Sang po* always have a small tab in the center for easy lifting. Some *sang po* have long straps attached to the four corners so that they could be tied under the portable food tables or trays on windy or rainy days. Because strict Confucian rules of propriety between the sexes had to be observed during the Chosŏn dynasty, the men's quarters, or the *sarangch'ae* (outer quarters), were separated from the women's quarters, or the *anch'ae* (inner quarters), where the kitchen was located. Light material, such as ramie (*mosi*), was often used for summer; thick fabrics, sometimes padded with cotton, were favored for winter. Those *sang po* in constant use were usually lined with an added oiled paper to protect them from being soiled by food.

When small pieces of cloth in two or three colors were selected, the beauty created by judiciously balancing colors and forms—as in the patchwork *pojagi* shown in plates 7 and 8—is often reminiscent of the abstract compositions of Piet Mondrian (1872–1944) and Paul Klee (1879–1940). Long before these Western painters were renouncing the art of illusionism and discovering true reality in rectilinear purism based on a severely limited vocabulary of forms and colors, Korean women had discovered the beauty in abstract two-dimensional designs as a result of experimenting with pure geometric forms and colors.

The surprisingly advanced and refined aesthetic sensibilities of Korean women are reflected in patchwork *pojagi* with irregular patterns (plates 9, 10). Those made in regular patterns evoke a sense of quietude and order, whereas those made in irregular patterns exude a feeling of adventure and excitement. Two-dimensional abstract designs of breathtaking beauty have been created on these patchwork *pojagi* by fitting together different sizes of asymmetrical shapes. The resulting designs are unusually bold and completely modern in feeling, reminiscent of an abstract cityscape (plate 9) or seascape (plate 10), although the unknown women makers of these patchwork *pojagi* must have only been trying to create the most pleasing designs possible that would agree with their own esthetic sensibilities.[14]

Next to patchwork wrapping cloths, embroidered *pojagi*, or *su po,* used by ordinary people merit our attention because they are equally outstanding works of art from an esthetic as well as an historic perspective. The embroidered wrapping cloths were usually made for happy occasions, such as betrothals and marriages. The embroidered motifs are based usually on trees, flowers, birds, clouds, fruits, dragons, phoenixes, or ideographs. They are represented without restraint, making the designs often burst forth with a sense of abandon. *Su po* made in the Kangnŭng area in the central east are especially spectacular because of the jubilant natural forms embroidered in brilliant colors (plates 11, 12). The *pojagi* were frequently in the form of *yemul po* (*yemul* = ceremonial or special object), which enclosed gifts from the bridegroom's family to the bride; *yedan* (ceremonial silk) *po*, for enclosing the gifts the bride's family sent to the groom's family; and *norigae* (personal ornaments) *po*; and *kirŏgi* (goose) *po*, or wrapping cloths for a wedding goose.

The embroidered wrapping cloths that have attracted more attention than all other *su po* are *kirŏgi po*, due perhaps to their romantic connotations. They were used to wrap a wooden goose presented by the bridegroom to the bride's family to be placed on the central table during the traditional Korean wedding ceremony, symbolizing the groom's pledge to be faithful and a good provider (plates 13, 14). The most frequently used motifs for *kirŏgi po* were trees and flowers, followed by fruits, butterflies, or birds. In Korea, trees have had sacred symbolism from the earliest times. In the foundation myth of Korea, the celestial prince Hwan'ung comes down with his followers to Mt. T'aebaek "to a spot under a tree by the Holy Altar"[15] The famous gold crowns of the Silla Kingdom (57 B.C.–A.D. 668) are decorated with a stylized tree motif symbolizing the tree of life. Flowers represent wealth, prosperity, and honor, while fruits symbolize abundance in material things and male offspring. Birds and butterflies represent happiness and joy.

The fabric on which embroidery was done was either cotton or silk. *Su po* were always embroidered with twisted strands of thread and always lined. During the Chosŏn dynasty, a design worked out by each maker was first drawn on thick Korean paper. Each design was then placed over the fabric and the embroidery was stitched over the paper, which provided extra padding under the embroidered designs. The parts of the paper not covered by the embroidery fell off easily due to needle marks made around each design. Blue, green, red, pink, orange, yellow, black, and white comprised the dominant palette, making the design burst forth with a feeling of exuberance and abandon. The *kirŏgi po* were not only lined and embroidered, but also often decorated with strands of rainbow-colored threads representing rice stalks, a symbol of the family's wishes for abundance in married life.

Although the design motifs are based on natural forms, they are flattened and simplified, so that they can easily be viewed as abstract designs. A tree spreads out its branches vigorously in all directions laden with broad leaves, as if to empower the whole world with energy and joy. In this imaginary land of hope and happiness, tree leaves come in rainbow colors, and small birds perched on the branches are also yellow, orange, red, pink, or blue, representing the embroiderer's wishes for the recipient's happiness and prosperity in her new married life. Embroidered wrapping cloths encouraged the full use of the makers' imaginative talent, which is already seen in their composition and forms as well as in their use of color. Tree branches, for instance, grow as though they are not bound by earthly logic, and the leaves metamorphose into birds. The colors of trees, leaves, birds, flowers, or other forms in the compositions are not only completely arbitrary but full of excitement and vitality because they represent the land of the makers' imagination, which is free from established rules.

The creative talents of Korean women are best illustrated in the patchwork and embroidered wrapping cloths. These unknown women, who lived in an extremely rigid society, delighted in their creative activity, often discovering their hidden talents while working on their projects. Their strong emotions as well as their good wishes for the recipients of these wrapping cloths show through the exuberant colors and designs of their patchwork and embroidery. These women made vibrant colors an important part of their lives, reflecting their own energy and vitality in the celebration of life and their ardent wishes for joy and happiness. Their creativity and originality shine through in exciting two-dimensional designs of balanced colors and forms, and in their exuberant embroidered designs that give free play to their inspiration and imagination. These wrapping cloths are the artistic gifts from the unknown Korean women artists to the world.

1. Sang po, satin-weave silk with patchwork design, early twentieth century, 102 x 102 cm, Asian Art Museum of San Francisco, Gift of Mrs. Ann Witter, 1998.57.

2. Sang po, silk with patchwork design and border (*myŏngju*), early twentieth century, 64.5 x 62.5 cm, Asian Art Museum of San Francisco, Gift of Dr. Forrest Mortimer, 1993.5.

3. Sang po, silk (*sa*) with self-patterned design, early twentieth century, 53.5 x 53.9 cm, Asian Art Museum of San Francisco, 1993.6, Gift of Dr. Richard Hahn.

4. Sang po, silk (*sa*) with self-patterned design, early twentieth century, 38.2 x 35.3 cm, Asian Art Museum of San Francisco, 1993.7, Gift of Mr. & Mrs. Edward K. Kang.

5. Yuji sang po, self-patterned silk (*sa*) with patchwork design and lined with oiled paper (*yuji*), nineteenth century, 49.5 x 49 cm, The Museum of Korean Embroidery, no. 8.

6. Sang po with sashes, from *Crafts of the Inner Court*, Seoul:
Museum of Korean Embroidery, 1987, p. 128.

7. Ch'ŏn po, ramie (*moshi*) with patchwork design, nineteenth century, 41 x 41 cm, Museum of Korean Embroidery, no. 63.

8. Ot po, ramie (*moshi*) with patchwork design, nineteenth century, 58 x 59 cm, Museum of Korean Embroidery, no 70.

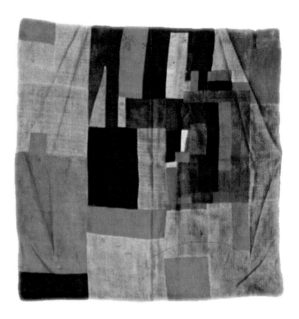

9. Ot po, silk (*myŏngju*) decorated with patchwork design, nineteenth century, 85 x 85 cm, Museum of Korean Embroidery, no. 57.

10. Ot po, unpatterned and self-patterned silk (*myŏngju* and *sa*) decorated with patchwork design, nineteenth century, 74 x 75 cm, The Museum of Korean Embroidery, no. 53.

11. Yemul po, silk (*tan* and *myŏngju*) with embroidered design of pomegranate, tree, butterflies, and birds, nineteenth century, 39 x 36 cm, The Museum of Korean Embroidery, no. 80.

12. Yemul po, cotton (*myŏngju*) with embroidered design of pomegranate, tree, birds, and butterflies, nineteenth century, 41 x 42 cm, The Museum of Korean Embroidery, no. 86.

13. Kirŏgi po, silk with embroidered design of trees, pomegranate, and birds, nineteenth century, 42 x 40.6 cm, Asian Art Museum of San Francisco, gift of Mrs. Chung-Hee Kim, 1993.4.

14. Kirŏgi po, cotton with embroidered design of tree, pomegranate, and birds, late nineteenth–early twentieth century, 40.6 x 40.6 cm, Asian Art Museum of San Francisco, gift of the Korean Art and Culture Committee, 1995.78.

Notes

An earlier version of this chapter appeared in *Oriental Art* 45:4 (1999/2000): 52–58, and is used with permission of *Oriental Art*.

1. The exhibitions on Korean wrapping cloths include the following: *Han'guk ŭi mi* (Beauty of Korea: Traditional Costumes, Ornaments and Cloth Wrappings), Seoul: National Museum of Korea, 1988; Huh Dong-Hwa. *The Wonder Cloths*, Seoul: Museum of Korean Embroidery, 1988; Sheila Hoey Middleton. *Traditional Korean Wrapping Cloths*. Cambridge: Fitzwilliam Museum, 13 March–29 April 1990, Oxford: Ashmolean Museum, 9 May–1 July 1990; Yi Sŏng-mi, *Korean Costumes and Textiles*, New York: IBM Gallery of Science and Art, 14 April–13 June 1992; *Colors and Shapes: A Korean Tradition*, Azabu Bijutsu Kogei-kan, Exhibition catalog, 30 July–16 August 1992; Huh Dong-Hwa. *Yet chogak po chŏn* (Exhibition of Traditonal Patchwork Wrapping Cloths), Taejŏn Expo, 7 August–7 November 1993; Kumja Paik Kim and Huh Dong-Hwa, *Profusion of Color: Korean Costumes and Wrapping Cloths of the Chosŏn Dynasty*. Asian Art Museum of San Francisco, 28 February–30 April 1995; Seattle Art Museum, 9 September 1995–3 March 1996; Peabody Essex Museum, 25 April–22 July 1996.

2. Kim and Huh, *Profusion of Color*, 28.

3. Han, "Hanguk chasu yŏn'gu irhwan," 96; Kim and Huh, *Profusion of Color*, 28.

4. Huh, *The Wonder Cloths*, 276; Kim and Huh, *Profusion of Color*, 28 and plate 10.

5. Haboush, *The Memoirs of Lady Hyegyŏng*, 59; Choe-Wall, trans., *Memoirs of a Korean Queen, Lady Hong,* 7; Kim and Huh, *Profusion of Color*, 28.

6. Huh, *The Wonder Cloths,* 274; Yi Sŏng-mi, *Korean Costumes and Textiles*, 16; Kim and Huh, *Profusion of Color,* 28.

7. Yi , "Changsŏgak sojang Chosŏn wangjo karye togam ŭigwe ŭi misulsa-jŏk koch'al" ("An Art Historical Investigation on the Records of the Superintendencies of Chosŏn Dynasty Royal Wedding Ceremonies in the Changsŏ-gak Collection"), 33–115; Kim, *A Study of Pojagi*, 142–47, 274–76.

8. Yi, Kang, and Ryu, *Changsŏgak sojang karye togam ŭigwe*, 9–10, 119.

9. *Chosŏn wangjo sillok* 6:19:1439, 4:24:1495; Kim, "A Study of *Pojagi*," 113, 120.

10. Huh, *The Wonder Cloths,* 267–69; Kim and Huh, *Profusion of Color*, 29, 35.

11. Kim and Huh, *Profusion of Color*, 29, 35; Kim, "A Study of *Pojagi*," 82.

12. Dr. Marsha Weidner, at the symposium "Sparks of Creativity: Women in the Korean Humanities," held at The George Washington University in October 1998, pointed out wrapping cloths must have won respect for brides from their husbands' families. She also raised a question regarding the "ordinary people," that is, if the "ordinary people" included everyone outside the palace. In this chapter the term is used from the economic perspective, and therefore refers to everyone outside the palace except for the poor. Making patchwork and embroidered *pojagi* was one of the genteel activities initially encouraged for and enjoyed by the women of the *yangban* (gentry) class. But, by the eighteenth century there were many wealthy *chung'in* ("middle people")—the class to which belonged doctors, scribes, translators, engineers, artists, etc.—and *sang'in* or commoner families. The women of these newly prosperous families must have been encouraged to learn the habits of gentle-

women because the men of the *chung'in* and *sang'in* classes strove to be as learned and refined as men of the gentry class. There were many impoverished *yangban* families. Their women, in spite of their reduced financial state, clung more tenaciously to their *yangban* traditions. Each *pojagi* reflects its maker's skill as well as her aesthetic taste and talent. It does not tell whether it has been made by a woman of the gentry or common class, although the fabrics she uses might give a clue to her family's past or present financial status. The wrapping cloths were never made commercially.

13. As mentioned on page 164–65, *pojagi* are divided into two major groups: *kung po* and *min po*. They are further divided according to their construction, design, and function. Some of the names of popular *pojagi* are listed below:

> Construction: *hot po* (*hot* = single)—unlined *pojagi*. When pronounced, it becomes *hoppo*.
> *kyŏp po* (*kyŏp* = double)—lined *pojagi*.
> *nubi po* (*nubi* = to quilt)—quilted *pojagi*.
> *som po* (*som* = cotton)—*pojagi* padded with cotton.

> Design: *chogak po* (*chogak* = small segment)—patchwork *pojagi*.
> *hwagŭm po* (*hwagŭm* = painted gold)—gold-painted *pojagi*. For palace use only.
> *kŭmbak po* (*kŭmbak* = pressed gold)—gold-decorated *pojagi*. Initially they were only for royalty, but in the late-Chosŏn-dynasty, families with means also used them.
> *su po* (*su* = embroidery)—embroidered *pojagi*.
> *tangch'ae po* (*tangch'ae* = Tang colors)—painted *pojagi*; also called *inmun po*. For palace use only.

> Function: *ch'ŏn po* (*ch'ŏn* = fabric)—*pojagi* for fabrics.
> *norigae po* (*norigae* = ornament)—*pojagi* for ornaments, often embroidered.
> *kirŏgi po* (*kirŏgi* = goose)—*pojagi* for wedding geese, often embroidered.
> *ot po* (*ot* = clothing)—*pojagi* for clothing. When pronounced, it becomes *oppo*.
> *sang po* (*sang* = food table)—*pojagi* for the food table.
> *yedan po* (*yedan* = ceremonial silk)—*pojagi* for gifts from the bride's family, often embroidered.
> *yemul po* (*yemul* = ceremonial objects)—*pojagi* for gifts from the bridegroom's family, often embroidered.
> *yibul po* (*yibul* = bedding)—*pojagi* for bedding.

Although one *pojagi* may have more than one name, the commonly used name has to do with its function.

14. Both Dr. Marsha Weidner and Dr. Yi Sŏng-mi suggested that a comparative study on *pojagi* and American quilts would enable us to understand more fully their function, meaning, and cultural significance. Making *pojagi* was a solitary task as far as we know, whereas making American quilts usually was a group project. This topic deserves more study.

15. Lee, *Sourcebook of Korean Civilization*, 6.

References

Choe-Wall, Yang-hi, trans. *Memoirs of a Korean Queen, Lady Hong.* London. KPI, 1985.

Haboush, JaHyun Kim, trans. *The Memoirs of Lady Hyegyŏng: The Autobiographical Writings of a Crown Princess of Eighteenth-Century Korea.* Berkeley and Los Angeles: University of California Press, 1996.

Han, Sangsu. "Hanguk chasu yŏn'gu irhwan" (Survey on the Studies of Korean Embroidery). *Hanjung kogŭm chasu kyoryu chŏn* (Art of Embroidery: Relationship Between Korea and China Throughout Successive Periods), exhibition catalog. Seoul: Traditional Craftwork Museum, Kyŏngbok Palace, March 1991.

Han, Yonghwa. *Chŏnt'ong chasu.* (Traditional Embroidery). Seoul, Taewŏnsa, 1989.

Han'guk minjok munhwa taebaekgwasajŏn (Encyclopedia of Korean Culture), vols. 18, 22. Sŏngnam: Chŏngsin Munhwa Yon'guwŏn (Academy of Korean Studies), 1991.

Huh, Dong-Hwa. *The Wonder Cloths.* Seoul: Museum of Korean Embroidery, 1988.

———. *Yet Chogak po chŏn* (Exhibition of Traditonal Patchwork Wrapping Cloths), exhibition catalog (Taejon Expo), 7 August–7 November 1993.

Kim, Kumja Paik, and Dong-Hwa Huh. *Profusion of Color: Korean Costumes and Wrapping Cloths of the Chosŏn Dynasty,* exhibition catalog San Francisco: Asian Art Museum of San Francisco), 28 February–30 April 1995.

Kim, Soo Kyung. "A Study of Pojagi (Korean Wrapping Cloths) in the Late Chosŏn Dynasty (1724–1910)." Ph.D. diss, New York University, 1997.

Lee, Peter H. *Sourcebook of Korean Civilization,* vol. 1. New York: Columbia University Press, 1993.

Middleton, Sheila Hoey. *Traditional Korean Wrapping Cloths,* exhibition catalog. Cambridge, Fitzwilliam Museum, 13 March–29 April; Oxford, Ashmolean Museum, 9 May–1 July 1990.

Yi Sŏng-mi, Kang Sinhang, and Ryu Songok, *Changsŏgak sojang karye togam ŭigwe* (Records of the Superintendencies of Royal Wedding Ceremonies in the Changsŏgak Library Collection). Sŏngnam: Academy of Korean Studies, 1994.

Yi Sŏng-mi. "Changsŏgak sojang Chosŏn wangjo karye togam ŭigwe ŭi misulsajŏk koch'al" (An Art Historical Investigation of the Records of the Superintendencies of Chosŏn Dynasty Royal Wedding Ceremonies in the Changsŏgak Collection). *Changsŏgak Sojang Karye Togam Uigwe* (Records of the Superintendencies of Royal Wedding Ceremonies in the Changsŏgak Library Collection). Sŏngnam: Han'guk Chŏngshin Munhwa Yongguwŏn, 1994.

———. *Korean Costumes and Textiles,* exhibition catalog. New York: IBM Gallery of Science and Art, 14 April–13 June 1992.

9
Kim Iryŏp's Conflicting Worlds

Bonnie B.C. Oh

Preface

"Are you sure you are interested in studying Iryŏp no sŭnim's life after she entered the mountain?" a gray-robed, tall woman, with a powerful face and tonsured head, asked incredulously when I met her at a hotel coffee shop on a late June evening in the village of Tŏksan near the monastery of Sudŏksa. The woman asking the question was Wŏlsŏng (*sŭnim*),[1] Kim Iryŏp's *pŏpson* (lit. "grandson" in Buddhist tradition), a disciple. Wŏlsŏng sŭnim was with another nun, Chŏngjin, also a *pŏpson*, and four other novitiates. Disbelieving that someone from America should be interested in the deceased old nun, but nevertheless overjoyed, Wŏlsŏng sŭnim continued: "We are so glad and grateful that you are interested in Iryŏp *nosŭnim* ("old nun"). We have always believed that she deserved a serious study. She is too significant a figure in recent Korean history to be forgotten."[2] Wŏlsŏng and Chŏngjin were two of Kim Iryŏp's closest associates and disciples during her years at Sudŏksa. Wŏlsŏng sŭnim, who just turned sixty this year, did graduate work at Tong'guk University (a university of Sŏn Buddhism) in Seoul, and also in Japan, and edited, compiled, and published *Ŏnŭ sudoin ui hoesang* (Recollections of a Certain Nun) in 1960 and *Miraese ka tahago namtorok* (Until the End of the Future World and Beyond)[3] in 1974. The latter is a posthumously published two-volume collection of her *ŭnsa* (vocation master), Iryŏp sŭnim. Wŏlsŏng sŭnim went on, "She is truly a rare person not just in Korean history but in human history. She succeeded in organizing and ordering her spiritual life and thus succeeded in life itself. But it's a shame, so little is known about her after she joined the order."

Thus began our four-hour conversation, during which we didn't even stop to eat, in the coffee shop of the hotel in the village famous for hot springs. The six gray-robed nuns and I were the last customers when the café was closed at 11 P.M. I had asked all kinds of questions, quite boldly, I might add, including one about the existence of Iryŏp sŭnim's son, the artist-monk Ildang,[4] whom my husband and I visited the day before at Chikjisa, Kimch'ŏn, Kyŏngsang Pukdo. Wŏlsong and Chŏngjin sŭnim answered them frankly without any apparent attempt at deception while the four novitiates listened intently.[5] At the end of four hours, Wŏlsŏng sŭnim presented me the first of the above-mentioned two volumes, which were out of print. Upon seeing the six gray-robed women on a warm summer night in southern Korea, I became convinced of the value of my subject matter, and any doubts I had about the appropriateness of this paper's title was dispelled. I came to realize that Iryŏp sŭnim succeeded in overcoming life's conflicts by the end of her life. She devoted all of her Buddhist-period writing to spreading Buddhist teaching, which she considered as containing the ultimate secret of human life. This piece, therefore, despite its title, is not about the conflicting worlds of Kim Iryŏp, but of how she succeeded in reconciling them.

Introduction

Kim Iryŏp (1896–1971) was a prominent pioneering figure at the dawn of modern Korea. She was a feminist writer, an essayist, a poet, and a Buddhist nun. In her lifetime of seventy-five years, she wrote fifty-eight poems, sixteen novellas, and countless essays and reflective short pieces. Based on the sheer quantity of her writing alone, she should have been taken more seriously as a writer than has been the case. But her influence in modern Korean literature is not as great as her reputation (or notoriety). And many literary critics did not include her among the noted writers of the early twentieth century. Sŏng Rakhŭi suggested three reasons for Kim Iryŏp's exclusion from the literary circle: that Kim Iryŏp's writing was didactic; that she was a female; and that she became a nun.[6]

Kim Iryŏp wrote with messages on life's meanings even before she joined the religious order, and her writing was not considered pure literature.[7] As such, it did not sit well with her contemporary writers who advocated "art for art's sake" in 1920s Korea, partly as an escape from Japanese persecution.[8] Then, she was not just a writer, but a female writer who attempted to promote women's rights, to raise women's consciousness, and to reform past and contemporary abusive customs affecting women of Korea, which threatened to disrupt men's lives. She even practiced what she preached by leading an unconventional lifestyle that was considered scandalous.[9] In an age with so few professional women, early female artists were seen through the colored prisms of men, who slandered them after earlier having encouraged them. Kim Tong In, one of the best-known writers of the time, even wrote a caricature, *Kim Yŏnsil chŏn* (Life of Kim Yŏnsil). It was a collective, satirical, condescending, and defamatory rendering of the lives of three prominent artistic women: Na Hyesŏk, the artist, Yun Simdŏk, the singer, and Kim Iryŏp, the writer. Then, suddenly and sensationally, Kim Iryŏp dropped out of the world and "entered the mountain (*ipsan*)"[10] to become a nun of Sŏn (Zen in Japanese) Buddhism and stopped publishing for thirty-one years.

Whatever others might have thought, however, Kim Iryŏp considered herself a writer, particularly a poet, before she became a nun, and writing was an important part of her life even after she joined the Buddhist order. But she always wrote with messages on life's meanings in mind and did not concern herself with critics. Much like Han Yongŭn, a writer/reformer monk who might have been a role model for her, Kim stood apart from the Korean literary scene, a sort of stranger, an outsider, to the circle known for its close-knit exclusiveness of dilettante devotees of art for art's sake, who pretended to be oblivious to the world around them.[11] To her contemporaries, she was perhaps their most unusual feminist—one who turned Buddhist nun and, after being a reformer, then a writer, and an occasional one at that. Obviously such an iconoclast could not be considered a serious writer. As a writer, she was a loner left to do whatever she pleased. No serious writer would write in so many different genres—essays, poetry, novellas, and random recollections. She simply did not fit in with other literary figures.

Kim Iryŏp's pre-Buddhist life represented a paradigm of the first generation of women intellectuals of Korea. She was outspoken against social ills, led an unusual life, and was ostracized by society, but she ultimately overcame criticisms, unlike two of her close friends, artist

Na Hye Sŏk and novelist Kim Yŏnsil, and survived to be admired as a great woman, perhaps by becoming Buddhist clergy. I have written and published about Kim Iryŏp as a feminist and as a pioneer reformer in colonial Korea—her life and work before she became a Buddhist nun in 1928 at the age of thirty-three.[12] This article is a sequel to my earlier work—about the later, Buddhist period of her life, a total of forty-four years. Though spanning four times the years of the earlier part of her adult life, her Buddhist phase is less known and deserves examination beyond what it generally has received.

Kim Iryŏp's writing summons conflicting images to ordinary people in contemporary Korea. I was quite surprised how many people recognized her name. Many have at least heard of her. They know that she was a *sŭnim*, that she made Sudŏksa a tourist attraction in South Korea, that, in fact, it was she many tourists wanted to catch a glimpse of during her lifetime rather than the noted monastery itself, and that she died a *Sŏnsa*, Sŏn master (Zen Buddhist teacher),[13] the title usually reserved for an accomplished male monk. But the name, Kim Iryŏp, also invokes a portrait of a bespectacled, handsome, and modern young woman, pursued by men, but ultimately lonely, forlorn, and scandalized for having failed in marriages and love affairs. Some people remember her, wrongly, only as the lover of the person who gave her the pen name, Iryŏp ("one leaf"), and that individual was none other than the even more well-known and controversial "father" of modern Korean literature, Yi Kwangsu. Accompanying these contradictory sketches is a common assumption that she became a nun, as many Korean women had before, to escape and forget her disappointments in life.

It is true that she had a series of disappointing love affairs and marriages, which were rare and scandalous in 1920s Korea, and certainly they played a part. But to attribute her decision to ascend the mountain entirely to disappointing love affairs is mocking her intelligence as a modern, educated woman and that of women in general.

Why Did Kim Iryŏp Become a Buddhist Nun?

Whenever Kim Iryŏp was asked her reasons for becoming a nun during her novitiate years, she would often repeat the question and then answer: "Why am I practicing Buddhism? "Why shouldn't I?"

Just before she made the final *ipsan* decision, she wrote a short piece entitled "Na ŭi norae" ("My Song").[14] This was a declaration of her pledge to universalize Buddhist teaching, and, in fact, a profession of why she was contemplating becoming a nun.

I sing a song.

> Upon the sound of my song,
> The numbers of time and limits of space disappear.
> I'd like to sing a song freely,
> Completely free of even the beautiful musical melodies and beats . . .
> It's not a song of love, it's not a song of sorrow, it's not even a song of
>   inspiration.

> I would simply like to sing the mysterious verse of complete ecstasy.
> Then, even the decomposed soil and dried-up tree barks would be moved.
> Even immovable rocks would smile.
> The sound of my song would resonate throughout the wide earth . . .

> I would like to sing life after life, generation after generation, to fill the
>   universe.
> Then, even those who turned deaf ears would be moved by my song.
> Ah—, I would like to sing—until the future world ends and beyond—
>   forever.

Her "song" disclosed her dream to propagate her newfound faith. It was a combination of idealistic goals, personal aspirations and an accident of fate that led an iconoclastic feminist to Buddhism: a high-minded hope to spread Buddhist teaching to save humanities, combined with her personal desire to redeem her life in order to discover self and meaning of life. Just then, an opportunity presented itself to guide her to a road she had not conceived of only a few years earlier.

In the mid-1920s, Kim was disillusioned with her life, which she viewed as filled with loneliness and suffering. After she had lost all her immediate family members, and failed in several marriages and romances—making her a rootless, drifting solitary being—she had thrown herself into various activities as a modern feminist: to writing, to reform projects and to the education of women, and to leading a life that she considered honest and true to her beliefs—the lifestyle of a liberated woman. But such a philosophy of life brought nothing but grief and notoriety. Thirty years after she became a nun, she reflected:

> I do not consider my life experience (of that time) shallow. Compared with those who suffered most, it may be infinitesimal (as but "a hair of nine cows.")[15] But troubles and anguish of the past thirty years of my earlier life were not insignificant for my mental and physical well-being.

Even now, I have no blood relative, no one who would feel conjugal love toward me, I have no worldly possessions, neither a thatched roof hut, nor a silk garment, nor a silver ring. Nobody has a life as·simple as mine. In this process of elimination of fame and wealth, I have experienced no less pain and suffering than others.[16]

Since she had suffered, she understood others' pains and commiserated with fellow human sufferers and hoped to do something about them. In a piece, "Puldo rǔl takkǔmyǒ" (While Studying the Buddhist Way), dated 1935, Kim cited her favorite passage in the 80,000-chapter *Tripitaka*:[17]

> Human beings have countless agonies.
> One must sever them—as with a knife.
> If I am lucky to receive great virtue,
> I wish to save millions of creatures languishing in suffering.

To save multitudes in anguish was her great wish (*taewǒn*), which she wanted to accomplish above all else. If she could not attain it in this life, then in the next life, and then the next life and so on, until the future world ended and even further, "miraese ka tahago namtorok," in other words, forever.[18] Until such time, she would strive to achieve this goal of saving suffering humanity and at the same time finding her "self," her "great self." Only then would she succeed in attaining her goals: ending her own suffering, saving herself, and finding her true self.

An accident of fate also intervened. Kim Iryǒp became involved in the 1920s with a magazine, called *Yǒsi* (As Is), whose office was located across the hall from the Pulgyosa (Buddhist Publishing Company).[19] She became acquainted with the company staff and published several articles in the magazine, visiting the office frequently. Born and raised as a Christian, she had been taught to regard Buddhism as a superstitious cult of immoral believers, and she was hardly interested in Buddhism at that time. But when she made the staff's acquaintance through her work for the Buddhist *Yǒsi*, she became impressed with their courteous demeanor, their peaceful and trustworthy appearance. She became so fond of them that, even after the magazine folded, she continued to get together with them.[20]

It was during this time that she met a Mr. B.,[21] her one and only true love, who abruptly left her in 1925(?) to become a monk, from which she never recovered. They were in touch with each other, however (albeit between long intervals), all her life, and were informed of each other's activities.

She began learning Chinese from Master Kwon Sang No through Buddhist canons and came to realize that there was something mysteriously vast and profound in Buddhism. She began to think of learning all she could and of propagating that learning to others.[22] At the moment of her grief over lost love, her desire to learn more about Buddhism, her wish to find herself, and her will to save multitudes of others who were suffering—all came together. She came to the conclusion that only through Buddhism could she accomplish all of them and the writing would become her means.[23]

Korean *Sŏn* Buddhism and Kim Iryŏp

The school Kim Iryŏp joined was *Sŏn* Buddhism, known for its emphasis on meditation. *Sŏn*, as it is known in Korea, existed on the Korean Peninsula as early as the end of the seventh century, almost simultaneously with the beginning of its Chinese counterpart, *Ch'an*, and became a discernible force within the Korean Buddhist tradition by the end of the ninth century.[24] In contemporary Korea, it is called *Chogyejong*, or the Chogye school.

There are two different accounts of its origin in Korea. According to one theory, the contemporary *Sŏn* tradition owes its genesis to the eminent Koryŏ monk, Chinul (1158–1210),[25] the founder of Songgwangsa, who combined *Sŏn* with the doctrinal teachings of the more scholastic schools of Buddhist thought and who brought *Sŏn* into the mainstream of Korean Buddhism. From this beginning, *Sŏn* tradition grew to dominate Korean Buddhism.[26] The other explanation is that Monk Towoe established it by combining several sects during the reign of King Hyŏndŏk (809–26) of the unified Silla period. And, at the end of the Koryŏ dynasty, Monk T'aego brought further unification, moving the sect's headquarters to T'aego Temple (Susongdong, Seoul) as the center of Korean Buddhism.[27]

Korean *Sŏn* Buddhism attained its supremacy by absorbing and subsuming other branches into what came to be known as the indigenous Chogye school of Korean Buddhism. *Chogye* is the Korean pronunciation of *Ts'ao-ch'i*, the name of the mountain where the sixth patriarch of Chinese Ch'an, Hui-neng, resided, adumbrating the fundamental *Sŏn* stance of Korean Buddhism.[28]

The Korean *Sŏn* Buddhist school, like Ch'an in China and Zen in Japan, emphasized meditation. As a religious practice, meditation was not peculiar to *Sŏn*, but no other school attached such near-exclusive importance as *Sŏn* did to meditation, not only as a method or means for intuiting Ultimate Truth, but also as an end in itself, as "the Truth realized in action."[29] Iryŏp sŭnim resonated with this doctrine and stated, "theory and doctrine are nothing but a finger pointing at true self (*pona*)," in which they exist.[30]

Sŏn Buddhism believes in an intuitive approach to enlightenment, for "Buddha-nature" is inherent in the minds of all sentient beings; this nature can readily be seen through meditative introspection.[31] "By Buddha-nature is meant the Buddha-mind in its highest attributes and true essence, which transcends all distinctions of [. . .] specific characters"[32] and the mind that human beings have originally.[33] So the mind controlled the body, Iryŏp sŭnim believed, and "human problems can easily be solved for happiness or unhappiness is determined by one's mind."[34]

Initially, human beings were in the state of "greater self" (*taea*), capable of noticing this nature, of general love (*pakae*), equal love (*p'yŏng-ae*), and merciful love (*chaae*), but they had regressed to "lesser (small)–self" (*soa*) and were incapable of the love of greater self. According to Kusan, a twentieth-century Korean head monk of Song'gwangsa[35] who was Buswell's master, the mind also subsumed all things in existence, from one's own body, to the earth, humankind, and all the animals. The entire universe was, therefore, no different from one's own mind. The world of appearances, therefore, is but a product of the imagination. Reflecting this *Sŏn* belief, Iryŏp sŭnim pointed out the utter futility of judging people by appearance when she alluded to the time when she was severely criticized for leaving a loveless marriage.[36]

Owing to its virtual omnipresence, the mind could also be called the "greater self" (*taea*). All things are in a state of interrelationship, one with the other; there was no self or soul that could be conceived separately from anything else. Hence, through *Sŏn* practice the student was to realize a universal "ecology" of mind, in which "this world, mankind and all the animals are no different from oneself."[37] This is precisely the "greater self." And as it is not possible to separate any component from the rest of the world, both objects and the relative self cannot really exist. Therefore, the "greater self" is precisely "no-self"(*mua*).[38]

Because *Sŏn* Buddhism believed that enlightenment was not something that needed to be attained or created but was the fundamental element underlying everyone's existence, a person had to be taken through the process of transition—which the meditation practice provided—during which her/his true status would be revealed to her/him (self-realization). This process was necessary because the individual had so thoroughly convinced her/himself that s/he was not worthy of enlightenment.[39] Because one did not know that originally one was a Buddha, one could not live like a Buddha. But within oneself, there was limitless possibility, similar to a Buddha's.[40]

The length of time needed for self-realization might vary; some novitiates would not take their final vows for they did not feel worthy or prepared to take the final step. In other cases, an aging nun or monk would feel that her/his time was running out and would devote all available time and energy to attain or to retrieve the source of enlightenment buried in her/him. According to Wŏlsŏng sŭnim, Iryŏp sŭnim seemed to have felt that way. After turning sixty, she concentrated entirely on meditation, staying up in the sitting position even during the night.

Kim Iryŏp as a Buddhist Writer

Yim Jungbin, a literary critic, said in "Kim Iryŏp non" (On Kim Iryŏp) that Iryŏp sŭnim wanted to share her enlightenment and she put Buddhist homily into her writings wherever she could. Her urge to spread her newfound belief was so strong that she continued to write even after becoming a nun despite her pledge to her ŭnsa, Man'gong sŭnim, that she would not write.[41] This is where she differed from other Korean Buddhist clergy and where she exhibited her creativity. She wrote not only in han'gŭl (Korean alphabet) but also in various literary styles—poetry, essays, and autobiographical recollections.

As a sŏnsa, Iryŏp sŭnim wrote to popularize Sŏn Buddhist doctrine, but three particular themes stand out in her post-conversion writings: To end suffering, to search for self and for meaning of life, and to bring salvation to the suffering multitude—the very same three motivations that led her to Buddhism.[42]

In the early years of her religious life, she continued to write poetry, her favorite genre. Seventeen of twenty-three poems were written in 1932, four years after she entered the mountain. That was obviously the pivotal year. According to Buswell, it takes about three-and-a-half years before one can be ordained as a regular priest or nun—six months as haengja ("postulant") and three years as a novitiate. During this time, one could easily leave Buddhism, but thereafter it would become more difficult.[43]

Thus, in 1932, Iryŏp was in her mid-30s and was still struggling at the crossroads of life before she took the road not taken—and one of no return. These poems continue to have romantic themes but with Buddhist messages. Novelist Pak Chong Hwa wrote on the occasion of Iryŏp sŭnim's posthumous publication of *Miraese* in 1974 that her postconversion poems had a similar flair to that seen in Han Yongun's poems.[44] Yearning for lost love was still there, but, unlike her earlier poems, there was a sense of peace for she had now (in 1932) acquired the Buddhist perspective of transcending narrow human love and boundaries, artificially created by human beings. A 1932 poem read:

> Things cast shadows.
> My approaching lover makes a rustle.
> Peach blossoms smile silently
> But in the winter mountain, plum blossoms bloom,
> Who could deny that spring and winter are one?

Another poem of that year, "Nim ege" ("To My Lover"), clearly exhibited the signs of Buddhist thinking.

> Trusting your words.
> My young soul struggles to trek on the road you showed me.
> But it's hard to tell when I'll reach where you are
> For I do not even know the way.
>
> Was it 1,000 years or 10,000 years ago that you called me?
> When I hear your voice inside me,
> I feel as though I'm going to see you right here,
> And I get lost in (religious) ecstasy,
> But when I return to reality, I am still where I was.[45]

The lover of whom this poem sings is no longer the secular lover but is now the Buddha of eons ago, who called her during one of Iryŏp's former lives. He seemed so close and yet was so far away. She might have been thinking of her lost love, who now appeared as the Buddha.

If the above two poems betrayed vacillation and confusion between Iryŏp sŭnim's worldly lover and religious deity, the next poem demonstrates her complete abandonment to and reliance on the religion. In "Kwi ŭi" (Conversion; lit. "return to reliance"), she confessed:

This confused and bewildered body
Has converted to Buddhist teaching.
I can't be happier, for I now
Study the sacred knowledge.
But I do not have good ears, and
Must rely completely on thee.[46]

After the bumper crop year of poems in 1932, Iryŏp sŭnim seldom wrote poetry again and concentrated on short, reflective pieces, many of which were autobiographical. When one looks at *Na ŭi hoesang rok* (My Recollections), it becomes clear that she was keenly interested in discovering herself and explaining her motivations for becoming a nun. The main title of *My Recollections* is "Chilli rŭl morŭmnida" (I Do Not Know the Truth [Ultimate Truth]) and is divided into forty-nine headings, which occupy more than 100 pages of the first volume of *Miraese*. The subjects range from her personal accounts, her Christian family background, her parents' life stories, close friends' anecdotes, childhood memories, her native village, and her love affairs, to such more public-oriented topics as her controversial views on chastity, religion, and even the difficulties of reaching Buddhahood.

Then, there are the many and more serious essays, written for the direct purpose of spreading *Sŏn* Buddhism. Many of these were discovered after her death and edited in the second volume of *Miraese* under the heading of *Pop'o rok* (The Records of Words of Buddhism), which has a main subtitle of "Ilch'ehwa ŭi kil" (The Way Toward Unity). *Pop'o rok* occupies the first 150 pages of the second volume. A sampling of titles of parts would reveal the issues with which Iryŏp sŭnim was preoccupied: "Life," "Reality and Human Beings," "Thought, Dream, and Reality," "Toward Rebuilding Buddhist Organizations," "Mind," "Return to Void," "Prayer," "Meditation and Enlightenment," "Self-Discovery," "The Way to Eternal Life," "Unifying Soul," and "Life Without Suffering."[47] In many of these, she emphasized the need to become one with the universe, or *Ilch'ehwa,* and to become like Buddha—the one who was able to part with human anguish and to achieve peace of mind. "All solutions existed in the ability to become one."[48]

Both genres (poetry and prose) of her writings reveal her firm belief in the twin *Sŏn* doctrines that enlightenment was innate in the minds of all sentient beings, and that mind initiated all action and was the master of the body. Iryŏp sŭnim taught that, to attain the twin objectives, one needed to practice meditation in order to be able to sever ties with the world, to have no attachments, to empty one's mind, and to return to the void. These were the ways of liberation—from the pain of life and death.[49] Then, one's mind would be able to control the body; it could also subsume all things in existence, from one's own body, to the earth, humankind, and all the animals. Thus, the entire universe was but a reflection of one's own mind. These messages were so precious and she was so convinced of their correctness in solving human problems that she felt great urgency in sharing them with others. In other words, she had to sing her "song" for eternity.[50] Her song, of course, was her writing and she was driven to write.

According to Wŏlsŏng, Iryŏp sŭnim found it extremely difficult to cease writing suddenly, for, by the time she came to the temple, writing had become so much a part of her life that she wrote secretly and without light, deep into the night—only by moonlight in the summer and by the reflection of snow in the winter—or she then simply scribbled in complete darkness. After she passed away, Wŏlsŏng found many hidden manuscripts, which were hard to decipher because they had been written in the dark.[51]

At the end of her life, Iryŏp sŭnim pointed out the difficulties of attaining what she had been preaching and emphasized the need for incessant effort. She confessed: "Buddhist teaching saved me from my crises, but I have not yet reached the stage of great courage due to innumerable past residues, which, even at age seventy, could not completely be removed. I have not thoroughly emptied myself to recover my real self (pona)."[52] Fearing, however, that people, preoccupied with gaining salvation, might neglect life, she urged people to lead a meaningful life for it will not return as it is. "One could not end life," she commented. "Life is like a drama with one act ending and another one beginning."[53]

So how did Iryŏp sŭnim try to reclaim what existed innately inside her, the source of holiness, the enlightenment, or the Buddha-nature or Buddha-mind? She did so through Sŏn practices, which she taught and practiced with all her mind, soul, and body. She was so totally committed to meditation and so intent on succeeding to regain the Buddha-nature that existed in her that she remained in meditative posture continuously for nearly ten years toward the end of her life. About three years before her death, the lower half of her body became so atrophied for lack of use and movement that she could not walk, and they had to help her to get up with support at her sides.

Conclusion

At first glance, Kim Iryŏp's life seems full of contradictions. She was born into a Christian family but converted to Buddhism. She yearned for a happy family life but abandoned her two marriages within only a few years. She was bereft of her entire immediate family when she was only twenty; she was desperate for companionship but departed the secular world for that of a solitary meditative nun. She sought to be recognized by her literary peers for her writing, but she was a permanent outsider. Her professional life before and after she became a nun seems especially contradictory, but her earlier life constituted a foundation on which she built the later phase.

Yim Jungbin compares Iryŏp sŭnim's life with a lotus blossom, a flower which grows and blooms in the mud. Iryŏp sŭnim arose like a white lotus blossom from the mud, which can be compared with the youthful period of her life and which was necessary for the later stage. Because of her troubled past, she was able to abandon the "lesser self" of her youth and find enlightenment in the state of Sŏn.[54] Soong chongjung (head of Chogyejong) remarked in the introduction to *Miraese*:

> There is no saint who is a saint from the beginning. Everyone has human frailties. One who overcomes that becomes a saint. The issue is how to win over past mistakes. If a person wants to become truly great, one must experience difficulties and pass through the process of trial and ordeal and roam and pass the passages of obstacles. With that in mind, Iryŏp sŭnim's accomplishments are truly great. The first part of her life was indeed full of difficulties, but she made that as the basis for attaining Buddhahood and perfecting virtue. She was thus able to spend the rest of her life in pursuit of truth [as a religious ascetic.][55]

A comment like that reminds one of St. Augustine, one of the greatest saints of Catholicism, whose *Confessions* were the unsparing and humble revelations of Augustine's past sins and his search for redemption. Such baring of souls by the religious is very much in the tradition of mysticism[56] of world religions such as Christianity and Buddhism. Iryŏp sŭnim is almost repetitious in recalling her past (sins) in her writings as if she were in a confessional with the earnest hope that they be properly forgiven so that she could be certain of the love Buddha (God) has for her.[57]

The Buddhist phase of her life was a journey during which the former Iryŏp died and a new, hopeful Iryŏp was born to embark on the road to discover the "greater self." By discarding the love of the secular world, her world was opened up to that of "greater love." That does not mean that she forgot her entire past. Her past was recast in wider and deeper context, giving different perspectives. Iryŏp sŭnim's writings recollecting the later stages of her life are teachings of Buddhism and have a characteristic of Buddhist missionary literature.[58]

In poems of part-romantic, part-Buddhist themes, some literary critics consider Kim Iryŏp to have succeeded in the tradition established by Han Yongun,[59] also a literary Buddhist monk, who, by writing in *han'gul*, brought Korea's Buddhist literature into modern times.[60] This is quite a compliment, albeit a posthumous one, from mainline literary figures. The literary acclaim she pursued in her youth came late—decades after she became a nun. When her *Ch'ŏng ch'un ŭl pulsarŭgo*[61] was published in 1960 and 1962, it was a huge success. But, by that time, the kind of critique her writing received mattered little to her, for she had entered a stage where she could not be destroyed by slanderous criticism.[62] Han, like Kim Iryŏp, explored the mystery of love persistently and completely as no other modern Korean writer had. That is what made Han a poet and a novelist of love, a rarity in his generation and in the whole range of modern Korean literature.[63] But Kim Iryŏp went further—she unabashedly brought her own life into her writing and used herself as a source for examples to make her point. For instance, by recasting her pre-Buddhist life in inspirational writings, she taught the importance of self-worth, self-confidence, self-awareness, self-awakening, and self-realization—the messages she specifically aimed at women. Rather than distancing herself on the mountain as a nun, Iryŏp sŭnim reached out, through her writing, and identified herself with other women (and men) of all walks of life, uniting herself with ordinary people, which was consistent with her belief of *Ilch'e hwa*, or becoming one—with people and the universe.

Iryŏp sŭnim's prose serves as inspirational literature from which one can derive refinement, faith, and enlightenment. It is also a road map to attain greater love. In this genre, she used metaphors by creatively and selectively drawing on Korean myths, fables, and historical legends, which is very much in the tradition of the world's religious writing.

Asked what the greatest legacy of Iryŏp sŭnim was, Wŏlsŏng pointed out three particular points: First, she popularized Buddhist teaching by writing in plain language and *han'gŭl*. Second, she brought respect to

Buddhism. And, most important, she enhanced the position of Buddhist nuns to an immeasurable degree. That she was an educated feminist reformer before becoming a nun is in itself a phenomenon that people recognized. But she went further; she emphasized nuns' education, raised funds for the purpose by writing the script for, and even producing, a Buddhist play, *Yi Ch'a Don ŭi chugŭm* (The Death of Yi Ch'a Don), and succeeded in erecting a modern building for the nuns' sole use. By becoming a Buddhist nun, she undoubtedly abandoned all her worldly aspirations, but, in the end, she succeeded in fulfilling her secular, feminist goal of lifting up women not only to the level of men but even beyond. She showed people in general how to recover their inner perfect self, their Buddhahood, and attain enlightenment, which is the end of suffering and source of happiness and life until *miraese ka tahatorok*, the end of the world to come, and beyond.

On her last birthday, she reportedly said, "having learned from life's experiences, having forgotten all past anguish, having surrendered completely to Buddha, I am living peacefully and happily, without pain."[64] Indeed, the joy and peace she attained are forever commemorated in Hwanhidae (Hall of Exultation), a nuns' hermitage at Sudŏksa. Iryŏp sŭnim's smiling life-sized portrait is hung on the wall of the large main room, used as a reception area, and in the courtyard stands a five-story stone pagoda erected two years after her death. Looking at her face with its faint smile and at the stone tower and thinking about passages from her poems and prose, I felt touched by her spirit and holiness. As Master Unho remarked in the congratulatory remark in *Miraese*, reading Iryŏp sŭnim's life stories can become an occasion for drawing near to Buddhist philosophy.[65]

Kim Iryŏp's conflicting worlds have become one, *ilch'ehwa*, reconciled in every aspect. In the process, she created a whole body of popular Buddhist literature, easily accessible to ordinary people. Whether it is pure literature or not, creating a body of religious literature easily understandable to ordinary people is in itself creative. In her writings, we experience Iryŏp sŭnim's flashes of holiness as well as sparks of creativity.

Notes

1. I use the term *sŭnim* to refer to Kim Iryŏp after she became a nun and to other nuns and monks. Koreans refer to all Buddhist monks and nuns as *sŭnim*, a term of

respect that is a contraction of *song*, the Sino-Korean transliteration of *sangha* (congregation of monks), combined with the honorific Korean suffix *–nim*. Korean monks use the term *chung* when referring to themselves; this is a Korean word that derives from a Sino-Korean term meaning "congregation," or by synecdoche just "monk." Buswell, *Zen*, 69.

2. Interview 23 June 1998 at Tŏksan Hotel, Tŏksan Ch'ungch'ŏng Namdo, near Sudŏksa. According to temple records, Sudŏksa was founded in the A.D. 590s, the late Paekche period. It is one of the five main temples of Korea, where there is a comprehensive training center comprising a meditation hall, a monks' college and a center for studying monastic rules. The main hall was built in 1308, one of only a few to survive through successive invasions Korea endured. *Exploring Korean Buddhist Temples* (Seoul: Korean National Tourism Organization, n.d.).

3. Kim Iryŏp, *Miraese*.

4. The monk Ildang at Chikjisa, Kimch'ŏn—Kyŏngsang Pukdo—is reportedly Iryŏp sŭnim's son, born of a union with a Japanese man in 1922 during Iryŏp's stay in Japan. Ildang sunin authored a two-volume autobiographical work about his relationship with Kim Iryŏp. Kim T'aeshin, *Rahula ŭi samogok*. He also has a book that combines his "mother's" poems with his paintings, *Tugogan jŏng* (Leaving Love Behind).

5. The two nuns told me that, during Iryŏp sŭnim's lifetime, there was absolutely no mention of her son despite the late nun's considerable candor about her former secular life and that there was no extant proof that Monk Ildang is her son. But they have come to terms with him and have given him the benefit of the doubt. I will not deal with the question of Iryŏp's son in this paper.

6. Sŏng, *Asea yŏsŏng*, 307–26.

7. Ibid., 307.

8. Ibid., 54–5.

9. Sŏng, *Asea yŏsŏng*, 307–8.

10. *Ipsan* refers to becoming a Buddhist cleric. The expression probably comes from the fact that most Buddhist temples and monasteries have been located deep in the mountains due to the Yi policy of suppressing and driving Buddhism out of cities.

11. Yu, *Han Yongun*, 11.

12. Oh, "Kim Iryŏp: Pioneer Writer/Reformer," 9–30.

13. A nun or monk, inspired by his/her contemplation, who would continue on for the rest of her/his career as a meditation monk and achieves a measure of recognition for the quality of her/his practice, eventually becomes a *Sŏn* master (*Sŏnsa*) at a major training monastery. Buswell, *Zen*, 70.

14. Kim, *Miraese*, 1:32.

15. A colloquial Korean expression.

16. Kim, *Miraese*, 1:472–74.

17. The work of the Koryŏ period, consisting of 83,000 wood carvings of Buddhist canons, currently enshrined in Haeinsa, Kyŏngsang Pukdo, northeast of Taegu.

18. Kim, *Miraese*, 1:472.

19. Kim, "Pulmun t'ujok yi junyŏn e" (1930) in *Sudŏksa ŭi noŭl*, 1976.

20. Kim, *Sudŏksa ŭi noŭl*, 44–45.

21. This Mr. B., according to Wŏlsŏng sŭnim and as I suspected, is Hon. Paek Sŏng-uk, a prominent educator who served as the president of the Tong'guk University in Seoul, Korea and as a government minister.

22. Kim, *Sadŏksa ŭi noŭl*, p. 46.

23. Kim, *Miraese*, 1:321–22.
24. Buswell, *Zen*, 149.
25. Buswell, *Tracing Back the Radiance*.
26. Buswell, *Zen*, 149.
27. Yi, "Wŏrha chongjong ŭi," 283–95.
28. Buswell, *Zen*, 22.
29. De Bary, Chan, and Watson, *Chinese Tradition*, 346–47.
30. Kim, *Miraese*, 2:51,74.
31. De Bary, *Chinese Tradition*.
32. Ibid., 347.
33. Batchelor, *Lotus Flowers*, 109.
34. Kim, *Miraese*, 2:51.
35. A temple in Chŏlla Namdo, a short distance southeast of the city of Kwangju, site of the only Buddhist training center for foreigners.
36. Kim, *Miraese*, 1:465.
37. Buswell, *Zen*, 154.
38. Ibid.
39. Ibid., 25, 152.
40. Batchelor, *Lotus Flowers*, 109.
41. Because obeying one's master was supposed to be absolute in Korean Buddhist tradition, one could only imagine Iryŏp sŭnim's inner conflict between her desire to write and her obligation to obey her master.
42. See above, 7.
43. Buswell, *Zen*, 76–86.
44. Kim, *Miraese*, 1:22.
45. Ibid., 1:54–55.
46. Ibid., 1: 62.
47. Ibid., 2:31–153.
48. Ibid., 2:126.
49. Ibid., 1:325.
50. Ibid., 1:329.
51. Interview with Wŏlsong, Tŏksan Hotel, 23 June 1998.
52. Kim, *Miraese*, 2:153.
53. Ibid.,1:332,351; 2:153.
54. Kim, *Sudŏksa ŭi noŭl*, 11–12.
55. Soong Chongjong, "Kanhaeng sa," in Kim, *Miraese*, 1:20.
56. Gardiner "Introduction," *Confessions*, xii.
57. Ibid.
58. Yim, *Noŭl*, 14–15.
59. Pak Chang hwa, in Kim, *Miraese*, 1:22.
60. Yi, "I chaek ŭl naemyŏ," 5.
61. This is the later title of the same earlier publication, *Ŏnu sudoin ŭi hoesang* (Recollections of a Certain Nun) (1960), *Ch'ŏngch'un ul pulsarŭgo* (After Torching the Youth), Seoul: Munsŏn'gak, 1962. The edition with the second title was an immediate success, going through many editions. Money from the sale of the book enabled Sudŏksa to purchase land, which considerably eased the poverty of the monastery.
62. Yi, "I chaek ŭl naemyŏ," 9.

63. Yu, *Han Yong-un*, 17, 83.
64. Interview with Wŏlsŏng sŭnim, 23 June 1998.
65. Unho, "Ha sa" (Congratulatory Note), in Kim, *Miraese*, 1:18.

References

Batchelor, Martine. *Walking on Lotus Flowers: Buddhist Women Living, Loving and Meditating*. London: Thorsons, 1996.
Buswell, Robert E., Jr., trans. *Tracing Back the Radiance: Chinul's Korean Way of Zen*. Honolulu: University of Hawaii Press, 1991.
————. *The Zen Monastic Experience: Buddhist Practice in Contemporary Korea*. Princeton, NJ: Princeton University Press, 1992.
De Bary, William Theodore, Wing-tsit Chan, and Burton Watson, comps. *Sources of Chinese Tradition*, vol. 1. New York: Columbia University Press, 1960, 1963.
Gardiner, Harold C.S.J., Introduction to *the Confessions of Saint Augustine*. Translated by Edward B. Pusey. New York: Pocket Books, 1957.
Kim, Iryŏp. *Miraese ka tahago namtorok* (Until the End of the Future World), 2 vols. Seoul: Inmul Yŏn'guso, 1974.
————. *Ch'ŏngch'un ŭl pulsarŭko* (After Torching the Youth), 2d ed. Seoul: Pomusa, 1993.
————. *Haengbok kwa pulhaeng ŭi kalp'i eso* (Between Happiness and Despair). Seoul: Huimun Ch'ulp'an Sa, 1964.
————. *Sudŏksa ŭi noŭl* (In the Shade of Sudŏksa). Seoul: Pomusa, 1976.
Kim T'aeshin. *Rahula ŭi samogok* (Rahula's Songs of Yearning for Mother), 2 vols. Seoul: Hankilsa, 1991.
Oh, Bonnie. "Kim Iryŏp: Pioneer Writer/Reformer in Colonial Korea." Royal Asiatic Society, Seoul branch, *Transactions*, vol. 71 (1996): 9–30.
Sŏng, Rakhŭi. "Kim Iryŏp munhak-ron" (On Kim Iryŏp's Literature). *Asea yŏsŏng yŏn'gu* (Journal of Asian Women) 17 (December 1978): 307–26.
Yi, Eun Yun. "Wŏrha chungjong ŭi salm kwa chŏrhak" (The Life and Philosophy of Wŏrha). *WIN* (March 1998): 283–95.
Yi, Ki Hong. "I chaek ŭl naemyŏ" (On the Occasion of Publishing This Book). *Tangsin ŭn na e ge muoshi doe ŏt sap ki e* (I Don't Know What You Are to Me), Kim Iryŏp poetry collection. Seoul: Munhwa Sarang, 1997.
Yim, Jungbin. "Kim Iryŏp non" (On Kim Iryŏp), *Kim Iryŏp, Sudŏksa ŭi noŭl* (The Twilight of Sudŏk Temple). Seoul: Pomusa, 1976.
Yu, Beongcheon. *Han Yongun and Yi Kwangsu: Two Pioneers of Modern Korean Literature*. Detroit: Wayne State University Press, 1992.

10
Dialectics of Life

Hahn Moo-Sook and Her Literary World

Yung–Hee Kim

Hahn Moo-Sook (Han Musuk, 1918–1993) debuted in 1943, toward the end of Japanese colonial rule (1910–1945), when her first full-length novel, *Tŭngpul tŭnŭn yŏin* (A Woman Holding a Lamp), written in Japanese, won the first prize in the fiction contest held by *Sinsidae* (New Age) magazine.[1] Soon after this breakthrough, Hahn ventured into the field of drama, when she wrote two award-winning plays one year after another, a one-act play, "Maŭm" (The Heart, 1943), and a four-act play, "Sŏri kkot" (Frost Flowers, 1944).[2] These works signaled Hahn's early success in experimenting in genres other than the novel[3] and served as a concrete indication of her multifaceted literary talents. Hahn established another literary milestone when her second full-length novel, *Yŏksa nŭn hŭrŭnda* (History Flows), received the top prize in the competition held by the newspaper *Kukche sinbo* (International News) in 1948.[4] Throughout her career Hahn tried her hand at several other genres, and her versatility is displayed in a wide spectrum of works, ranging from literary criticism to public lectures, travelogues, broadcasts, and interviews.[5] The only genre she little touched is poetry. In the end, Hahn's reputation rests on her achievement as a writer of short stories and full-length novels.[6]

It is surprising as well as enlightening to learn that Hahn Moo-Sook's literary career was actually her second, or even fortuitous, choice of vocation. Born of a modern, Japan-educated father and a book-loving, classically schooled mother, Hahn was noted for her artistic talent from a very young age and enjoyed a privileged childhood and adolescence, compared with her contemporaries. Encouraged and nurtured by her parents and teachers, she had long harbored aspirations to become a painter.[7] The illness to which she was prone in her youth, however, frequently prevented her from regular school attendance, which finally culminated in her four-year confinement at home beginning in 1936, her high school senior year; this illness forced her to give up her long cherished dreams of pursuing art and even pursuing higher education.[8]

Even so, Hahn's artistic accomplishment was publicly recognized in 1937 when she was commissioned to draw illustrations for the woman novelist Kim Malbong's (1901–1961) first novel, *Millim* (The Jungle, 1935–36; 1937), serialized in *Tonga ilbo* (Tonga Daily)—an unprecedented honor for a nineteen-year-old high school student.[9]

Ironically, Hahn's prolonged bout with poor health in solitary isolation at home provided her with ample opportunity to immerse herself in literature, allowing her to roam the world of imagination and to develop independent and original thinking. An avid reader from youth, Hahn began to devour books from her father's study, reputed for its wealth of Chinese classics and Western literary masterpieces.[10] Among these Hahn found the novels of Thomas Mann and Russian masters, especially Dostoyevsky, most fascinating.[11] As she recalled later, this total absorption in reading was a desperate gesture—an expression of raging thirst for life, truth, knowledge, and action in the face of possible death.[12] In this connection, the literary critic Yu Chongho insightfully remarked that Hahn Moo-Sook's engrossment in literature in those days was not a teenager's passing infatuation, but was grounded in the intense corporeal need forced upon her by her physical ailment.[13] And this complete immersion in reading unwittingly laid the foundation for her eventual writing career.[14]

According to Hahn, what actually drove her to creative writing was the hopelessly self-negating married life she had to lead as the wife, mother, and daughter-in-law of an extremely conservative Korean household, which demanded that she submit to the gender expectations of her patriarchal society.[15] Given her background of being reared in a progressive, Western culture-exposed family atmosphere in which her individuality and artistic gifts were fostered and treasured, her arranged marriage into an orthodox, Confucian family with its fortune in decline proved to be little short of a culture shock.[16] Hahn's married life was an endless continuation of self-abnegation, serving every need of the Confucian-steeped extended family in conformance to traditional womanly ideals in the most exemplary manner imaginable. Oppressive conventions, suffocating repetition of empty rituals, difficulties stemming from differences in value systems between her and her in-laws, and unending onerous domestic chores in the end took a severe toll on her—both physically and emotionally.

These conflicts, frustrations, and despair drove her to question the meaning of her life. She felt culturally and intellectually starved and utterly shortchanged.[17] These negative circumstances, however, also aroused in her an irrepressible desire to lead a self-determined life as a worthy human being. She felt she had so much to relate—all those suppressed emotions— and writing meant releasing them.[18] Thus was born her first novel, the result of her pure, desperate desire to reaffirm and validate her existence.[19] In this sense, Hahn's literary career was launched purely on her own volition and in the absence of mentors, regular training, or even literary friends—a unique distinction she had been clearly aware of.[20]

Unlike many of her colleagues, Hahn Moo-Sook had initially pursued her literary career largely detached from established literary organizations or group activities, common for the majority of Korean writers, and especially noticeable among male authors. Even her first novel's success was a secret kept strictly between her and her husband for fear of her in-laws; she could not even attend the award ceremony.[21] It was only after the publication of her second novel, *Yŏksa nŭn hŭrŭnda*, that Hahn finally made her formal association with members of the Korean literary establishment.[22] Considering her personal circumstances, such reserve is readily understandable. As Hahn's retrospect of her career suggests, even when she felt creative urges, she often had to suppress them to fulfill her familial roles.[23] She even observed that gifted and carefree artists made her feel like an incompetent and ordinary housewife, though she couldn't help but feel a strong consciousness as a writer and a sense of distance in the presence of complacent professional housewives.[24] This complex position, which Hahn defined as that of an outsider[25]—suspended between the private and public realms and between creative pulses and domestic obligations—must have been a source of tension and conflict throughout her writing career; but this state also seems to have served as the inspiration and impetus for her literary production.[26]

We customarily associate the name Hahn Moo-Sook with traditional Korean upper-class culture, which emphasized formality, decorum, restraints, frugality, propriety. Undoubtedly, the widely circulated information on her ultra-Confucian married life contributed to her being labeled a traditionalist. Her expertise in age-old ceremonial protocol, rites, and rituals; mastery of the vocabulary and lexicon exclusive to the *yangban* (nobility) class; accurate knowledge of traditional customs, seasonal observations, and human relationships; and her love of detailing the cuisine, clothing, and Korean-style houses of the gentry unquestionably qualified Hahn as an authentic connoisseur and guardian of the fast-disappearing Korean cultural legacy.

And yet Hahn Moo-Sook has also been identified as a discerning literary arbiter who promoted harmony and balance between the presumably opposing cultural entities—Korean and non-Korean.[27] Though she is remembered today as a committed validator of Korean cultural heritage, her literary reputation also lies in her acknowledgment of the necessity of accommodating elements of modern Western culture within the Korean traditional framework.[28] Some scholars even praise her works as significant contributions to transcending the unfortunate disjunction between tradition and modernity often encountered in modern Korean literary history.[29] Hahn's strenuous effort to negotiate the diametrically opposed forces that had shaped her own life—her premarital upbringing and education carried on in a rather open, Western-oriented atmosphere and her married life in a rigidly Confucian, traditional family with its obligatory mandates—and to bring them into a harmonious and felicitous whole may have contributed to her formation of such an ideological stance.

This eclecticism or integrative stance is not limited simply to Hahn's affirmation of both the indigenous and foreign cultural traditions. It extends to many other areas of concern in her works, which deal with different conceptual dyads, such as love/hate, joy/sorrow, happiness/misery, the sacred/the profane, transgression/redemption, past/present, life/death. She finds that these seeming dichotomies exist not as disparate elements operating independently with rigidly marked boundaries and fissures between them but along one continuum, converging and interacting with each other, and even containing one another. In Hahn's vision of life, therefore, there prevails an aura of mysticism, a sense of

tolerance, and reverence for life that evinces the worth of human existence for what it is, as is revealed in her remark: "What exists is precious, and everything is good as it is."[30] In fact, in her major works, it
is not unusual to see the protagonists experience an epiphany in which
their conflicts and quandaries are sublimated, providing the characters with moments of intuition leading to personal emancipation or
redemption.

My study here focuses on Hahn's acclaimed short stories, such as
"Wŏrun" (The Halo Around the Moon, 1955) and "Ch'ukche wa
unmyŏng ŭi changso" (The Site of Festival and Fate, 1962),[31] and the
novel Sŏngnyu namujip iyagi (The Tale of the House with Pomegranate
Trees, 1964). These works demonstrate that the author's vision of life is
one of holistic approaches; that is, it sanctions life in its entirety without
devaluing one facet in favor of others. These narratives provide evidence that Hahn sees life as a multifarious entity wherein frailty, bro-
kenness, misfortune, and heartaches are found side-by-side with inner
strengths, the desire for reintegration, the will to amend, and healing
and regenerative powers. This means that for Hahn the configuration of
human life consists in dialectic interactions of these seemingly binary
opposites, and that the meaning of life derives from accepting and, ultimately, celebrating them as interlocked and integral parts of human existence. Ultimately, Hahn projects the idea that the ideal of human life
lies in overcoming the rigid duality of good and evil, purity and defile-
ment, success and failure, health and sickness, new and old, tradition
and modernity, indigenous and foreign, and other such strict dichotomi-
zations or compartmentalizations of reality, thereby obtaining exultant
experiences of transcendence and liberation.

Hahn's reconciliatory perspective of life finds its compelling expression in "Wŏrun." Centering on a sixty-two-year-old childless, judgmental, thrifty but financially secure widow, Mrs. Hong, the narrative
demonstrates the sterility and destructiveness of moral rigidity and self-
righteousness, which emphasize only a partial truth of life by rejecting
the rest of it as invalid or simply wrong. And by having the heroine
come to a profound understanding of her myopic view of life, the story
articulates the essential positive effect of tolerance and of discarding
exact moral categorization.

Mrs. Hong has basically been imprisoned by the ideology of prim
widowhood and puritanical sexual morality. Married at nineteen and
widowed at twenty-two, she knew little about conjugal love, especially

because of the sexual taboo imposed on her out of concern for her tuberculosis-stricken husband. Her only memories of her marriage consist of her ritual of dedicating a bowl of pure water every midnight for her husband's recovery and a brief, yearning encounter between her and her husband, which transpired when she put her hands on his burning forehead just before his death. Ever since, through forty years of widowhood, Mrs. Hong has regarded "sexual acts, be they among animals or vegetation, somehow sinful, like living itself."[32]

A domineering figure, dubbed as "Tiger Grandma" by others, Mrs. Hong exacts obedience and subservience from her social inferiors. She is harsh and abusive toward her maid, Kŭmsun; she had scared away her adopted son and his good-natured and meek wife from her house; and the orphaned eight-year-old nephew under her care cringes in her presence. There is an implied irony in that the narrative begins with its first sentence saying that the overbearing Mrs. Hong is about to take over an orphanage the next day. Above all, she maintains an attitude of moral superiority and intolerance for disorder. To Mrs. Hong, the young female boarder renting a backroom in her house—an unwed mistress with a meek and guilt-ridden demeanor—is nothing but an object of contempt, although the quiet, unassuming woman is an ideal tenant, invariably paying her rent on time. Mrs. Hong's disdain toward the young woman becomes almost a physical loathing after she accidentally witnesses the single woman's carrying on with her man in broad daylight.

Mrs. Hong doesn't even realize that the young woman is pregnant until the latter goes into labor, and this development makes Mrs. Hong extremely upset, especially because her own maid and another older female boarder at her house, Ongnye's mother, make so much fuss over the young woman. Ongnye's mother, a middle-aged woman, by virtue of having given birth to seven children, plays the role of midwife in total disregard of Mrs. Hong's authority or her feelings as landlady. Upon visiting the young female boarder's room, however, Mrs. Hong, contrary to her expectation, finds nothing degrading or indecent there; instead, she detects in the scene "an aura of awe-inspiring reverence, which makes one fiercely tense, while reminding one of a festival ritual" (p. 235). Furthermore, the profile of Ongnye's mother assisting the woman appeared to Mrs. Hong utterly grave and dignified.

As Mrs. Hong catches sight of the moon, with a halo around it, reflected on the water in the coarse pottery bowl prepared for the birthing woman's use and listens to the woman's moaning, she is struck by an uncanny similarity between the woman's giving life and her husband's death—the same groans and the same moon with a halo in early summer. At the same time, the death of the dayflies, which moments ago formed a thick mating column in the garden, awakens in Mrs. Hong a profound sense of mystery of how life and death are enmeshed. This realization leads her to a better understanding of the behaviors of Ongnye's mother and her maid, which had earlier provoked such irritation and anger in her:

> Now she seemed to have some understanding about the attitude of Ongnye's mother and Kŭmsun this evening. Weren't they participating in "life?" Because of that, didn't they put on airs and behave so brazenly? (p. 240)

It seems as if it no longer matters to Mrs. Hong whether the young woman is an unmarried mistress or whether the man, who is going to be the father of the baby, has not come to see the woman giving birth. She embraces the young woman's shame, muted suffering, and indignity of the illegitimate liaison. The arrival of the newborn with a piercing cry coincides with Mrs. Hong's final inner transformation:

> At that moment, in her mind, she put her palms together in front of the coarse pottery water-bowl in which the halo-moon was reflected, as if it were pure sacral water. (p. 240)

Here, the figure of Mrs. Hong—finding herself in awe of the process of procreation and the sacredness of life—stands for an equation of birth with death, reverence for life, obliteration of moral superiority, and even suspension of social hierarchical distinctions.

Suddenly Mrs. Hong is overwhelmed by fatigue, symptomatic of her letting go of and release from the "tiredness of her lifetime" (p. 240) as a prisoner of the tyrannical principle of sexual prudery and of the self-limiting and destructive artificiality resulting from fastidious, prejudicial, and rigid marking of life's boundaries.

In a similar manner, reconciliation with and acceptance of life's many unfoldings and circumstances is articulated in Hahn's "Ch'ukche wa unmyŏng ŭi changso." The narrative exemplifies the necessity of accepting imperfect and dark sides of human existence such as failures, sickness, uncertainties, anxiety, fears, and even death, for what they are and discovering beauty, value, meaning, and truths in unlikely places (hospitals), people (dying patients), and conditions (imminent death). While illustrating such thematic concerns, the story also presents the possibilities of turning life's negativity into positivity and thereby finding the meaning of human life in its most paltry form and manifestation.

As with the preceding story, "Ch'ukche wa unmyŏng ŭi changso" sets up two women, Chŏn Okhŭi and Song Miyŏn, as counterpoints, and through their interactions the narrative communicates its themes. The heroine, forty-nine-year-old Chŏn Okhŭi, is a terminal cancer patient in a charity hospital. She hides a scarred past: her first love, an anti-Japanese underground freedom fighter, died in a Japanese prison, and, after his death, still unwed, she delivered his stillborn child. With no job and no relatives to support her, she has eked out an existence relying on favors from others; she habitually made hollow claims of her connections with people of high social standing and power, which no one believed. Her dismayed and exasperated friends dumped her in the charity hospital and, without her knowledge, made secret arrangements with the hospital to have an autopsy performed on her after her death. On the other hand, Song Miyŏn, the twenty-year-old nurse who befriends Chŏn Okhŭi, is a pristine, tenderhearted, inexperienced woman and an orphan of the Korean War. The lonely Miyŏn falls in love with a thirty-one-year-old reticent, noncommittal young architect, Hyŏnmin, the son of a wealthy businessman. Although perplexed by her own attraction toward him, Miyŏn sees in him an escape from her monotonous and desolate life in the hospital dormitory.

The epitome of human failure, Chŏn Okhŭi, however, recovers a sense of wholeness and self-worth before her death. This is made possible by her genuine concern to intervene on Miyŏn's behalf and to prevent the naïve, young woman from repeating her own past mistake:

> "Miss Song! Be careful! Women have only one chance for victory or defeat. You shouldn't be defeated by anyone. Never by either your passion, your lover, or yourself!" What's more, she shouted in her heart: "Look at me! Me!"

> This was a scream uttered by Ms. Chŏn Okhŭi for the first time in her life. It was a cry looking straight at her naked self.[33]

Chŏn Okhŭi even makes Miyŏn her double—as if her failed life could be redeemed through the young woman, an obsessive feeling she has never had in her life—and is determined to make it perfect the second time around:

She had a kind of illusion that her life was allowed another chance through Miyŏn. Her own life, full of vanity, humiliation, disdain, and privation shouldn't be repeated in the life given the second time around. If the same disgrace and misery come upon her, she will again be crumbling and tearing apart such a precious second life granted to her. (p. 66)

So resolved, Chŏn Okhŭi tries to shield Miyŏn from the misdirected rage of a fellow female patient, a factory worker who had lost her arm at her workplace and who is bitter about the hospital's slighting of its charity patients. In this process of protecting her young protégée, Chŏn Okhŭi becomes exposed to the stark truths about her own horrifying and shocking personal situation: that she is a terminal lung-cancer case and that, without her consent, an autopsy is scheduled upon her death. This appalling revelation, however, prompts Chŏn Okhŭi to look at herself with no illusion from a "perspective of bidding final farewell to life, which makes the outside scenery truly beautiful" (p. 76). With her imminent death as an illuminator of her past, she succeeds in obtaining insights into the identity of death and life and makes peace with herself, as is revealed in her internal monologues:

Death is not something that happens instantly, but is an inherent component of life. So, human beings die minute by minute, and every instant might be a small fraction of death [. . . .] Confronting her approaching death, she felt as if she had gained wisdom.

Chŏn Okhŭi felt that she was now placed in the privileged state that death grants. Just as every fruit on a tree has its own kernel, it seemed as if everyone had his or her own different death. For her, who has lived her life pestering others shamelessly and inexcusably, the frame of her body, which was barely over five feet tall, was the whole content and the certainty of her life. Nothing beyond that mattered to her. But then, who knows whether in the beginning everyone had an equal share of everything? Ever since Chŏn Okhŭi stopped talking about her nonsensical hopes and plans, she began to look like a thoughtful person. It seemed as if wisdom, which had been squashed under the weight of her unscrupulousness, began to take back its old place little by little. (p. 76)

This newly salvaged wisdom, which allows Chŏn Okhŭi to see death as coterminous with life—an inevitable process within life itself— makes her recognize the value of life as a gift given to everyone equally and universally—except that she has squandered hers senselessly and disgracefully by masquerading her fake persona and unscrupulously imposing on others and selfishly demanding their goodwill. Such honest and open confrontation with and evaluation of her self and life provides Chŏn Okhŭi with personal growth and depth, which she had never experienced before.

As Chŏn Okhŭi takes a last look at life, she feels no more qualms about Miyŏn's affairs. Now that Chŏn Okhŭi has accepted the totality of life, she is convinced that her act of love, which was her greatest transgression, should be celebrated even though it had proved to be the ultimate ruin of her honor and happiness. In this light, Chŏn Okhŭi is persuaded that her life, with all its flaws, blemishes, and tragedy, is to be acknowledged as authentic and not to be lived otherwise and that her concern about Miyŏn is unwarranted and needs to be relinquished:

> She doesn't know whether Miyŏn has given her virginity to the young man. But that will happen eventually anyway; and granted that the climax of carnal desires and ecstasy is directly linked to a woman's destiny finally leading to autopsy, "love-making" should be a site of festival that confirms human sense of belonging, just as some poet has said.

> Chŏn Okhŭi acutely realized that, even if she were given another life, she would really be repeating the same stupidity and the same mistakes, and would have taken the same painful road. This was not an affirmation of life by justifying one's failures, but an awakening, which only a human being facing death could have. (p. 78)

This self-acceptance grants Chŏn Okhŭi a release from her botched, counterfeit past, leading her to graceful calm, unaffectedness, and peace she had never known before. Her ultimate act of self-affirmation translates into her figurative adoption of Miyŏn as her surrogate daughter, which bestows on herself a maternal role—a privilege long denied her:

> Chŏn Okhŭi shivered with an indescribable emotion. A soft voice naturally flowed out of her. With each word following the other like snow piling up quietly, she said:

> "Won't you mind me calling you by your name Miyŏn? My baby."

> Miyŏn, startled by these unexpected words, turned her head from looking at Changgyŏngwŏn Palace. A smile floated on Chŏn Okhŭi's face. (p. 78)

With this utterance on her last breath, Chŏn Okhŭi meets her death, having experienced redemption in her own way, albeit for a brief duration, of her life that had been a transparent fabrication and an empty show, full of self-deception, pretensions, loneliness, degradation, and rejection. By presenting this portrayal of a dying social pariah who comes to terms with her life and retrieves a measure of dignity, Hahn Moo-Sook legitimizes the validity and meaning of human existence, even in the most seemingly vulnerable, wretched, and marginalized cases.

Hahn's novel *Sŏngnyu namujip iyagi* is a fuller enunciation of the theme of the acceptance of the multi-dimensionality of life and human relationships and of the beauty and significance when such diversity, differences, and conflicts are allowed to coexist, serving as mutual complements and enhancing the value of one another. The novel is basically a gothic tale of betrayal set against the backdrop of a traditional-style Korean house. Infidelity, adultery, fraud, treachery, murder, and death, based on love triangles, are staged in this setting, further complicated by contention between traditional and nontraditional elements. Numerous characters and incidents related to this story line converge on the protagonist, Song Yŏngho—the U.S.-educated, thirty-two-year-old son of Korean expatriates in Hawaii and a recent arrival in Seoul as an aspiring president of a mining company. Placed at the center of this vortex, Song Yŏngho functions as a catalyst and, in the end, succeeds in bringing about reconciliation and healing among those around him. He accomplishes this feat through his decision to accept the cacophony of broken trust, guilt, and dishonor, and with a determination to build his future on the redeemed past of his elders and their traditions.

The only son of Korean parents who had immigrated to Hawaii after engaging in anti-Japanese resistance activities in China during Japanese colonial rule, Song arrives in Korea in May in the early 1960s motivated by a desire to serve Korea—the poverty-ridden land that his kindhearted, beautiful, and devout mother loved so much—"by exploring God's yet undiscovered gift to it."[34] His attempt to take root in this newly adopted country leads him to buy a house, a traditional Korean house (ninety-nine *kan*),[35] nicknamed "the house with pomegranate trees" because of these rare trees growing in the garden. Located in a dead-end alley, this house—"with no name-plate on its gate, with one of the fluorescent lights on the frame of the gate broken" (p. 12), and yet with an immaculately manicured garden accentuated by pomegranate trees[36]—serves as a metaphor for Korean traditional culture in disarray and fast vanishing. This household—a masterless old aristocratic family with its fortune in decline—consists of five specter-like residents: Chŏng Sŏnyŏng (the twenty-two-year-old daughter of the deceased owner of the house and a college student majoring in painting); Sŏnyŏng's aged, skeletal uncle (Ch'unggwŏn, her father's younger brother); her elderly grandmother; Pangkol Aunt (the cousin of Sŏnyŏng's father); and Chuksunkol Grandfather (a gardener who religiously tends the pomegranate trees).

After Song Yŏngho buys the house out of consideration for the financial difficulties of Sŏnyŏng's family, he lets them stay in the inner quarters (at least until his parents' upcoming visit), while taking up the outer section of the house facing the garden as his own living quarters. These two parts of the house are completely separated by a fence, connected only by a small gate that opens into the garden; there is virtually no direct communication between the two quarters.

Despite its imposing façade, beautiful garden, and intricate interior structure, the house is rumored to have been haunted even before it had been occupied by Sŏnyŏng's family. The house has been marred with eerie stories of two previous owners: scandals of adultery, suicide, bankruptcy, and deaths caused by fire. Sŏnyŏng's household has had its own share of tragedy there: the deaths of her mother, older brother Int'aek, and, most recently, her father, for whom Sŏnyŏng is still wearing mourning clothes. Sŏnyŏng, although attached to it, feels "the house is cursed and detestable and ought to be burned down" (p. 20). In this house, shrouded in death-like silence, the elderly Pangkol Aunt and Chuksunkol Grandfather dutifully carry on their work as its unfaltering stewards. Almost invisible, the aunt, who makes her existence known indirectly through her instructions to the maid, is the keeper of the internal and spiritual side of the culture and orchestrates behind the scenes family ceremonies, business matters, and even traditional foods, medicine, and clothes.

On the other hand, the tight-lipped elderly Chuksunkol Grandfather is a loyal custodian of the external and physical side of the high culture, as indicated by his selfless dedication to the care of the garden, especially the pomegranate trees which are emblematized in this story as the "trees of the Orient" (p. 169). Sheltered in this last stronghold of a dying elite Korean tradition, Sŏnyŏng alternately appears and disappears like a shadow. She is proud but self-effacing and aloof; elegant, reticent, possessing a suggestive beauty; and yet fragile and vulnerable, not unlike the pomegranate trees, which require painstaking care, protection, and attention—in short, she represents the epitome of Korean tradition at its most refined, delicate, and classical. Casting a dark shadow and complementing Sŏnyŏng as the product of the same culture, her aged, invalid uncle lives as a fossilized specimen of a deadening weight of the past.

Understandably, Song Yŏngho is struck by the impenetrable mystery surrounding the house and feels "a kind of superstitious premonition that deceptions will inevitably be disclosed in this house" (p. 26). As he tries to familiarize himself with his new environment, Yŏngho senses a gap between the two cultural worlds he has been exposed to: "the Hawaiian sun is multi-colored, whereas the sun he looks at in Korea is white" (p. 64). Nevertheless, gradually he is attracted toward the unapproachable, cold beauty of Sŏnyŏng, who resents the current living arrangements and even shows hostility toward Song Yŏngho whenever he is permitted to catch a glimpse of her. The haughtiness and strict ceremoniousness with which Sŏnyŏng's family treats him provokes in Song Yŏngho discomfort and a sense of dismay: "The groundless superiority and pride of these people, rotten to their bones in utterly rotten feudal ideas, made him sick in the stomach" (p. 71). The legal owner of the house, Song Yŏngho, feels like an outsider or even an intruder, convinced that he will never become its master just as his dream told him: "The owner of this house is somewhere else; don't hurry, he will come around the time when the pomegranates ripen" (p. 71).

Thus, the house, separated into two quarters, becomes the battleground for two conflicting cultures represented by Sŏnyŏng and Yŏngho, respectively: tradition-rooted patrician family vs. transplanted expatriates; bankrupt old gentry vs. new money and power; conventional, static, and conservative ethos vs. Western, enterprising, and venturesome mindset. As JaHyun Kim Haboush observed, "Song Yŏngho . . . seems to embody modernity and the future Korea while Sŏnyŏng . . . represents tradition and the past Korea."[37]

As the narrative unfolds, even more complicated relationships are revealed, involving a number of love triangles, breaches of faith, and victimization that affect the lives of its characters. Sŏnyŏng, the prim classical beauty, attracts Song Yŏngho, while she herself is attracted to Pak Ch'anggŭn, her brother's old friend and a man of numerous sordid love affairs. In the meantime, U Chaemin, Chuksunkol Grandfather's grandnephew and an orphaned son of a tenant farmer, yearns for Sŏnyŏng from afar due to his self-consciousness of class barriers between her and himself. U Chaemin is in turn pursued by Aeja, his next-door neighbor and a college junior majoring in painting, who proves to be an illegitimate daughter of Sŏnyŏng's father, Chŏng Ch'unghwi, and her mother, a *kisaeng* (a lower-class woman of entertainment). Furthermore, Pak Ch'anggŭn destroys the trust of Chŏng Ch'unghwi by having a clandestine relationship with his mistress, which sickens Int'aek and triggers his suicide, disguised as a mountain-climbing accident. In the end, Aeja's mother, herself a victim of financial fraud by her acquaintance, is killed in a car accident.

Among these entangled pairs, Sŏnyŏng and Aeja emerge as clearly drawn opposites. For instance, the group art exhibition, to which both Sŏnyŏng and Aeja submit their paintings, juxtaposes the two women and brings out their contrasting traits. Sŏnyŏng's purely abstract painting with a classical ambience about it sharply contrasts with Aeja's applied decorative art with practicality in mind. The reserved attitude of Sŏnyŏng, who waits for Pak Ch'anggŭn at the show, suffering in silence from his indifference to her, runs counter to Aeja's frank and assertive approach to Chaemin, even in disregard of his true feelings. The Sŏnyŏng/ Aeja polarity/double produces a remarkable effect when the secret of Aeja's parentage—she is Sŏnyŏng's half-sister, born two months later— are divulged. Their antithetical positionality is described as the contrast between "a white, noble, frail flower in a deserted garden ever growing emaciated with no one to take care of it," (p. 132) which symbolizes Sŏnyŏng, and "the weeds, which have been hidden in the shadow, growing in wild profusion with vitality once they have found their outlet," which stand for Aeja (p. 132).

Such antipodal characteristics between the two female characters are further highlighted when Aeja moves into the "pomegranate house" after her mother's death and is pitted against Sŏnyŏng. Aeja's unrestrained young voice rings out from the usually hushed house, whereas Sŏnyŏng keeps to her usual shadow-like self. While Sŏnyŏng determinedly attempts to drag her infirm uncle, Chŏng Ch'unggwŏn, from the garden and sunlight into the inner quarters, Aeja tries to take him out to the garden (p. 133). When Aeja finds a job as an interior decorator, Sŏnyŏng shuts herself up in the house, spending time looking at Western paintings and sketches. In all, the two women feature contrasting and opposing points of the narrative: formal aestheticism of tradition vs. informal pragmatism of the new age; conservatism vs. adventurism; self-destructive withdrawal to the past vs. the will to fashion the future;

maudlin, introverted sensibility vs. genial, common-sensical reasoning. And yet, as observed by Song Yŏngho, these two women, who represent polar differences, need to be accepted for who they are:

> Sŏnyŏng, respectably raised in the sunlight of a traditional household of long standing, somehow seemed to retain an elegant shadow, whereas, Aeja, who was brought up to be the so-called child of "shadow" as the daughter of a *kisaeng*, looked as if she were overcoming the strong sunlight shining upon her.

> This was a contrast between great but ordinary common sense that asks "one to live" and a narrow, lonely road, which demands "one to stand out." Facing these two, Song Yŏngho felt compelled to stand on the side of common sense, but at the same time, he clearly recognized himself helplessly longing for that lonely beauty. (p. 134)

As Song Yŏngho's adjustment to and even enjoyment of the traditional lifestyle of the "pomegranate house" progressively develops, his initial feelings of cultural obstruction and alienation recede. He now considers the pomegranate trees (Sŏnyŏng) more to his liking than the hibiscus of Hawaii (his American girlfriend, Beth) (p. 119). His acculturation to the things of Korea—Koreanization, so to speak—begins. In the meantime, Sŏnyŏng goes through her own form of cultural alteration, presented in her critical encounter with an American soldier who mistakes her for a prostitute. The immaculate cultural homogeneity and orthodoxy she represents is almost compromised in that incident, but its impact brings about Sŏnyŏng's outlook on human reality and contributes to expanding its scope and dimensions. In that perilous and pivotal moment, Sŏnyŏng intuits that women of the night who are engaged in the most profane, carnal transactions on the streets of Seoul also participate in the sacred, just like the Babylonian brides-to-be she read about in a book who dedicated to gods the money they got from selling their virginity the night before their wedding (p. 146). She comes to realize the arbitrariness and distortion, and even falsehood, embedded in inflexible categorizations and value-laden judgments of human activities and modes of thinking. After this eye-opening experience, Sŏnyŏng starts to come out into the garden and sits there, where the pomegranates begin to ripen—a signal that she has begun to free herself from negative caveats of old traditions and head for emotional balance and poise and even toward modern individuation. When Song Yŏngho locates Sŏnyŏng standing under the ripening pomegranate tree in her house, he confesses to himself his love for her (p. 155). The following observation by JaHyun Kim Haboush clarifies the significance of the personal evolution and transformation involving Song Yŏngho and Sŏnyŏng:

> Song Yŏngho and Sŏnyŏng must deal with their interior dualities. Yŏngho feels a certain absence and incompleteness; only by coming to Korea, buying a Korean house, and falling in love with Sŏnyŏng does he feel he has become whole [. . . .] Similarly, his love for Sŏnyŏng is also a longing to connect to, or even to repossess, the Korean past from which he has been severed. Sŏnyŏng on the other hand has to overcome an obsession with her past, represented by her infatuation with Pak Ch'anggŏn, her dead brother's friend, before she can accept Yŏngho and march toward the future.[38]

The dramatic disclosure of the secrets of Aeja's parentage and Pak Ch'anggŏn's affair with her mother further illustrates the confused and complicated mess of human relationships in the "pomegranate household." The philandering of Sŏnyŏng's father proves to be a betrayal to both Sŏnyŏng and Aeja and makes him a father figure acceptable to neither of them (p. 153). This long-hidden, conjugal deception and familial double-dealing, however, contributes to Song Yŏngho's deepening understanding of life's complexity and the need for accepting the seemingly less commendable facets of life and even acknowledging their positive sides, as his conversation with Chaemin and his subsequent musing reveal:

> "Human beings may finally acquire their true strength to resist the outer world by experiencing betrayal," said Yŏngho.
> Chaemin remained silent.

> "It's because we are all born of betrayals. Don't you think so? I think life will be eventually betrayed by death, and living always contains death," said Yŏngho (p. 154).

> Yŏngho continued in thought, "To be betrayed and to betray—maybe, human ties grow more resilient and stronger by such breach of faith," [. . .] and "the right way to live life perhaps lies in restarting from betrayal or transcending it" (p. 155).

Here, Yŏngho's interpretation of "betrayal" as one of the fundamental, inborn human conditions and his suggestion that the catastrophes resulting from such tragic inevitability be transformed into a trajectory for a better and more constructive life serves to prefigure a forthcoming monumental issue of betrayal involving his parents and even his own birth.

Sŏngnyu namujip iyagi comes to its climax and closure with a spectacular revelation of horrifying, ugly, and ultimate truths about the mysteries surrounding the "pomegranate house." This turning point occurs when Song Yŏngho's parents finally arrive from Hawaii at the house in late autumn after thirty-some years' absence from their homeland. Within a few days after the couple's arrival, Sŏnyŏng's uncle, the old, invalid Chŏng Ch'unggwŏn, is killed at night by a fire accidentally set during his wrestling with Song Yŏngho's father, Song Hosang, who attempts to murder the old man. This incident proves to be the result of another longstanding love triangle thus far hidden. It turns out that Chŏng Ch'unggwŏn's amnesia is the result of Japanese police torture caused by the betrayal of his dear friend and fellow anti-Japanese resistance freedom fighter, Song Kyŏngbin (who later changed his name to Song Hosang), who, out of desire to take Chŏng's sweetheart, Pak Hyeryŏn, as his wife, betrayed Chŏng to Japanese police in Shanghai. The fact that amnesiac Chŏng can often call out the name of Hyeryŏn, who eventually married Song Hosang, is rooted in this tragic past indelibly engraved in his memory. Song Hosang, stunned and panic-stricken by his totally unexpected confrontation with his tainted past in the ghostly figure of Chŏng, sets out to commit an even more heinous crime than his first and loses his life as well. Thus, just like Sŏnyŏng or even Aeja, Song Yŏngho is also a victim of his father's wrongheaded passion, judgment, and action. The "pomegranate house," a cursed house, has indeed lived up to its name, a space where moral corruption, depraved human desires, and misguided decisions were played out to their worst.

With the eventual gruesome death of Song Hosang from severe burns, the moral and spiritual chaos created by the older generation is cleared. On the ruins of this sinister, macabre, and degenerate heritage, which seemed to have required a purification by fire, Song Yŏngho is determined to build a new, euphonious future. His commitment is based on an open-minded and inclusive endorsement of life, accommodating the dissonance of friction, cruelty, and evil as well as good, truth, and harmony, as he proclaims to the survivors of the family calamity:

> I am going to rebuild a house on this burnt site. I would accept the evil will, if it still exists in this house. I have long been picturing a world

where evil and good coexist. Just like Noah's Ark, where together with human beings, all kinds of animals, fish, and seeds were included and waited for a new world, I am going to dedicate myself to this house and to this world. Don't you think that the existence of evil evidences the existence of happiness and goodness? God permitted both evil and good. I will affirm life by following such mysterious providence. I detest the word "fate," but it seems to me that living a truthful life means to get deeply hurt by that fate. (p. 196)

With this public statement of his all-encompassing and eclectic validation of life, Song Yŏngho also asserts his true ownership of the house—a symbolic claim of mastery over life—for the first time:

Up to now, strangely enough, I could not feel that I was the owner of this house. I have felt uneasy as if I were a boarder of this family. I thought it was because I didn't know my homeland well enough. But now I see that this house, called by the Manager Chŏn a "cursed house," was possessed by evil will, and I have vaguely submitted myself to it without clearly grasping its meaning. Now, I finally realize that I am the owner of this house. This realization does not come from the fact that I bought the house with my money. Rather, this stems from my consciousness that I own the house without being enslaved to it. (p. 197)

With the arrival of autumn, the pomegranates fully ripen, and the "pomegranate house," as foreshadowed in the beginning of the narrative, finally finds its authentic master in Song Yŏngho. He represents the healing and restorative power of an all-inclusive stance toward life in which conflictual forces and opposing positions are equally vouchsafed and find their proper place and significance.

In the concluding part of *Sŏngnyu namujip iyagi*, the love tension among the members of the younger generation involving Yŏngho, Sŏnyŏng, Chaemin, and Aeja stabilizes, as Chaemin becomes more sympathetic toward Aeja after learning about her parentage and background. With the exodus of Pak Ch'anggŭn from the narrative complication by his emigration to Brazil, which coincides with Song Yŏngho's proposal to Sŏnyŏng to share the house, the novel concludes the final pairing of Yŏngho/Sŏnyŏng and Chaemin/Aeja. This ending provides an appropriate and clean resolution of personal frictions among the contemporaries of Song Yŏngho's generation and a sense of equilibrium and symmetry to the narrative—a marked contrast to and difference from the twisted and unsettled personal networks of his parents. Most significantly, the anticipated marriage between Song

Yŏngho and Sŏnyŏng is symbolic of the coming of "modernity based on an acceptance of tradition and the unity between the past and future."[39]

Some critics register their impatience or complaints about Hahn Moo-Sook's perceived complacent anchoring in the realm of "personal/private art" rather than the pursuit of "literary activities with a sharp, social consciousness as a writer," and they characterize this orientation as a limitation in her literary achievement.[40] Other critics, however, point out that the strengths in Hahn Moo-Sook's works come from her comprehensive, ideological syncretism in which a variety of religious or philosophical forces form a felicitous harmony and coexist without mutual negation or rejection.[41] It has therefore been proposed that her works should be appraised as such, without being subjected to currently domineering, monolithic critical standards of realism or social engagement.[42]

Unquestionably, Hahn Moo-Sook's works discussed here eloquently exemplify the crux of her view of life as well as her literary vision. The distinguishing hallmark of the oeuvre of Hahn Moo-Sook is the acute awareness of the enduring presence and power of Korean traditional culture, which operates expressly in the lives of modern Koreans. In fact, a significant number of her works are poignant elegies dedicated to the passing of the exquisite and ageless beauty of Korean classical traditions.[43] In this sense, few Korean writers have surpassed Hahn's virtuosity in capturing and conveying the essence of orthodox Korean high culture. Still, her critical acumen saw the danger of the constricting and negative weight of tradition. Furthermore, she advocated the need for negotiating an opportune and active coalescence between the West and the East, tradition and change, past and present, and other such dichotomies, as she believed each of these entities would illuminate and often enhance, rather than cancel out, the other.[44] This striving for dialectical synthesis, quest for wholeness, and all-embracing appreciation of life epitomize the literary consciousness of Hahn Moo-Sook, who constantly found human life a mysterious and inexhaustible treasure-house for her literary exploration.

Notes

Unless otherwise noted, all works were published in Seoul.

1. The Japanese title of the novel is *Tomoshibi o motsu hito*. Because *Sinsidae* magazine folded soon after sponsoring the competition, Hahn's novel was never published; but recently Hahn's handwritten manuscript was unearthed in her family archive in Seoul and photocopy volumes were reproduced by Kaika Shobō (Japan,

Fukuokashi, 2000). As the daughter-in-law of an extended family, Hahn had to write the novel at night when everyone else was asleep. Regarding the difficult circumstances under which the work was written, see Hahn Moo-Sook, "Na ŭi mundan sasimnyŏn hoego" (Recollection of My Forty-Year Literary Career), in *Hahn Moo-Sook munhak chŏnjip* (Collected Works of Hahn Moo-Sook, hereafter, *Chŏnjip*) (Ŭllyu Munhwasa, 1993), 10: 278; also see a dialogue between Hahn Moo-Sook and the writer Han Mal-sook (Han Malsuk), her younger sister, "Uri nŭn han kil kajok," (We Are Family Members Traveling the Same Road), in *Chŏnjip* 10: 307.

2. These plays won competitions sponsored by Chosŏn Yŏn'gŭk Yŏn'guhoe (or Hyŏp'oe); see Hahn Moo-Sook, "Na ŭi mundan sasimnyŏn hoego" in ibid., 10: 278; also see Yi, "Han'guk," 288. Both these plays were lost during the Korean War, and the author herself reportedly did not have copies of these works; see Yi, "Han'guk."

3. See the remark made by Hong Yunsuk in a roundtable discussion by Korean modern women writers titled "Yŏryu munhak osimnyŏn ŭl hoegohanda" (Recollecting Fifty Years of Women's Literature), *Yŏryu munhak* (Women's Literature)1 (1968): 183. The first modern woman playwright in Korea was Sim Chaesun, wife of Yu Ch'ijin, who wrote "Chulhaengnang e sanŭn saramdŭl" (People Living in the Front Wing of the House, 1935), published in *Chosŏn ilbo* (Chosŏn Daily); see ibid.; also see Yi, "Han'guk," 566.

4. This event led to her introduction to major Korean writers such as Cho Yŏnhyŏn, Hong Hyomin, Ch'oe Chŏnghŭi, and others: See Hahn, "Na ŭi mundan sasimnyŏn hoego," *Chŏnjip*10: 280. The novel was serialized in *T'aeyang sinmun* (T'aeyang Newspaper; later to become *Han'guk ilbo* [Han'guk Daily]) in 1948 since *Kukche sinbo* was discontinued.

5. Her collected works, *Hahn Moo-Sook munhak chŏnjip*, were published in ten volumes by Ŭllyu Munhwasa in 1992–93.

6. During her career, Hahn produced five full-length novels, three novellas, thirty-seven short stories, and numerous critical articles and lectures/speeches. See Kang, "Hahn Moo-Sook," 173.

7. In 1926, when Hahn was eight years old, her painting was admitted to the World Children's Painting Exhibition held in Berlin; see Hahn, "Pulssi" (Kindling to Make a Fire), *Chŏnjip* 8: 19.

8. Hahn was a senior at Pusan Girls' High School when she contracted tuberculosis. (Hahn's family had been living in Seoul for generations, but her father's profession took them to Pusan, where she spent most of her growing years.) Her struggle with the illness lasted till 1940, which ended in her giving up her plans to enter college to major in painting—most possibly, at the Ueno Art School in Tokyo—for good; see Hahn, "Kŭl ŭl ssŭgi kkaji" (Until I Began Writing), *Chŏnjip* 9: 378. Her despair and frustration at the time is vividly described in her essay, "Pulssi," in *Chŏnjip* 8: 15–16.

9. See Hahn, "Na ŭi mundan sasimnyŏn hoego," in ibid., 10: 278. The novel began its serialization on 26 September 1935 in *Tonga ilbo*, and the illustrations were provided by the painter Yi Sangbŏm (Ch'ŏngjŏn, 1897–1972), one of the masters of the first generation of modern Korean painters. But, with the Japanese ban on the newspaper, the novel stopped sometime in 1936 after a year of serialization. Then with the resumption of the publication of the newspaper, the novel reappeared in the 1 November 1937 issue and this time, Hahn Moo-Sook was asked to draw the

illustrations. She worked on the project about three months until the novel ended with its 293rd installment on 7 February 1937. Thus, through her art, she had had early connections, however tangential, with the writer's world.

10. As a child, she was a zealous reader of Greek myths, Bible stories, *The 1001 Nights*, and Andersen's and the Grimm brothers' fairy tales; see Hahn, "Kŭrim e ŭi yŏlchŏng i munhak ŭro" (From Passion for Painting to Literature), *Chŏnjip* 9: 368.

11. See *Chŏnjip* 9: 369–70. Her only older brother, a college student in Tokyo at the time, was greatly influential in Hahn's development of interest in Western literature.

12. Ibid., 369.

13. Yu, "Sam," *Chŏnjip*, 6: 321.

14. In the long run, those early years of training and practice in art account for Hahn's exquisite esthetic consciousness and sensibility, demonstrated in her portrayals of characters (especially females) and in the strikingly detailed descriptions of settings in her short stories and novels. In some cases, her indulgence in such sketches becomes the cause of diversion or distraction, as they take on a life of their own beyond their direct relevance to the context in which they appear. Hahn's enduring passion for painting is well attested in her three personal art exhibitions held in 1976, 1985, and 1990, which also included paintings and calligraphy of her husband, Kim Jin-Heung (Kim Chinhŭng).

15. Hahn, "Na ŭi mundan sasimnyŏn hoego," *Chŏnjip* 10: 279–80. Hahn touched upon this personal situation in a number of her other essays and journal interviews; the following are representative, all included in Hahn's *Chŏnjip*: "Yŏngnan kkot hyanggi ka pŏnjinŭn ap'ŭm sok esŏ" (In the Midst of Pain Where the Fragrance of Orchids Pervades), 7: 67–70; "Kŭrim sonyŏ ŭi tokpaek i" (Monologue of a Girl Painter) 7: 71–72; "Tasi toragadŏrado" (Even if I Go Back Again), 7: 252–78; "Pulssi" (Kindling to Make a Fire) 8: 15–37; "Na ŭi munhak sŭsŭngdŭl" (My Literary Mentors), 8: 42–50; "Kŭrim e ŭi yŏlchŏng i munhak ŭro" (From Passion for Painting to Literature), 9: 367–71; "Kŭl ŭl ssŭgi kkaji"(Until I Began Writing), 9: 372–79; "Sam ŭi konoe sagiryŏ munhak t'aekhaetta" (I Chose Literature to Alleviate My Life's Agony), 9: 431–36; and "*Mannam, Yŏksa nŭn hŭrŭnda* ŭi chakka Han Musuk ssi: U Yŏngmi pyŏnjip wiwŏn kwaŭi taedam" (Hahn Moo-Sook, the Author of *Mannam* and *Yŏksa nŭn hŭrŭnda*: An Interview with the Editor, U Yŏngmi), 10: 321–27.

16. Hahn's marriage in 1940 at twenty-two, soon after her recovery from tuberculosis, was arranged between her father and her father-in-law (who were childhood school friends), much to her dismay and protest; see "Chŏnbo hanjang ŭro" (Because of a Telegram), *Chŏnjip* 7: 260–64. At this time, through the good offices of the writer Kim Malbong, Hahn had been offered an opportunity to go to England to study painting, sponsored by a British woman missionary stationed in Korea; see *Chŏnjip* 7: 259–60.

17. See Hahn, "Pulssi," *Chŏnjip* 8: 33.

18. Ibid.

19. See Hahn, "Sam," *Chŏnjip* 9: 435.

20. Ibid.

21. Hahn, "Pulssi," *Chŏnjip*, 8: 36. Hahn's husband was the sole, dedicated supporter of her creative writing at this time.

22. Hahn, "Na ŭi mundan sasimnyŏn hoego," *Chŏnjip* 10: 280.

23. Hahn, "Tasi toragadŏrado," *Chŏnjip* 7: 252.

24. Hahn, "Isop ŭi kkamagwi" (Aesop's Crow), *Chŏnjip* 7: 117.

25. Ibid.
26. Hahn, "Tasi toragadŏrado," *Chŏnjip* 7: 252.
27. Hong, "Kyunhyŏng," 33.
28. Ibid., 73.
29. Ibid., 74.
30. Hahn, "Urisai modŭn kŏsi" (Everything Between Us), *Chŏnjip* 6: 42.
31. Hahn says that the title of this short story was a line from Rainer Maria Rilke's poem, "A Letter to a Young Poet"; see "Na ŭi mundan sasimnyŏn hoego," *Chŏnjip*, 10: 282.
32. "Wŏrun" (The Halo Around the Moon), *Chŏnjip* 6: 232.
33. "Chu'kche wa unmyŏng ŭi changso" (The Site of Festival and Fate), *Chŏnjip* 6: 65–66.
34. See *Chŏnjip* 4: 105.
35. One *kan* equals thirty-six square feet. During the Yi dynasty (1392–1910), the government made the ninety-nine-*kan* house the largest sized that could be owned by non-royal members of the kingdom.
36. The descriptions of the house and the garden in this novel are concrete examples of Hahn Moo-Sook's virtuosity in the art of background sketches.
37. Comments made by JaHyun Kim Haboush on my paper at the 1998 Hahn Moo-Sook Colloquium in the Korean Humanities, The George Washington University, Washington, D.C., 24–25 October 1998. I am indebted to Professor Haboush's insightful analysis, which helped me in further elaborating my study.
38. Ibid.
39. Ibid.
40. Chŏng, "Hahn Moo-Sook," 87.
41. Hong, "Kyunhyŏng," 74.
42. Ibid., 72.
43. Some of Hahn's representative works in this category include: *Yŏksa nŭn hŭrŭnda* (History Flows), "Yusuam" (The Hermitage of Running Water, 1963), "Isajong ŭi anae" (Isajong's Wife, 1978), "Saeng'in son" (The Sore Finger, 1981), "Songgot" (A Drill, 1982), and *Mannam* (Encounter, 1986).
44. Don Baker, commenting on my paper, first observed the influence on Hahn of the "yin-yang philosophy of complementary opposites, which has prevailed in China and Korea for centuries." From this perspective, Baker identified Hahn's distinguishing concerns in her works as follows: "Hahn's stories are filled with hints of yin and yang, the mutually generating binary dyads of Neo-Confucianism. That is why it would not be misleading to call her a Confucian writer. In line with Hahn's embrace of intertwined opposites, it would be appropriate to describe her as a Catholic Confucian writer." Don Baker's comment, presented at the 1998 Hahn Moo-Sook Colloquium in the Korean Humanities, The George Washington University, Washington, D.C., 24–25 October 1998.

References

Unless otherwise noted, all were published in Seoul.
Chŏng Chaewŏn. "Hahn Moo-Sook tanp'yŏn sosŏl yŏn'gu" (On Hahn Moo-Sook's Short Stories). Master's thesis, Yonsei University, 1994.

Hahn Moo-Sook. "Chŏnbo hanjang ŭro" (Because of a Telegram). In *Hahn Moo-Sook munhak chŏnjip* (Collected Works of Hahn Moo-Sook; hereafter, *Chŏnjip*) (Ŭllyu Munhwasa, 1993), 7: 257–64.

———. "Ch'ukche wa unmyŏng ŭi changso" (The Site of Festival and Fate). *Chŏnjip* 6: 43–79.

———. "Isajong ŭi anae" (Isajong's Wife). *Chŏnjip* 6: 269–88.

———. "Isop ŭi kkamagwi" (Aesop's Crow). *Chŏnjip* 7: 115–17.

———. "Kŭl ŭl ssŭgi kkaji" (Until I Began Writing). *Chŏnjip* 9: 372–79.

———. "Kŭrim e ŭi yŏlchŏng i munha kŭro" (From Passion for Painting to Literature). *Chŏnjip* 9: 367–71.

———. "Kŭrim sonyŏ ŭi tokpaek i" (Monologue of a Girl Painter). *Chŏnjip* 7: 71–72.

———. *Mannam* (Encounter). *Chŏnjip* 3.

———. "Na ŭi mundan sasimnyŏn hoego" (Recollection of My Forty-Year Literary Career). *Chŏnjip*10: 278–86.

———. "Na ŭi munhak sŭsŭngdŭl" (My Literary Mentors). *Chŏnjip* 8: 42–50.

———. "Pulssi" (Kindling to Make a Fire). *Chŏnjip* 8: 15–37.

———. "Sam ŭi konoe sagiryŏ munhak t'aekhaetta" (I Chose Literature to Alleviate My Life's Agony). *Chŏnjip* 9: 431–36.

———. "Saeng'in son" (The Sore Finger, 1981). *Chŏnjip* 6: 289–315.

———. "Songgot" (A Drill, 1982). *Chŏnjip* 9: 293–318.

———. *Sŏngnyu namujip iyagi* (The Tale of the House with Pomegranate Trees). *Chŏnjip* 4: 11–198.

———. "Tasi toragadŏrado" (Even if I Go Back Again). *Chŏnjip* 7: 252–78.

———. "Urisai modŭn kŏsi" (Everything Between Us). *Chŏnjip* 6: 11–42.

———. "Wŏrun" (The Halo Around the Moon). *Chŏnjip* 6: 228–40.

———. *Yŏksa nŭn hŭrŭnda* (History Flows).*Chŏnjip* 1.

———. "Yŏngnan kkot hyanggi ka pŏnjinŭn ap'ŭm sok esŏ" (In the Midst of Pain Where the Fragrance of Orchids Pervades). *Chŏnjip* 7: 67–70.

———. "Yusuam" (The Hermitage of Running Water). *Chŏnjip* 4: 199–257.

Hahn Moo-Sook and Han Malsook (Han Malsuk)."Uri nŭn han kil kajok" (We Are Family Members Traveling the Same Road." *Chŏnjip* 10: 304–11.

Hahn Moo-Sook munhak chŏnjip (Collected Works of Hahn Moo-Sook). 10 vols. Ŭllyu Munhwasa, 1993.

Hong Kisam. "Kyunhyŏng kwa chohwa ŭi wŏlli—Hahn Moo-Sook munhak ŭi munhaksajŏk ŭimi" (Principles of Balance and Harmony—Literary and Historical Significance of Hahn Moo-Sook's Literature). In *Hahn Moo-Sook munhak yŏn'gu* (On Hahn Moo-Sook's Literature), edited by Hahn Moo-Sook Foundation. Ŭllyu Munhwasa, 1996, pp. 32–74.

Kang Nan'gyŏng. "Hahn Moo-Sook yŏn'gu" (A Study of Hahn Moo-Sook). In ibid, pp. 173–333.

Kim Yung-Hee. "Hahn Moo-Sook." In Jane Eldridge Miller, ed., *Who's Who in Contemporary Women's Writing*. London: Routledge, 2001, p. 133.

"*Mannam, Yŏksa nŭn hŭrŭnda* ŭi chakka Han Musuk ssi—U Yŏngmi pyŏnjip wiwŏn kwaŭi taedam" (Hahn Moo-Sook, the Author of *Mannam, Yŏksa nŭn hŭrŭnda*: An Interview with the Editor, U Yŏngmi). *Chŏnjip* 10: 321–27.

Yi Inbok. "Han'guk yŏsŏng ŭi saengsa kwan kwa sun'gyŏl ŭisik—Hahn Moo-Sook ŭi tanp'yŏn sosŏl ŭl chungsim ŭro hayŏ" (Korean Women's View of Life and

Death and Consciousness of Purity—Focusing on Hahn Moo-Sook's Short Stories), *Asea Yŏsŏng Yŏn'gu* (Studies on Asian Women) 17 (1978): 285–304.

"Yŏryu munhak osimnyŏn ŭl hoegohanda" (Recollecting Fifty Years of Women's Literature), *Yŏryu munhak* (Women's Literature) 1 (1968): 174–84.

Yu Chongho. "Sam ŭi chinsil kwa sŭlp'ŭm" (Truths and Sorrows of Life). In *Hahn Moo-Sook munhak chŏnjip* 6: 319–33.

Yu Minyŏng. *Han'guk hyŏndae hŭigoksa* (History of Modern Korean Drama). Hongsŏngsa, 1982.

Glossary

Place Names, Bibliographical and General Terms

Akchang kasa 악장가사 (樂章歌詞) 16th c.? *Anthology of Music.*

Andong 안동 (安東) A county and city in the Kyŏngsang Province.

Andong chach'ŏng 안동자청 (安東紫靑) Crimson and Blue Colors.

chaae 자애 (慈愛) Merciful love/benevolence.

Chat'an ka 자탄가 (自歎歌) "Song of Laments."

chemun 제문 (祭文) Funeral oration.

Chikchisa 직지사 (直指寺) Chikchi Temple.

Chogak po 조각보 (chogak = small segment) Patchwork *pojagi.*

Chogyejong 조계종 (曹溪宗) The largest Buddhist sect in South Korea.

Ch'ohan ka 초한가 (楚漢歌) "Song about Chu and Han."

ch'ŏn po 천보 (ch'ŏn = fabric) *pojagi* for fabrics.

Ch'ŏngju Han 청주한 (淸州韓) Prominent aristocratic descent group
of late Koryŏ and early Chosŏn.

chŏngp'yo 정표 (旌表) State recognition of persons exemplifying
cardinal Confucian virtues, usually by erecting honorary gate in
front of their homes.

chŏngsa 정사 (正史) Official dynastic history.

Chŏngsok Ŏnhae 정속언해 (正俗諺解) Korean language
translation of Yuan dynasty morals handbook, Zhengsu;
translated and published by Kim An'guk 김안국 (金安國)
in 1518.

Ch'ŏnjŏn 천전 (川前) village near Andong, Kyŏngsang Province.

Chosŏn 조선 (朝鮮) Korean dynasty (1392-1910).

Chosŏn ilbo 조선일보 (朝鮮日報) Chosŏn Daily Newspaper.

Chosŏn kŏn'guk ka 조선건국가 (朝鮮建國歌) "Song of Establishing
the Chosŏn state."

Chosŏn yŏn'gŭk yŏn'guhoe/hyŏphoe 조선연극연구회/협회
(朝鮮演劇研究會/協會) Established in 1940. Association for
the Study of Korean Drama.

Chu 楚 Chinese state of the Spring and Autumn and Warring States
periods.

Chuja kahun (C. Zhuzi jiaxun, Family Precepts of Master Chu)
주자가훈 (朱子家訓).

Ch'unch'ŏn 춘천 (春川) A town in Kangwŏn Province.

Chŭngbo munhŏn pigo (Revised Reference Compilation of Documents
on Korea) 증보문헌비고 (增補文獻備考).

dexing 德性 Moral nature.

Haebang ka 해방가 (解放歌) "Song of Liberation."

Haedong manhwa 해동만화 (海東漫話) "A Talk about the Land in the
East of the Sea."

Haenam 해남 (海南) A town on southwestern coast of Korea.

haengja 행자 (行者) A postulant.

Hahoe 하회 (河回) A village near Andong, Kyŏngsang Province.

Han 漢 [K. Han (한)] Chinese dynasty (B.C.E. 206-C.E. 220).

Han'guk ilbo 한국일보 (韓國日報) Korean Daily Newspaper (1954 to
the present).

han'gŭl 한글 The Korean alphabet; see *Hunmin chŏng'ŭm.*

Hanjung mallok 한중만록 See Chapter 6.

Hanjungnok 한중록 (閑中錄) See Chapter 6.

hansi 한시 (漢詩) Korean poem in classical Chinese that follows all the
rules of Chinese versification.

Han'yang ka 한양가 (漢陽歌) "Song of Metropolis."

hot po (*hot* = single) [pron. *hoppo*] 홋보 Unlined *pojagi.*

huanghu 황후 (皇后) Empress.

hun'gu 훈구 (勳舊) "Meritorious subjects": Powerful group of officials
made up largely of merit subjects and their descendents in late
fifteenth and early sixteenth century Chosŏn.

Hunmin chŏng'ŭm 훈민정음 (訓民正音) Correct Sounds for Educating
the People: Korean phonetic writing system invented in the 15th
century, also known as *Ŏnmun*; Now generally known as
han'gŭl.

hwajŏn 화전 (花煎) Flower cake.

Hwajŏn ka 화전가 (花煎歌) "Songs of Enjoying Flowers."

hwanggŭm po 황금보 (*hwanggŭm* = painted gold) Gold-painted *pojagi.*

Hwanhŭidae 환희대 (歡喜臺) Hall of Ecstasy.

hyobu 효부 (孝婦) Filial daughter-in-law.

hyŏn'gŭm See *kŏmun'go.*

ibul po 이불보 (*ibul* = bedding) *pojagi* for bedding.

ilch'ehwa 일체화 (一體化) Becoming one with the universe [Buddhist].

Imha 임하 (臨河) Village near Andong, Kyŏngsang Province.

ipsan 입산 (入山) Entering the Buddhist order [Lit. entering the mountain].

Iryun haengsil to 이륜행실도 (二倫行實圖) Illustrated Examples of Relations between Elder and Younger and between Friends; morals handbook published by Kim An'guk in 1518.

junzi 君子 [K. kunja (군자)] Superior man.

kasa 가사 (歌辭) Literary genre.

kayagŭm 가야금 (伽倻琴) A Korean twelve-stringed zither.

kayo 가요 (歌謠) Literary genre.

kirŏgi po 기러기보 (*kirŏgi* = goose) *pojagi* for wedding geese.

kisaeng 기생 (妓生) Professional (beauty) entertainers, who traditionally had skills in performing arts, games, and poetry.

Kohŭng Yu ssi 고흥유씨 (高興柳氏) Family Yu from Kohŭng.

kŏmun'go 거문고 [Also called *hyŏn'gŭm* 현금 (玄琴) and *hyŏnhakkum* 현학금 (玄鶴琴)] A long, six-stringed zither originating from the Koguryŏ dynasty (37 BC-668).

Kukche sinbo 국제신보 (國際新報) International Newspaper. Published in Pusan in 1947 to become the leading regional newspaper, but was absorbed into *Pusan ilbo* (Pusan Daily) in 1980.

kŭmbak po 금박보 (*kŭmbak* = pressed gold) Gold-decorated *pojagi.*

Kŭmgye 금계 (金溪) Village near Andong, Kyŏngsang Province.

Kwandong pyŏlgok 관동별곡 (關東別曲) A *kasa* by Chŏng Ch'ŏl, 1580.

kwiŭi 귀의 (歸依) Conversion (to Buddhism)/ return to reliance.

kwŏn 권 (卷) Volume.

Kyenyŏ ka 계녀가 (誡女歌) "Song of Admonitions for Women."

Kyohun ka 교훈가 (敎訓歌) "Song of Edification."

Kyŏnggye ka 경계가 (警誡歌) "Song of Admonitions."

Kyŏngju 경주 (慶州) The ancient capital of Silla kingdom.

Kyŏngminp'yŏn 경민편 (警民編) "Warning the People"; morals handbook published by Kim Chŏngguk (金定國) in 1519.

Kyonyŏ ka 교녀가 (敎女歌) "Song of Instructing Women."

Kyonyŏ sa 교녀사 (敎女詞) "Song of Instructing Women."

kyŏp po 겹보 (*kyŏp* = double) Lined *pojagi*.

Kyubang kasa 규방가사 (閨房歌辭) "Kasa of the Inner Rooms."

Kyujung haengsil ka 규중행실가 (閨中行實歌) "Song of Moral Conduct in the Inner Rooms."

Kyujung kado 규중가도 (閨中歌道) "Songs of the Inner Rooms."

kyujung kasa 규중가사 (閨中歌辭) "Kasa of the Inner Rooms."

Kyujung yoram 규중요람 (閨中要覽) "Manual of the Inner Rooms."

lienü 烈女 [K. yŏllyŏ (열녀)] Virtuous woman. See yŏllyŏ.

Lienü chuan 烈女傳 [K. Yŏllyŏ chŏn (열녀전)] Five Biographies of Faithful Women; morals handbook from Han dynasty.

Liji 禮記 [K. yegi (예기)] Book of Rites.

Manjŏnch'un 만전춘 (漫殿春) "Spring Pervades the Pavilion," a Koryŏ song.

Miam ilgich'o 미암일기초 (眉巖日記草) Diary written by Yu Hŭich'un 유희춘 (柳希春), 1513-1577.

Millim 밀림 (密林) (Dense Forest) (September 1935-December 1938, serialized in *Tong'a ilbo*). A novel by female writer Kim Malbong (1901-1962).

Ming 明 [K. myŏng (명)] Chinese dynasty (1368-1662).

Mingxin (明鑑) [K. *Myŏnggam* (명감)] [= *Mingxin baojian*].

Mingxin baojian 명심보감 (明心寶鑑) [K. *myŏngsim pogam* (명심보감)] (Precious Mirror for Illuminating the Mind); Confucian morals primer believed to have been compiled in 14th century.

mua 무아 (無我) (Buddhist) Selflessness.

Myŏnggam 명감 (明鑑) [Ch. *Mingxin*].

Myŏngsim pogam 명심보감 (明心寶鑑) [Ch. *Mingxin baojian*].

Naebang kasa 내방가사 (內房歌辭) Kasa of the Inner Rooms.

Naegan 내간 (內簡) Private letter.

Naehun 내훈 (內訓) (Instructions for Women); morals handbook compiled by Queen Sohye. See Chapter 2.

naejo 내조 (內助) Help women provide their husbands.

namjon yŏbi 남존여비 (男尊女卑) Lit. "elevation of man and subjection of woman."

Namyang Hong 남양홍 (南陽洪) Prominent aristocratic descent group of late Koryŏ and early Chosŏn.

Neixun 內訓 Instructions for Women; morals handbook compiled by Ming empress Wen.

Neize 內則 [K. Naech'ik (내칙)] Chapter from the *Liji*.

norigae po 노리개보 (*norigae* = ornament) *pojagi* for ornaments.

nubi po 누비보 (*nubi* = quilt) Quilted *pojagi*.

Nüjiao 女教 [K. Yŏgyo (여교)] Teachings for Women; Chinese moral handbook.

Ŏnmun 언문 (諺文) "Vernacular Script"; Another name for the Korean alphabet.

Ŏnmun samgang haengsil to yŏllyŏdo 언문삼강행실도열녀도 (諺文三綱行實圖烈女圖) Vernacular Illustrations of Faithful Women from Illustrated Exemplars of the Three Bonds; published in 1481.

Onyang 온양 (溫陽) Hot springs in west central Korea.

ot po (*ot* = clothing) [pronounced *oppo*] *pojagi* for clothing.

Ŏu yadam 어우야담 (於于野談) *Ŏu's Unofficial Accounts* (1621) by Yu Mong'in 유몽인 (柳夢寅) 1559-1623.

P'aegwan chapki 패관잡기 (稗官雜記) *The Storyteller's Miscellany* by Ŏ Sukkwŏn 어숙권 (魚叔權) 1525-1554.

Paekche 백제 (百濟) Korean kingdom (?-660).

pagae 박애 (博愛) Benevolence/ philanthrophy.

P'alsŏndae 팔선대 (八仙臺) Eight Fairies Rock.

P'apy'ŏng Yun 파평윤 (坡平尹) Prominent aristocratic descent group of the late Koryŏ and early Chosŏn.

p'iri 피리 Korean flute.

pojagi 보자기 Korean wrapping cloths.

Poksŏn hwaŭm ka 복선화음가 (福善禍淫歌) "Song of Blessing, Virtue, Calamity, and Indecency."

pona 본아 (本我) True Self.

Pop'o rok 보포록 (寶布錄) The records of the words of Buddhism.

p'ungryu (Ch. Fengliu) 풍류 (風流) Carefree, aesthetic style of life, transcending the stock emotional response. Almost always associated with poetry, music, wine and female (*kisaeng*) company.

p'yŏngae 평애 (平愛) Equal love.

P'yŏngyang 평양 (平壤) Ancient capital of Koguryŏ and the current capital of North Korea.

Quli 曲禮 [K. *Kongnye* (곡례)] Chapter from the *Liji*.

Samgang haengsil to 삼강행실도 (三綱行實圖) Illustrated Exemplars of the Three Bonds; morals handbook published in 1431.

samjong 삼종 (三從) "Three Obediences (for a woman)."

sang po 상보 (*sang* = food table) *pojagi* for the food table.

sarim 사림 (士林) (Confucian scholars in seclusion) A group of morally high-minded scholars in late fifteenth and sixteenth century Chosŏn.

seja pin 세자빈 (世子嬪) Crown prince's consort.

sijo 시조 (時調) Traditional Korean short-form poetry.

Sillok 실록 (實錄) See Chosŏn wangjo sillok *Veritable Records of the Chosŏn dynasty.*

Sinsidae 신시대 (新時代) (*New Age*; 1941-1944) A monthly magazine of general cultural interest published in Seoul.

Sirhak 실학 (實學) Practical Learning.

soa 소아 (小我) Lesser/small self.

Sohak [Ch. Xiaoxue] 소학 (小學) *Lesser/Minor Learning.*

Sok samgang haengsilto 속삼강행실도 (續三綱行實圖) Continued Illustrated Examplars of the Three Bonds; morals handbook published in 1514.

Sŏkpyŏl ka 석별가 (惜別歌) "Song of Painful Parting."

som po 솜보 (*som* = cotton) *pojagi* padded with cotton.

Sŏn (Skt. Dhyana, Ch. Chan, Ja. Zen) 선 (禪) Buddhist sect.

Song　宋　[K. Song (송)]　Chinese dynasty (960-1279).

Sŏngho sasŏl 성 호 사 설 (星湖塞說)　*Collected Essays of Sŏngho* (Yi Ik), 1579-1624.

Sŏngju 성 주 (星州)　County and city in Kyŏngsang Province.

sŏnsa 선 사 (禪師)　Sŏn (Buddhist) master.

sosŏl 소 설 (小說)　Narrative/novel.

sŏwŏn 서 원 (書院)　Private academy.

Ssangbyŏk ka 쌍 벽 가 (雙璧歌)　"Song of a Pair of Jade Discs."

su po 수 보 (繡褓) (*su* = embroidery)　Embroidered *pojagi*.

Sŭngjŏngwŏn 승 정 원 (承政院)　Royal Secretariat.

Sŭngjŏngwŏn ilgi　승 정 원 일 기 (承政院日記)　Diary of the Royal Secretariat: 3047 books covering the years of 1624-1894 are extant.

sŭnim 스 님　Honorable monk.

taea 대 아 (大我)　Greater Self.

T'aep'yŏng hwajŏn ka 태 평 화 전 가 (泰平花煎歌)　"Song of Enjoying Flowers in a Time of Great Peace."

taewang taebi 대 왕 대 비 (大王大妃)　Grand queen dowager; primary consort of deceased king.

taewŏn 대 원 (大願)　Great Wish.

T'aeyang sinmun 태 양 신 문 (太陽新聞) (Sun Times) A newspaper published in Seoul in 1949; later taken over by *Han'guk ilbo* on June 8, 1954.

tangch'ae po 당 채 보 (唐彩褓) [*Tangch'ae* = Tang colors] Painted *pojagi*.

tŏksŏng 덕 성 [Ch. Dexing (德性)]　Moral nature.

Tomoshibi o motsu onna 灯 を 持 つ 女　*A Woman Holding a Lantern.* First novel by Hahn Moo-Sook.

Tonga ilbo 동 아 일 보 (東亞日報)　Tonga Daily Newspaper (1920-1940; 1945 to the present).

Tongguk sinsok samgang haengsilto 동 국 신 속 삼 강 행 실 도 (東國新續三綱行實圖) New Continued Exemplars of the Three Bonds in Korea; morals handbook published in 1614.

Tongnip ka 독 립 가 (獨立歌)　"Song of Independence" by Tosan 도 산 (陶山).

Tosan 도산 (陶山) Village near Andong, Kyŏngsang Province.

turumari 두루마리 Scroll.

ŭnsa 은사 (恩師) Mentor.

wangbi 왕비 (王妃) Royal consort.

wanghu 왕후 (王后) Deceased queen.

Wei 衛 Chinese state of Spring and Autumn period.

wŏnsang 원상 (院相) High officials advising Queen Chŏnghŭi during her regency

Xiaoxue [K. Sohak (소학)] (小學) *Lesser Minor Learning*; basic Confucian morals primer complied by Zhu Xi in 1189.

Xiaoyi 小儀 Chapter from the *Liji*.

yadam 야담 (野談) Unofficial version of historical tale.

yangban 양반 (兩班) Socio-political elite status group.

Yangban kasa (Nobleman's kasa) 양반가사 (兩班歌辭).

Yean 예안 (禮安) Now Tosan, a district in Kyŏngsang Province.

yedan po 예단보 (禮緞褓) (*yedan* = ceremonial silk) *pojagi* for gifts from the bride's family.

yemul po 예물보 (禮物褓) (*yemul* = ceremonial objects)—*pojagi* for gifts from the bridegroom's family.

Yŏch'ik 여칙 (女則) (Rules of Conduct for Women).

Yŏgyo 여교 (女敎) See *Nüjiao*.

Yŏktae ka 역대가 (歷代歌) "Song of Successive Dynasties."

yŏllyŏ 열녀 (烈女) Faithful (virtuous) woman.

Yŏllyŏ chŏn 열녀전 (烈女傳) Morals handbook from Han dynasty depicting faithful women. See *Lienü chuan*.

Yŏn'an Yi ssi 연안이씨 (延安李氏) Family Yi from Yŏn'an.

yong 용 (用) Function; second part of Neo-Taoist/Confucian pairing of tiyong (體用 essence and function) [K. ch'eyong (체용)].

Yŏngnam 영남 (嶺南) The region of southeastern Korea.

Yŏngjo sillok 영조실록 (英祖實錄) Veritable records of King Yŏngjo.

Yŏsi 여시 (如是) *As Is*, a literary magazine.

Yŏson hunsa ko 여손훈사고 (女孫訓辭考) Instructions to the Grand-Daughter.

Yuan 元 [K. Wŏn (원)] Mongol dynasty in China (1260-1368).

yulsi 율시 (律詩) (Ch. lüshi) Regulated verse, a strict verse form that developed in Tang China.

Zheng 鄭 [K. Chŏng (정)] Chinese state of the Spring and Autumn period.

Zhou 周 [K. Chu (주)] Chinese dynasty (B.C.E. 1134-250).

Names

An Ch'angho 안창호 (安昌浩) 1878-1938. See Tosan.

Ansun (queen) 안순왕후 (安順王后) (?-1492) Primary consort of King Yejong, daughter of Han Paengnyun.

Changsun (queen) 장순왕후 (章順王后) (1445-1461) Consort of King Yejong, daughter of Han Myŏnghoe.

Chasan (prince) 자산군 (者山君) Title for king Sŏngjong before he became crown prince.

Cheng Yi (1033-1107) 程頤 A Song dynasty philosopher.

Chengzu 成祖 (r. 1403-1424) Ming emperor (r. 1403-1424).

Chini 진이 (眞伊) [= Hwang Chini 황진이 (黃眞伊)]

Chinul 지눌 (知訥) (1158-1210) An eminent Koryŏ monk.

Ch'oe Ch'iwŏn 최치원 (崔致遠) (857-?) Famed Silla scholar-poet.

Ch'ŏlchong (king) 철종왕(哲宗王) r. 1849-1863.

Chŏng Ch'ŏl 정철 (鄭澈) (1536-1593) Official and famed poet.

Chŏnghŭi (queen) 정희왕후(貞熹 王后) (1418-1483) Primary consort of King Sejo; acted as regent for youthful King Sŏngjong.

Chŏngjo (king) 정조 (正祖) r. 1777-1800.

Ch'ŏngsŏn 청선(淸璿) Prince Sado's second daughter born of Lady Hyegyŏng.

Chŏngsŏng (queen) 정성왕후 (貞聖王后) Yŏngjo's first legal wife.

Chŏngsun (queen) 정순왕후(貞順王后) (1745-1805) Consort of King Yŏngjo; acted as regent for youthful King Sunjo.

Ch'ŏngyŏn 청연 (淸衍) Prince Sado's first daughter born of Lady Hyegyŏng.

Deng (empress) 鄧 (皇后) Consort of Han dynasty emperor Hedi (和帝 r. 88-105).

Du Fu (712-770) 杜甫 A Tang poet.

Fanji 樊姬 Wife of King Zhuang.

Gao (empress) 高 (皇后) (d. 1382) Consort of Ming emperor Taizu.

Hahn Moo-Sook / Han Musuk 한무숙 (韓戊淑) (1918-1993). See
 Chapter 10.

Han Ch'ihyŏng 한치형 (韓致亨) 1434-1502.

Han Ch'iin 한치인 (韓致仁) 1421-1477.

Han Ch'irye 한치례 (韓致禮) ?-1499.

Han Ch'iŭi 한치의 (韓致義) 1440-1473 .

Han Hwak 한확 (韓確) 1403-1456.

Han Mahlsook/ Han Malsuk 한말숙 (韓末淑) (1931-) A novelist and
 Hahn Moo-Sook's younger sister.

Han Myŏnghoe 한명회 (韓明會) 1415-1487.

Han Myŏngjin 한명진 (韓明縉) ?-1454.

Han Paengnyun 한백륜 (韓伯倫) 1427-1474.

Han Yongun 한용운 (韓龍雲) 1879-1944.   Famed independence
 activist and Buddhist monk and writer/poet of early 20th century
 Korea.

Hideyoshi. See Toyotomi.

Hŏ Kyun 허균 (許筠) 1569-1618. See Chapter 4.

Hŏ Nansŏrhŏn 허난설헌 (許蘭雪軒). See Chapter 4.

Hŏ Yŏp 허엽 (許曄). See Chapter 4.

Hŏndŏk (king) 헌덕왕 (憲德王), r. 809-826 (Silla).

Hong Kyŏngson 홍경손 (洪敬孫) 1409-1481. See Chapter 6.

Hong Nagim 홍낙임 (洪樂任). See Chapter 6.

Hong Ponghan 홍봉한 (洪鳳漢). See Chapter 6.

Hong Ŭng 홍응 (洪應) 1428-1492.

Hŏnjong (king) 헌종 (憲宗) r. 1834-1849.

Hwadam 화담 (花潭) pen name of Sŏ Kyŏngdŏk. See Chapter 5.

Hwang Chini 황진이 (黃眞伊) See Chapter 5.

Hyegyŏng[gung Hongssi] 혜경[궁홍씨] (惠慶[宮 洪氏]) Lady Hong
 of the Hyegyŏng Palace. See Chapter 6.

Hyojang 효장 (孝章) (prince) [=진종 (眞宗)] King Yŏngjo's son,
 1719-1728.

Hyujŏng 휴정 (休靜) 1520-1600. Buddhist monk noted for his
     scholarship and his leadership of an army of monks at the time
     of Toyotomi Hideyoshi's invasion of 1592. Also known as Sŏsan
     taesa.

Insu 인수 (仁粹) Early title for Queen Sohye.

Insun (queen) 인순왕후 (仁順 王后) 1532-1575 Regent for youthful
     King Sŏnjo.

Inwŏn (queen) 인원 (仁元) Sukchong's third legal wife.

Kim Iryŏp 김일엽 (金一葉) [Original name, Kim Wŏnju 김원주
     (金元周)] 1896-1971. See Chapter 9.

Konghye (queen) 공혜왕후 (恭惠王后) (1456-1474) Consort of King
     Sŏngjong.

Kongmin (king) 공민왕 (恭愍王) r. 1351-1374.

Kwŏn Yŏngch'ŏl 권영철 (權寧徹) See Chapter 7.

Li Bai (701-762) 李白 A Tang poet.

Munjong (king) 문종 (文宗) r. 1450-1452.

Munjŏng (queen) 문정왕후 (文定王后) (1501-1565) Regent for
     youthful King Myŏngjong.

Myŏngdŏk (queen) 명덕왕후 (明德王后) (?-1380) Mother of King
     Kongmin, known for her participation in political affairs.

Myŏngjong (king) 명종 (明宗) (r. 1545-1567) .

Myŏngsuk (princess) 명숙공주 (明淑公主) (?-1482) Daughter of
     Queen Sohye

Na Hyesŏk 나혜석 (羅蕙錫) (1896-1948) First Korean woman painter
     in Western oil medium and writer.

Ŏ Sukkwŏn 어숙권 (魚叔權) fl. 1525-1554. Author of *P'aegwan
     chapki.*

Qu Yuan (340-278 B.C.) 屈原 A great politician and poet in the
     Warring States Period (476 BC - 221 BC).

Sado (crown prince) 사도(세자) (思悼[世子]) Lady Hyegyŏng's
     husband. See Chapter 6

Sejo (king) 세조 (世祖) r. 1455-1468.

Shun 舜 Legendary Chinese sage-king.

Sim Chaesun 심재순 (沈載順) The first modern Korean woman
     playwright.

Sima Wen 司馬溫 (Sima Guang 司馬光, 1019-1086) Prominent Song dynasty official and scholar.

Sin Saimdang 신사임당 (申師任堂) Painter/poet, mother of Yulgok. See Chapter 3.

Sŏ Kyŏngdŏk 서경덕 (徐敬德) 1489-1546. See Chapter 5

Sohye (queen) 소혜왕후 (昭惠王后) 1437-1504. Compiler of *Naehun*. See Chapter 2.

Song, Madam 송씨 (宋氏) 1521-1578. Wife of Yu Hŭich'un with the maiden name of Song.

Song Siyŏl 송시열 (宋時烈) 1607-1689. Famed Confucian scholar and official.

Sŏngjong (king) 성종 (成宗) r. 1469-1494.

Sŏnhŭi 선희 (宣禧), lady. Yŏngjo's secondary consort and Prince Sado's mother.

Sŏnjo (king) 선조 (宣祖) r. 1567-1608.

Sŏkpyŏl ka 석별가 (惜別歌) "Song of Painful Parting."

Sŏsan taesa 서산대사 (西山大師) Grand Sŏn Master Sŏsan; see Hyujŏng.

Sunjo (king) 순조 (純祖) r. 1800-1834.

Sunshu Ao 孫叔敖 Minister who assisted King Zhuang of Chu.

Sunwŏn (queen) 순원왕후(順元王后) (1789-1857) Regent for youthful king Hŏnjong (1834–1849).

Taisi 太姒 Consort of King Wen of Zhou.

Taizu (太祖) Founding emperor of Ming dynasty, r. 1368-1398.

T'oegye 퇴계 (退溪) penname of Yi Hwang 이황 (李滉), 1501-1570.

Tŏkchong 덕종 (德宗) Yi Chang, son of king Sejo; named crown prince but died before succeeding to throne; husband of Sohye.

Tosan 도산 (島山), pen name An Ch'angho. A chief strategist and architect of the Korean nationalist movement, a worldwide network of underground and exile activities.

Towŏn (prince) 도원군 (桃源君) Title of Tŏkchong before he was named crown prince

Toyotomi Hideyoshi [K. P'ungshin sugil (풍신수길)] (豊臣秀吉) 1536-1598. After unifying Japan, unsuccessfully invaded Korea in 1592 to 1598.

Wen (empress) 文 (皇后) (d. 1407) Consort of Ming emperor Chengzu

Wŏlsan (prince) 월산군 (月山君) (1454-1488) Son of Sohye

Yao 堯 [K. Yo (요)] Legendary Chinese sage-king.

Yejong (king) 예종 (睿宗) r. 1468-1469.

Yi Ch'adon 이차돈 (李次頓) A Silla monk and Buddhist martyr 503-527.

Yi Chang 이장 (李暲) See Tŏkchong.

Yi Hangno 이항노 (李恒老) 1792-1868.

Yi Hwang (1501-1570) 이황 (李滉) See T'oegye.

Yi Hyŏnbo 이현보 (李賢輔) 1467-1555.

Yi I 이이 (李珥) [penname, Yulgok 율곡 (栗谷)]   1536-1584. Neo-Confucian scholar/philosopher.

Yi Ik 이익 (李瀷) 1682-1764.

Yi Kwangsu 이광수 (李光洙) [= Ch'unwŏn 춘원 (春園)] writer 1892-?

Yi Kyubo 이규보 (李奎報)   1168-1241.

Yi Sangbŏm 이상범 (李象範) [= Ch'ŏngjŏn (青田)]   1897-1972. One of the leading modern Korean painters.

Yi ssi hoesim kok   이씨회심곡 (李氏悔心曲) "Lady Yi's Song of Longing."

Yi Tal 이달 (李達) See Chapter 4.

Yi T'oegye 이퇴계 (李退溪) 1501-1570 [= Yi Hwang 이황 (李滉)].

Yi Tŏngmu (1741-1793) 이덕무 (李德懋).

Yŏngjo (king) 영조 (英祖) r. 1724-1776.

Yu Chunggyo 유중교 (柳重教)   1832-1893.

Yu Hŭich'un 유희춘 (柳希春) 1513-1577. Prominent scholar-official, author of *Miam ilgich'o* 미암 일기초 (眉巖日記草), Diary of Miam from 1568 to 1577.

Yu Jianhua (兪劍華) Compiler of *Zhongguo meishujia renming cidian* (中國美術家人名辭典) (Dictionary of Chinese artists), Shanghai, 1981.

Yu Mong'in 유몽인 (柳夢寅) See *Ŏu yadam.*

Yu Sŏngnyong 유성룡 (柳成龍) 1542-1607.

Yu T'aejwa 유태좌 (柳台佐) Neo-Confucian scholar, dates
unknown.

Yulgok See Yi I.

Zhuang (king) 莊 (王) Chu king.

Zhu Xi (1130-1200) 朱熹 [K. Chu Hŭi (주희)], Song dynasty
philosopher.

The Editor and Contributors

The Editor

Young-Key Kim-Renaud [kimrenau@gwu.edu] received a Ph.D. in Linguistics from the University of Hawaii. She is Professor of Korean Language and Culture and International Affairs and the Chair of the East Asian Languages and Literatures at The George Washington University. She is the initiator and co-convener of the Hahn Moo-Sook Colloquium in the Korean Humanities series at GW. She is a past President of the International Circle of Korean Linguistics. Kim-Renaud's publications include *Korean Consonantal Phonology* (1974), *Studies in Korean Linguistics* (1986), *Theoretical Issues in Korean Linguistics* (1994), *The Korean Alphabet: Its History and Structure* (1997), *King Sejong the Great: The Light of Fifteenth Century Korea* (1992, 1997, 1998, translated into Korean 1998 and into German 2002). home.gwu.edu/~kimrenau, myprofile.cos.com/kimreny76

The Contributors

John Duncan [duncan@humnet.ucla.edu] received a B.A. in Korean History from Korea University in Seoul, and a Ph.D. in Korean History from the University of Washington. He is currently Director of the Center for Korean Studies and Associate Professor of East Asian Languages & Cultures and History, UCLA. Previously he taught at the University of Washington, Boise State University and Harvard University. He is interested in cultural and institutional history of traditional Korea and Confucianism in Korea. His recent publications include *Rethinking Confucianism: Past and Present in China, Japan, Korea, and Vietnam*, co-edited with Benjamin Elman and Herman Ooms (2002); "The Problematic Modernity of Confucianism: The Question of Civil Society in Chosŏn Dynasty Korea" (2002); *Origins of the Chosŏn Dynasty* (2000); and "Hyanghwain: Migration and Assimilation in Chosŏn Dynasty Korea."

JaHyun Kim Haboush [jkh25@columbia.edu] received her Ph.D. from Columbia University where she is currently King Sejong Professor of Korean Studies. She has previously taught at the University of Illinois at Urbana-Champaign. Her major publications include *A Heritage of Kings: One Man's Monarchy in the Confucian World* (1988), which is reissued as *The Confucian Kingship in Korea: Yongjo and the Politics of Sagacity* (2001), and *The Memoirs of Lady Hyegyong* (1996). She also edited *The Rise of Neo-Confucianism in Korea* (1985) and *Culture and the State in Choson Korea* (1999).

Sonja Häußler [Chusonja@aol.com] received her M.A. degree in Oriental Philology from Leningrad State University (1985) and her Ph.D. in Korean Language and Literature from St. Petersburg State University (1993). Since 1985, she has been Assistant Professor of Korean Literature and Culture at the Humboldt University in Berlin. Her major research focus has been on the literature and culture of the Confucian elite, especially the Confucian loyalists in the Early Chosŏn. She is currently preparing her *habilitation* on *Escapism and Social Responsibility. A Study on Kim Sisŭp's Literature and Thought.*

Kichung Kim [paikkim@aol.com] received a doctorate in English in 1969 from University of California at Berkeley, and has been a professor of English at San Jose State University since 1966. His essays on Korean literature have appeared in *Korean Culture, Korea Journal, Korean Studies,* as well as in other publications. His book, *An Introduction to Classical Korean Literature: From Hyangga to P'ansori* was published in 1996 by M.E. Sharpe, Inc.

Kumja Paik Kim [kkim@asianart.org] received her doctorate in Asian Art History from Stanford University and taught at San Jose State University from 1979 to 1989. She is Curator of Korean Art at the Asian Art Museum of San Francisco. Her articles have appeared in *Artibus Asiae, Oriental Art, Orientations, Korean Culture, Korea Journal,* and others. She has organized several exhibitions. Her most recent exhibition, "Hopes and Aspirations: Decorative Painting of Korea," was shown at the University of Michigan Art Museum at Ann Arbor.

Yung-Hee Kim [yunghee@hawaii.edu] is Professor of Korean Literature in the Department of East Asian Languages and Literatures at the

University of Hawaii at Manoa. After receiving her Ph.D. in Asian Studies from Cornell University, she taught at the Ohio State University from 1983 to 1996. Her research focus has been on modern and contemporary Korean fiction, especially women writers, from interdisciplinary perspectives based on her training in comparative literature and classical Japanese literature. Her major publications appear in *Korean Studies, Journal of Women's History, and Who's Who in Contemporary Women's Writing*. She has also been engaged in English translations of modern Korean short stories.

Bonnie B.C. Oh [OHB@georgetown.edu] is the University Faculty Ombuds Officer and Distinguished Research Professor of Korean Studies at Georgetown University. She has organized numerous conferences and lecture series, and edited newsletters in Korean studies. She is co-editor of *East Meets West, Jesuits in China, 1582–1773* (1988), and a contributor to the volumes, *Japan Examined: Perspectives on Modern Japanese History*, and *The Chinese and Japanese: Essays in Political and Cultural Interaction*. She is a co-editor with Margaret D. Stetz, *Legacies of the Comfort Women of World War II* (M.E. Sharpe, 2001) and the editor of *Korea Under the American Military Government, 1945–1948* (2002). She is currently engaged in a joint project with her husband, Dr. John K.C. Oh, Banigan Scholar Emeritus of Politics, The Catholic University of America, Washington, D.C. on "The Korean Embassy in the United States." www.georgetown.edu/sfs/programs/asia/faculty.htm, www.georgetown.edu/admin/ombuds

Kevin O'Rourke [seoulkor@hotmail.com] is an Irish priest (Columban Fathers) who has lived in Korea since 1964. He studied Korean literature at Yonsei University. He received his M.A. in 1970 and his Ph.D. in 1983. He came to Kyunghee University in 1977, where he is currently professor of English literature. He is widely known as a translator of Korean literary texts, classical and modern. *Tilting the Jar, Spilling the Moon*, a selection of Korean Poetry, published in 1993 by Daedalus, was greeted with acclaim and was a Poetry Book Society recommended translation. Daedalus subsequently published two more volumes, *Poems of a Wanderer* (Selected So Chongju poems) in 1995 and *Looking for the Cow* (an anthology of modern Korean poetry) in 1999. In 2002, Harvard University Press published *The Book of Korean Sijo*.

Yi Song-mi [yisongmi17@hanmail.net] is Professor of Art History and the Dean of the Graduate School of Korean Studies at the Academy of Korean Studies in Korea. She received her B.A. in Fine Arts from Seoul National University (1962), M.A. in Art History from University of California–Berkeley (1969), and Ph.D. in Art History from Princeton University (1983). She served as the director of the University Art Museum at Duksung Women's University and the president of the Art History Association of Korea. Recently she served as an advisor to the Metropolitan Museum of Art for its establishment of the Arts of Korea Gallery. She has published books and articles on Korean and Chinese art and culture in Korean as well as in English. Her most recent book in English is *Fragrance, Elegance, and Virtue: Korean Women in Traditional Arts and Humanities* (2002).

Index